Human Resource Management in Consulting Firms

Michel E. Domsch
Elena Hristozova
(Editors)

Human Resource Management in Consulting Firms

With 42 Figures

 Springer

Professor Dr. Michel E. Domsch
Dipl.-Oec. Elena Hristozova, M.E.S.

I.P.A. Institute for Human Resource
and International Management
Helmut-Schmidt-University
Holstenhofweg 85
22043 Hamburg
Germany

michel.domsch@hsu-hh.de
elena.hristozova@hsu-hh.de

ISBN-10   3-540-31137-8 Springer Berlin Heidelberg New York
ISBN-13   978-3-540-31137-9 Springer Berlin Heidelberg New York

Cataloging-in-Publication Data
Library of Congress Control Number: 2005938501

Springer is a part of Springer Science+Business Media

springeronline.com

© Springer Berlin · Heidelberg 2006
Printed in Germany

Hardcover-Design: Design & Production, Heidelberg

SPIN 11606727   43/3153-5 4 3 2 1 0 – Printed on acid-free paper

Preface and Acknowledgements

Consulting is a knowledge-intensive industry, in which human resources are considered to be the most important asset. This industry, which had been flourishing until recently, has attracted the interest of academia, private business, public authorities and even journalists. As a result, a broad range of issues related to this sector have been explored in detail. However, only a few contributions deal with personnel or human resource management.

There are two possible explanations for this lack. Due to its uniqueness and strategic importance, information about human resources has been treated by consulting firms with a great deal of confidentiality (Mohe 2004). This has been confirmed by our own experience. On the other hand, human resource management in consulting firms has just recently gained a more "explicit" and "formal" shape (Graubner and Richter 2003), thus making it a subject of researchers' and practitioners' interest.

Therefore the main intention of this book is to provide an insight into those areas as yet barely touched on by delivering a specific and fairly concrete idea about the role and different facets of human resource management in consulting firms. Although the present volume is addressed to a relatively broad audience, it is mainly aimed at the potential clients and applicants of consultancies and, of course, at scholars looking for empirical evidence with regard to the topic. Further, we can imagine that this book could be a useful source for professors teaching consulting firm management in a practice-oriented manner.

For the purposes of the present book we invited both HR professionals and managers from leading consulting firms as well as scholars investigating HRM within the consultancy industry. In the following, we will introduce the volume chapters and the relevant authors.

The Volume Chapters

All contributions reflect empirical evidence regarding personnel practice in leading consulting firms. The company reports have a common structure in which the first part presents the corporate background including size, clients and philosophy and the second part eider delivers an in-depth overview of the different HR processes or focuses on one concrete HR practice that is described in detail.

The first introductory chapter presents an integrative review of the role of human resource management in consulting firms. Starting from Ulrich's model regarding the roles of HR, Michel E. Domsch and Elena Hristozova, analyze the extant literature, focusing on particular personnel aspects arising from the specific business. The framework for the analysis serves also as a framework for the volume.

In the second introductory chapter Klaus Reiners focuses mainly on the importance of HRM in the consultancy industry. Starting with an overview of the recent developments on the consulting market in Germany, he derives the specific need for personnel management in this field of industry. In conclusion, he presents the whole range of basic and further training entities offered by the Federal Association of German Consultants.

The next part analyzes the role of HRM as a strategic partner and change agent. Central to this part is the report of Kienbaum Management Consultants focusing on the value-oriented culture of the company. Walter Jochmann shows how the HR core instruments are aligned with the corporate vision. The author stresses, in particular, Kienbaum's strategic competency management, performance management, corporate culture, and change management.

The chapters in the section "HRM as administrative expert" depict mainly the traditional role of HRM and reveal industry specific aspects regarding personnel functions such as recruitment, training and development, career development, knowledge management and so on. Most of these contributions are insider reports giving the reader a fairly concrete idea about HR systems and processes in leading consultancies.

To begin with the reader is provided with an in-depth overview of the current personnel practices in international consultancies. Michael Dickmann, Michael Graubner and Ansgar Richter compare HR practices in international consultancies with those in multinational organizations from other industries. Further, starting from the "Three-wave model" of Kipping, the authors distinguish between personnel practices in consultancies from the "second" and those from the "third" waves.

"Human Resource Management as Administrative Expert" contains two different kinds of contributions. While the cases of Booz Allen Hamilton, Metaplan, Roland Berger Strategy Consultants and BDSU deliver a broad picture of their personnel systems, Accenture and Lee Hecht Harrison focus on cases dealing with single practices regarding leadership development and knowledge management. The case in Chapter 9 focuses also on a concrete HR practice with regard to employer branding.

In Chapter 5 Rainer Bernnat and Angelika Sonnenschein use Booz Allen Hamilton's personnel background to present all the facets relevant to the corporate process of career planning. Further, the authors focus on HR-related corporate best practices such as mentoring programs, sponsorship programs and evaluation processes, all of which are aimed at the personal and professional development and career progression of the employees.

Chapter 6 reflects the theoretical background of Metaplan's consulting philosophy and HRM. Wolfgang Schnelle presents fairly concrete examples of personnel tools used within the corporate practice of recruitment and training.

For the case of Roland Berger Strategy Consultants, Burkhard Schwenker delivers a broad picture of the firm's specific HR systems and tools. Within the HR framework he focuses, in particular, on the basic principles on which HR work is built as well as on personnel processes and levers like selection, evaluation, compensation, and training and development. The author presents further initiatives aimed at additional skills and motivation enhancement.

Chapter 8 deals with HRM in "Junior Consultancies". Kathrin Günther, Frederike Harms, Mareike Schilling and Lorraine Schneider sketch briefly the phenomenon of Junior Enterprises in the European consulting arena. Based on different cases from their own practice regarding selection, employee commitment, training and alumni retention, the authors deliver a concrete and detailed idea of personnel work in Junior Enterprises.

As already introduced the final three chapters deal with specific aspects of single HR practices in consultancies, such as employer branding, leadership development and knowledge management. Stephan Erlenkaemper, Tom Hinzdorf, Katrin Priemuth and Christian von Thaden focus on the method of preference matching, a successful form of employer branding in consulting firms. Using the method of choice modeling as a basis, the authors explain the process of preference matching. Further, they deliver findings regarding the use of special software for the purpose of successful preference matching in consultancies.

In Chapter 10 Martina Beck and Ildiko Kreisz present Accenture's case regarding leadership development. The authors focus in particular on the corporate understanding of leadership, on the leadership competency matrix as a basis of the leadership development program, and on the basic elements of the program. The authors make explicit the integration of leadership development at Accenture into the other HR processes like performance management, recruitment and training.

Knowledge management is a topic very central to the consulting industry. Jane Aubriet-Beausire and Sophie Gaio deal with the personnel aspects of knowledge management at Lee Hecht Harrison. More concretely they stress the relationship between organizational learning and quality assurance, and how an organization can become a learning one. In this context, the authors present the practices of employee orientation and certification, as well as training and professional development.

The final two chapters reflect different aspects of the "employee-champion" role of HRM. Uta B. Lieberum investigates leading consultancies with regard to gender diversity management. She delivers empirical findings about the strategic importance of gender diversity and initiatives implemented in consultancies with regard to female promotion.

Maida Petersitzke and Elena Hristozova focus in their contribution on employability development. More concretely, the authors investigate both the organizational offers and the individual activity aspects of employability development. Their research is also aimed at defining employees' needs and expectations towards improving employability.

Finally, we would like to express our thanks to all authors for their efforts to respond to our expectations and suggestions. Our thanks go also to Springer Verlag for their patience and advice. We are also grateful to colleagues and students who have helped with the book.

The present volume was financially supported by Helmut-Schmidt-University / University of the Federal Armed Forces.

Michel E. Domsch and Elena Hristozova
Hamburg, January 2006

Contents

Part III: HRM as Employee Champion

List of Figures

List of Tables

Notes on Contributors

Introduction:

The Importance of HRM in Consulting Firms

1 The Role of Human Resource Management in Consulting Firms

Michel E. Domsch and Elena Hristozova

Helmut-Schmidt-University / University of the Federal Armed Forces Hamburg, Germany

1.1 Introduction

The importance of human resources for the consulting business is indisputable. The consulting business (see Appendix I to IV) is seen as a personnel intensive service (Fritzel and Vaterrodt 2002), the success of which depends to a great extent on the human resources and, more particularly, on the human capital of consultants (Höselbarth and Schulz 2005). This resource has been defined as *the most significant* or even the *only significant strategic and crucial factor of success* (Höselbarth and Schulz 2005; Robertson and Swan 2003; Franck, Opitz and Pudack 2002; Alvesson 2000).

Over recent years both academic and business interest in the consulting industry has grown rapidly. The most discussed topics within the relevant literature are the growth of the industry, its market development, the relationship between clients and consultancies, the evaluation criteria of consulting projects, and the criteria for selecting consultancies. In the recent years a further topic has become of central importance for consulting research, namely the issue of knowledge management in consulting companies (Mohe 2004; Engwall and Kipping 2002).

Although there is widespread interest in different topics with regard to consulting, and personnel has been defined as the most important resource within this field of industry, only few contributions deal with the issue of human resource management in consulting firms. One possible explanation for such a paradox could be the confidentiality of the consultancies regarding their internal issues (Mohe, 2004). Another explanation for the lack of (empirical) research done on HRM in consulting firms could be the hitherto existence of "less formal" and "explicit" HRM in this industry compared to other industries (Graubner and Richter 2003).

Today however, owing to challenges resulting from the clients' increasing demand for high quality service (Höselbarth and Schulz 2005; Graubner and Richter 2003) coupled with the current shortage of personnel (Bornmüller 2005; BDU 2004) there is a need for more awareness regarding the HR policies and practices as well as for a more proactive attitude towards their implementation (Graubner and Richter 2003).

The present volume aims at investigating specific aspects of the role of HRM in consultancies derived from the nature of consulting. In order to get a better understanding regarding the specific aspects of the topic, we first deliver an integrative review of the existing literature on HRM in consultancies.

1.2 A Framework for Literature Review

Ulrich (1993) differentiates four roles for the up-to-date HRM derived from two dimensions (see Figure 1.1.). The first dimension represents the focus of HRM and it ranges from *operational* to *strategic*. The second dimension reflects the HR activities and distinguishes between *managing HR processes* and *managing people*. Crossing these axes we arrive at the four roles of HRM: strategic partner, change agent, administrative expert and employee champion.

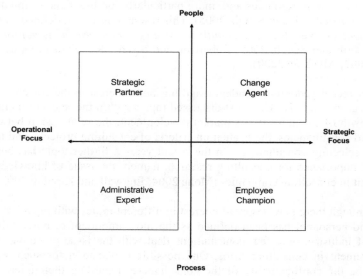

Fig. 1.1. HR Role Framework (Ulrich 1993)

HR as *strategic partner* is responsible for contributing to the organizational success, by developing and executing the HR strategies and practices. The role of *change agent* is aimed at managing transformation and change. HR professionals are both guards and the catalyst of organizational culture and the main contributors with regard to identification and implementation of change processes. The role of the *administrative expert* is actually the traditional responsibility of HRM, namely to cope with administrative tasks. In the context of this role HR must deliver efficient HRM processes for staffing, training, remuneration and promotion. HR as *employee champion* is responsible for managing employees' commitment and moral. In order to achieve it this role implies an engagement in day-to-day problems, concerns, expectations and needs derived from the workforce (Ulrich 2000). An empirical study of the roles of HRM (Conner and Ulrich 1997) confirms the existence of three of the four roles. The data does not discriminate between the roles of strategic partner and change agent. As a result, using Ulrich's conceptual framework and the findings of the study as a basis, we adopted for the purpose of our integrative review a slightly different framework (see Figure 1.2.). Furthermore, according to our understanding of personnel work HRM agents include not only the HR people, but also the management.

Fig. 1.2. A Framework for Analyzing HRM in Consulting Firms

Based on the above mentioned framework we run an integrative review within the literature on HRM in consulting firms with the purpose of answering the following questions: *Which specific aspects of the HRM roles in consulting firms are discussed within the extant literature?*

1.3 Results of the Review

As a result of the literature search we obtained 26 contributions (see Table 1.1.) that deal explicitly with different aspects of human resource management in consulting firms. From the total amount, 15 are research and 11 are practice-oriented articles. The contributors of the practice-related articles are either representatives of consulting companies reporting about concrete HR practices developed and implemented in their organization or scholars contributing to practitioners' magazines. There are 22 contributions originating from Anglo-Saxon magazines and 5 from German. With regard to the content, the issues range from ergonomics to aspects of organizational culture.

Table 1.1. Results of the Review

Reference	Strategic HRM / Change Agent	Recruitment	Selection	Socialization	Training	Career Development	Coaching and Mentoring	Performance Appraisal	Compensation and Benefits	Separation	Personnel Administration	Commitment and Moral	Personal and Family Needs
Alvesson 2000												X	
Armbrüster 2004			X										
Barkawi 2004		X											
Franck, Opitz and Pudack 2002			X										
Franck and Pudack 1999			X										
Fritzel and Vaterrodt 2002													X
Fuchs 1997						X							
Graubner and Richter 2003		X		X	X				X	X	X		
Hördt 2002													X
Höselbarth and Schulz 2005											X		
Hunter 1999						X							
Ibarra 2000							X						
Kubr 2002		X	X	X	X	X	X	X	X				
Langer 1998									X				
McMann 2000													X
Norman and Powell 2004	X												
Oertig and Stoll 1997						X	X						
Rasmussen 2004												X	X
Robertson and Swan 2003			X						X	X			
Saltzmann and Meyer 2004									X				
Sweat 2001											X		
Viator 2001	X												

1.4 HRM as Strategic Partner and Change Agent

Not surprisingly, there was only little evidence regarding the role of HR as strategic partner in consulting firms. The only report on this issue concerns the role reorientation of the HR department in Accenture, connected with a shift of operational responsibilities from the HR department to the line management. Due to this shift the HR department is freer to focus on strategic imperatives and thus to operate more strategically (Norman and Powell 2004).

In order to execute its new strategic role, HR has to develop new skills and attitudes to lead change, facilitate business growth and enhance innovation across the firm. Doing so, the HR starts a change process at the strategic level and executes simultaneously its role as a strategic partner and as a change agent (Norman and Powell 2004). More concretely, HR professionals in Accenture have to develop new skills like guiding and supporting rather than directing and giving answers. HR will use facilitation and coaching skills to lead change and add value to the business by building competence at senior director level. In order to ensure competence for its new roles, HR in Accenture has developed a special tool called "High impact Program for HR People". Central to this program are coaching, mentoring, problem sharing, networking and exchanging support (Norman and Powell 2004).

A further aspect of the role of change agent in consultancies is transformational leadership. This style of leadership refers generally to the ability of a leader to transform a subordinate's beliefs and values. Transformational leadership is considered to be an organizational mechanism for responding to increased economic competition and the demand for innovative services. Thus, supervisors in consulting companies are more likely to acquire transformational leadership skills than in other knowledge intensive services (Viator 2001).

1.5 HRM as Administrative Expert

In this part of our contribution we focus on different HR processes in consulting firms such as selection, training and development, separation and so on.

1.5.1 Recruitment

Against the background of the existing "war for talents", two specific aspects with respect to consulting firms appear. First, growth in the consulting industry can be achieved only by increasing the number of consultants. In this context consulting firms compete among each other, but also with other dynamic and forward-looking sectors (Barkawi 2004; Kubr 2002). The second aspect concerns the relevant labor market. As consulting firms cannot afford to recruit the "second best" people, the rejection rate is about 1 to 2 %. Thus, consultancies share the same narrow pool of "suitable" applicants. Additionally to this restriction, the "highest potentials" are aware of their high value and the broad range of options they have on the labor market (Barkawi 2004). Forced by such developments, consulting firms seek to make consulting careers attractive and by doing so to increase their employer attractiveness.

Since consulting firms recruit mainly from universities and business schools, the current profile of the potential employees they are trying to attract usually includes the following features: university degree irrespective of the field of study, and an age limited between 25 to 30 years (Kubr 2002). For several reasons consultancies avoid recruiting consultants at senior level. An exception can be made in special cases when senior people have to start new lines or head divisions (Kubr 2002). For the purpose of recruitment, consulting firms use two main sources: business enterprises and universities. The mostly used recruitment tools are job advertisements in business journals and management periodicals (Kubr 2002), and, more recently, career fairs.

Due to changes in the business environment and increased customer expectation, consultancies are forced to ensure the superior experience of their staff. Therefore, a more heterogeneous pool of applicants has to be addressed, where the applicants are older, more diverse and more experienced compared to the current practice (Graubner and Richter 2003).

1.5.2 Selection

Selection as a HR process contains two stages: the selection procedure when entering the organization and the continuous selection during the whole process of "climbing the pyramid". Franck and Pudack (1999) define the process of permanent selection as rank-order tournaments based on the "up or out" rule. These tournaments are very central to the consulting business in general, as they send several signals to different targets: customers, applicants and employees (Armbrüster 2004; Franck, Opitz and Pudack 2002; Franck and Pudack 1999). Figure 1.3. depicts the signaling effects resulting from a tough selection procedure and the recipients of these signals.

Fig. 1.3. Selection Signals Sent by Consulting Firms

As the effect of consulting services cannot be accurately estimated let alone proved, a firm's reputation is very central to this business. By executing rank-order tournaments, consultancies signalize a "high-quality guarantee" to their clients. The quality of the human capital is a sign of the service quality (Franck, Opitz and Pudack 2002). Further, high rejection rates signal *selectivity* and *rationality* to the business environment (Armbrüster 2004; Franck, Opitz and Pudack 2002; Franck and Pudack 1999). The signal of rationality can be explained with the existing symbolism regarding consultants as "analytically gifted employees" (Armbrüster 2004).

The tough selection procedure sends signals of "rationality", "analytically gifted people", "intellectual elitism", and "belonging to the best" also to their own employees. These symbols are part of the organizational culture in consultancies (Armbrüster 2004; Robertson and Swan 2003). In this context the importance of "organizational fit" should be mentioned (Robertson and Swan 2003). In order to ensure workforces "fit in", selection procedures are usually based on peer assessment (Robertson and Swan 2003; Kubr 2002).

A further effect of tough selection is the mechanism of self-selection among potential applicants. That is why management consultancies invest in "expensive" personnel marketing events, not only to attract applicants but also to generate long lists of applicants (Armbrüster 2004; Franck Opitz and Pudack 2002). The high rejection rates make consultancies highly attractive. This phenomenon can be explained with the fact that the best candidates on the labor market are forced to apply for a job in consultancies in order to ensure positive signals are sent to potential employers about their own human capital (Franck and Pudack 1999).

1.5.3 Training and Development

Training and Development as a HR process contains several sub- processes, some of which run simultaneously. These are socialization, training, career development as well as coaching and mentoring. In the following we will have a closer look at these processes in the particular context of consulting companies.

Training

Consultancies invest in training and development to satisfy the permanently increasing clients' expectations and to ensure employer attractiveness (Graubner and Richter 2004; Hunter 1999).

There are two central questions regarding the *intention* and *effectiveness* of training in consultancies. Is the training aimed at delivering knowledge or at developing skills? And is the training more effective when delivered in a group or to an individual? (Hunter 1999). Team work is the main production form in the consulting industry. Usually teams are mixed with consultants working together with customers. The human capital of the team is central for the generation of peer-effects in the learning and development (Franck, Opitz and Pudack 2002). Thus, the group dimension of exercises is very important for the training process in consultancies Hunter 1999).

The process of training can be divided into two main stages: initial training and other socialization activities for the new recruit aimed at integrating the new consultants into the particular consulting philosophy and handicraft as well as into the specific organizational culture. The second stage is the further training for operating consultants, including senior consultants, project leaders and partners.

Socialization and Initial Training

There is a range of different objectives a successful initial training has to fulfill: to ensure the ability of the new consultants to investigate existing situations; development and "sale" improvements; to establish relationship with the client implement changes, etc. (Kubr 2002). Typical components of the initial training process include training courses for new consultants, practical field training at the client organization and individual study. The individual study happens simultaneously to the other parts. In addition, there are two evaluation phases, one at the end of the course-training and one at the end of the field training (Kubr 2002).

Even if T&D policies of consulting firms tend to respect the diversity of the work force by offering different training activities (Kubr 2002), the redefinition of the workforce attracted - more diverse in terms of gender, age and experience – leads to an adjustment of the socialization activities (Graubner and Richter 2003). The traditional process of quick adaptation to the existing culture, supported only by a two-week boot camp has to be replaced with a continuous integration, requiring adaptation not only from the newcomers, but also from the existing members.

For that purpose one or two-day events involving employees with different tenures seem to be more efficient (Graubner and Richter 2003).

Further Training

The general practice in consultancies shows that training for junior consultants is more intensive than for the operating professionals (Hunter 1999), probably because senior consultants are thought to "know their trade" (Graubner and Richter 2003). However consultants' development is a continuous experience-driven learning process and the developmental needs for senior consultants, project leaders and partners should not be underestimated. There are two important reasons for redefining the attitude towards the training of operating consultants: the extremely short life-time of managerial concepts and techniques forces experienced professionals to update their knowledge and skills more frequently. Second, training can motivate these consultants (Graubner and Richter 2003; Kubr 2002).

Operating consultants can be present as always busy and often traveling individualists (Kubr 2002; Hunter 1999). In order to meet the needs of these often traveling professionals, multimedia, internet, and self-study formats can be offered as training methods. For enhancing cooperation and team work the firm can organize discussion forums, workshops, meetings and annual symposia (Hunter 1999).

The practice of *development centers* at KPMG takes into account the training needs of partners. The firm runs development centers at three levels. The target group of the third is partners. According to the internal rules of KPMG all partners have to be reselected every 7 years. As a result of this rule there is a continuous need for further development at the partner level. Central to this development centre are strategic issues and personal identification (Oertig and Stoll 1997).

Career Development

Career prospects are seen traditionally as the most important incentive for choosing consultancy as a profession (Graubner and Richter 2003). The current practice in consulting firms reveals career development as a 4 to 5 stage process (see Figure 1.4.) that usually takes about 6 to 12 years until the level of partner has been reached (Kubr 2002).

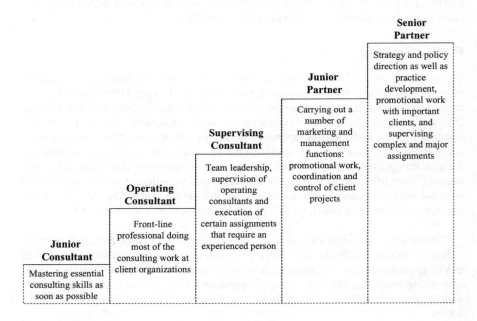

Fig. 1.4. Career Structure in Consulting Firms (Kubr 2002)

Successful junior consultants nowadays are no more willing to wait about 10 years in order to become partners (Ibarra 2000). Fast career progression positively motivates consultants and creates a dynamic and competitive working environment. However, such progression turns into an organizational challenge in turbulent times. As a consequence, consultancies can use some career alternatives as answer to the dilemma of fast progression (Kubr 2002).

One alternative could be to reorient the firm to more complex assignments and so to increase the demand for senior consultants without partnership (Graubner and Richter 2003; Kubr 2002). There are two further considerations regarding this initiative. As only few consultants can obtain a partnership, there is a need for developing other incentives in order to secure employer attractiveness. Secondly, since new recruits in the future will tend to be more experienced than now, career development will have to learn to integrate such newcomers who have already developed know-how (Graubner and Richter 2003).

Another alternative to formal career paths is provided by the practice of *"perspective groups"* in CSC Ploenzke Germany. This practice is based on an understanding of career in which the gaining of new competence is more important than promotion. The organization encourages multiple qualifications in order to enhance the shift from "specialists" towards "generalists" (Fuchs 1997).

Another very typical aspect of career found in consultancies is the process of career transfer. This practice is derived from the existing "up or out" rule whereby less successful employees are encouraged and supported by outplacement and alumni networks to continue their careers outside the consultancy (Kubr 2002).

Coaching and Mentoring

Coaching and mentoring are very central to successful career development. According to best practices in the consulting industry, partners and other senior consultants are responsible for the development of the junior consultants (Kubr 2002). The existence of a strong mentoring culture and a convenient ratio between senior consultants and mentees enhance the progress of the junior consultants (Graubner and Richter 2003). However, in some consultancies the career path from junior consultant to partner is considered as a natural process of selection; as a proof for endurance. This argument is also often the excuse for not offering coaching or mentoring (Ibarra 2000).

In the case of partner aspirants, partners have to be involved as mentors. An added value of this kind of mentoring is mentees can be brought together with as many senior consultants as possible. In this way the junior gains different experiences until he/she has found the most suitable mentor. Ideally speaking, the mentor programs should allow mentees to change their mentors if necessary (Ibarra 2000).

"Intervision" - a practice whereby two peers supervise each other on a regular basis, by using mutual criteria and principles – presents a possible alternative to time consuming mentor and coaching activities at senior level (Graubner and Richter 2003).

1.5.4 Performance Appraisal

Consulting companies conduct review processes where supervisors periodically evaluate the performance of the staff members with whom they work. In some cases groups of partners meet to discuss the consultants' performance and to rate them along several dimensions (Saltzman and Meyer 2004). There are two reasons why performance appraisal is particularly important for the development and promotion of consultants. Career patterns in consultancies require consultants to develop rapidly and second, the operational environment in which a consultant works changes frequently, e.g. a consultant can be a member of five or more different teams (Kubr 2002).

Two central aspects are typical with regard to performance appraisal processes in consulting firms: supervisors and consultants can discuss and agree upon the evaluation outcome and partners' group evaluation procedures exist (Saltzman and Meyer 2004; Robertson and Swan 2003; Kubr 2002). The main advantage of partners' group evaluation meetings is that they ensure the implementation of standardized evaluation criteria within the organization (Saltzman and Meyer 2004).

1.5.5 Reward Management

The general practice in consulting firms shows that merit pay is a relatively common tool, whereby the performance-related part of the compensation depends on the reaching of individual and/or group targets (Franck, Opitz and Pudack 2002; Robertson and Swan 2003). Usually the bonus paid to junior and operating consultants reflects the profitability of the firm as a whole, the individual fee-earning, and the new business generation. Due to their position as owners, partners participate in the profit and also receive compensation for their work as consultants (Kubr 2002).

Due to the specifics of consulting work, Kennedy Information has suggested several improvements regarding reward management in consultancies: non-billed time has to be taken into account; by converting partnerships into public companies the consultancy will be able to provide stock option incentives to employees; consultancies should create "near partner positions" that offer earlier equity- or profit sharing (Kubr 2002). Graubner and Richter (2003) suggest that the responsibility for the firms' future has to be shared among more senior consultants. This risk should no longer be compensated for by the premium resulting from partnership status, but by performance-related compensation, depending on the organizational performance.

1.5.6 Separation

Due to a strict "up or out" policy, separations are relatively central to HRM in consulting firms and not only in turbulent times. The average staff turnover (10 to 15%) in consultancies is relatively high compared to other sectors. Separation can also arise because of different views on consulting methods, on career advancement or preference for other careers. Many young people consider large consultancies as a kind of "business school" and join them without intending to stay (Kubr 2002).

Best practices regarding separation in consulting firms focus on maintaining good relations or even cooperation with former staff, based on regular and active communication (Graubner and Richter 2003; Alvesson 2000).

1.5.7 Personnel Administration

Considering the current consultancy practice with regard to personnel administration, we can notice the existence of three main tendencies: the shift of different administrative operations from HR departments to the line management or to the employees; the concentration of personnel data in integrative systems and tools; and the search for new ways to increase cost efficiency, for example via outplacement or shared personnel services.

The shift of operations such as personnel reporting or travel administration towards line management and employees is made possible by concentrating the necessary information in integrative systems and tools for the purpose of HR administration. Usually parts of a company's own service range, such personnel technology, is also offered today to the internal clients (Sweat 2001).

1.6 HRM as Employee Champion

The themes central to the role of HRM as employee champion in consulting firms are employee commitment, employee moral, loyalty and meeting employees' personal and family needs.

1.6.1 Employee Commitment and Moral

Due to their high intrinsic motivation and their professional identity as knowledge based workers, employees in consultancies are willing to work long hours. Thus, working hard and long hours may be part of their professional identity (Rasmussen 2004; Alvesson 2000). In the context of employee commitment the HRM in consultancies has to be aware of the fact that employees can be strongly committed to their tasks, customers and co-workers, but this does not mean that their commitment to the organizations is durable (Rasmussen 2004).

Further, HRM in consulting firms has to distinguish between short and long term employee commitment. At the beginning of their careers consultants can be considered underpaid. The willingness of consultants to accept low to medium pay while working long hours can be explained by their being offered interesting and challenging tasks, a very good social environment and the prospect of obtaining a partner position and so becoming overpaid (Rasmussen 2004; Franck and Pudack 1999). If the consultants are not able to reach the "partner level", they consider the missing salary as the "price" they have to pay to the consulting firm for obtaining the reputation of "belonging to the best" (Franck and Pudack 1999). However, these alternatives can work only in the short term. A long-term commitment to the organization includes professional development, challenging and interesting tasks, as well as work-life-balance. As long as consultancies are not willing to help employees meet their personal and family needs, consultants will be committed to their work, colleagues and probably clients, but not to the firm (Rasmussen 2004).

1.6.2 Personal and Family Needs

As already mentioned increased client expectations and changes in the business environment are forcing consultancies to recruit a more diverse workforce in terms of work experience, age and gender. The new background of the employees leads to new personal and family needs, where the HRM has to contribute to their satisfaction by developing and communicating work-life balance practice, mainly by avoiding excessive working hours. In this way consultancies will be able to attract and retain more experienced worker and women (Graubner and Richter 2003; Hördt 2002). Traditionally women are underrepresented in the consulting business. In order to benefit from a gender mix, HRM in consultancies has to implement additional measures regarding female promotion focused on removing the existing glass ceiling in this field of industry (Hördt 2002).

Job security is a need central to all employees irrespective of the industry they work in. The "job security" issue started to become relevant to the consulting business first in the recent past, when the demand for highly trained consultants decreased sharply (McMann 2000). Consultancies have realized that they do not want to lose their carefully selected and highly qualified human capital in which they have already invested a lot (Fritzel and Vaterrodt 2002). Further, downsizing leads to impending fear, uncertainty, and insecurity. As consequence, consulting firms are creatively exploring alternative approaches to downsizing and other non-traditional methods of maintaining staff capacity (McMann 2000).

Alternatives to downsizing in consultancies might include some of the following: a hiring freeze, overtime restrictions; part-time contracts for consultants; job sharing for back-office staff; and contractor pools of former consultants (McMann 2000). Flexible leave which enables employees to retain their connection with the company is another alternative created and implemented in Accenture. This practice is based on working flexibility and implies a longer timeout combined with partial remuneration. The main advantages of this practice are: noticeable personnel cost reduction, retention of highly qualified work force and highly motivated and committed consultants after their leave (Fritzel and Vaterrodt 2002).

1.7 Conclusion

In conclusion, it is important to mention that the HR systems and tools in consulting firms are tending to shift towards those in traditional industries (Graubner and Richter 2003). Nevertheless, we believe that the specifics of consulting services are quite distinctive and thus HRM in such companies will keep its unique features.

References

Alvesson M (2000) Social Identity and the Problem of Loyalty in Knowledge-intensive Companies. Journal of Management Studies 37 (8), pp. 1101-1123

Armbrüster T (2004) Rationality and Its Symbols: Signalling Effects and Subjectification in Management Consulting. Journal of Management Studies 41 (8), pp.1247-1269

Barkawi C (2004) Kampf um Kluge Köpfe. Staufenbiel Newsletter 2/2004, p.10

Conner J, Ulrich D (1996) Human Resource Roles: Creating Value, Not Rhetoric. Human Resource Planning, 19 (3), pp.38-51

Franck E, Opitz Ch and Pudack T (2002) Zum Kalkül der Personalauswahl in Topmanagement-Beratungen: Werden die besten Berater Partner?. Die Unternehmung: Swiss Journal of Business Research and Practice 56, pp.35-46

Franck E, Pudack T (1999) Unternehmensberatung und die Selektion von Humankapital. Freiberg Working Papers K99 A, 2536 (13)

Fritzel I, Vaterrodt JC (2002) Flexible Auszeit für Berater. management & training (2), pp.14-15

Fuchs J (1997) Karriere als Persönliche Kompetenzentwicklung. Personalwirtschaft (4), pp.12-14

Graubner M, Richter A (2003) Managing Tomorrow's Consulting Firm. Consulting to Management 14 (3) pp.43-50

Hördt O (2002) Frauen in der Unternehmensberatung: Empirische Analyse zur geschlechtsspezifischen Segregation, Deutscher Universitäts-Verlag GmbH, Wiesbaden 2002

Höselbarth F, Schulz J (2005) Personal-Controlling in Beratungsunternehmen. In: Stolorz Ch, Fohmann L (eds) Controlling in Consultingunternehmen. Gabler, Wiesbaden

Hunter RH (1999) The New HR and the New HR Consultant: Developing Human Resource Consultants at Andersen Consulting. Human Resource Management 38 (2), pp.147-155

Ibarra H (2000) Beratungsfirmen: Partner werden, das ist schwer. Harvard Business Manager (5), pp.78-92

Kubr M (2002) Management Consulting: A Guide to the Profession. International Labour Office, Geneva, 4th Edition

Langer S (1998) Compensation and Benefits in Consulting Firms. Journal of Management Consulting 10 (2), pp.27-30

McMann D (2000) Downsizing in the Consulting Industry. Consulting to Management 11 (2), pp.51-56

Mohe M (2004) Stand und Entwicklungstendenzen der empirischen Beratungsforschung. DBW (64) pp.693-713

Norman C, Powell A (2004) Transforming HR to Deliver Innovation at Accenture. Strategic HR Review 3 (3), pp.32-35

Oertig M, Stoll M (1997) Laufbahn mit Brücken und Pausen. Personalwirtschaft (4), pp.8-11

Rasmussen B (2004) Organizing Knowledge Work(ers): The Production of Commitment in Flexible Organizations. In: Carlsen A, Roger K, Krogh von G (eds) Living Knowledge: The dynamics of Professional Service Work. Palgrave Macmillan, Basingstoke, New York, pp.67-88

Roberston M, Swan J (2003) Control: What Control?: Culture and Ambiguity within a Knowledge Intensive Firm. Journal of Management Studies 40 (4), pp.831-858

Saltzman RM, Meyer JL (2004) A Consulting Firm Uses Constraint Programming to Plan Personnel-Review Meetings. Interfaces 34 (2), pp.106-112

Sweat J (2001) Glad We Thought of It. Informationsweek, September 2001, pp.93-96

Ulrich D (1998) A New Mandate for Human Resource. Harvard Business Review January-February 1998, pp.125-134

Viator RE (2001) The Relevance of Transformational Leadership to Nontraditional Accounting Services: Information Systems Assurance and Business Consulting. Journal of Information Systems 15 (2), pp.99-125

Appendices I, II, III and IV

Appendix I The Top 25 Management Consulting Firms in Germany, Ranked by Number of Employees

Rank 2004	Name	2004	2003	2002	2001	2000
1	McKinsey & Company Inc. Deutschland	1,750	1,770	1,812	1,768	1,660
2	Roland Berger Strategy Consultants	1,630	1,630	1,685	1,650	1,510
3	The Boston Consulting Group GmbH	1,050	1,050	1,100	1,150	1,000
4	Deloitte Consulting GmbH	646	677	683	456	435
5	Booz Allen Hamilton GmbH	430	410	384	365	340
6	Mercer Consulting Group GmbH	520	470	450	300	240
7	A.T. Kearney GmbH	440	510	543	620	616
8	Mummert Consulting AG	1,097	1,186	1,254	-	-
9	Bain & Company Germany Inc.	310	290	260	260	250
10	Droege & Comp. GmbH	285	280	280	315	290
11	Arthur D. Little GmbH	280	280	280	290	335
12	MC Marketing Corporation AG	225	190	160	150	132
13	Simon, Kucher & Partners GmbH	235	205	169	160	134
14	Horváth AG (Horváth & Partner Gruppe)	229	236	209	185	147
15	Management Engineers GmbH & Co. KG	142	132	125	105	105
16	Dornier Consulting GmbH	156	142	138	-	-
17	Kienbaum Management Consultants GmbH	165	158	195	189	165
18	Towers Perrin Inc.	145	140	140	140	120
19	Celerant Consulting GmbH	112	98	92	85	70
20	Kurt Salmon Associates GmbH	130	145	135	145	160
21	TMG Technologie Management Gruppe	80	80	70	-	-
22	Monitor Group	90	80	-	-	-
23	d-fine GmbH	109	102	-	-	-
24	RWE Systems Consulting GmbH	89	79	68	-	-
25	TellSell Consulting GmbH	40	35	-	-	-

Source: Lünendonk GmbH, 2005

Appendix II The Top 25 Management Consulting Firms in Germany, Ranked by Sales

Rank 2004	Name	2004	2003	2002	2001	2000
1	McKinsey & Company Inc. Deutschland	540.0	590.0	580.0	595.0	475.0
2	Roland Berger Strategy Consultants	530.0	318.0	526.0	511.0	433.0
3	The Boston Consulting Group GmbH	246.0	246.0	258.0	238.5	217.3
4	Deloitte Consulting GmbH	198.0	198.0	214.6	145.0	135.5
5	Booz Allen Hamilton GmbH	190.0	190.0	160.0	148.0	127.0
6	Mercer Consulting Group GmbH	167.0	167.0	125.0	106.0	93.0
7	A.T. Kearney GmbH	158.0	153.0	215.0	246.0	230.0
8	Mummert Consulting AG	147.0	143.0	-	-	-
9	Bain & Company Germany Inc.	130.0	130.0	110.0	105.0	97.0
10	Droege & Comp. GmbH	112.6	80.3	128.2	122.0	95.0
11	Arthur D. Little GmbH	72.1	72.1	85.0	89.5	100.3
12	MC Marketing Corporation AG	54.8	54.8	42.3	36.1	30.8
13	Simon, Kucher & Partners GmbH	46.5	36.0	30.1	29.0	24.1
14	Horváth AG (Horváth & Partner Gruppe)	46.5	33.7	40.5	30.0	21.0
15	Management Engineers GmbH & Co. KG	46.0	38.2	43.0	38.0	27.0
16	Dornier Consulting GmbH	43.6	32.6	-	-	-
17	Kienbaum Management Consultants GmbH	39.0	36.0	34.0	33.0	29.0
18	Towers Perrin Inc.	36.0	36.0	29.0	28.3	23.4
19	Celerant Consulting GmbH	28.1	24.6	24.0	18.3	14.5
20	Kurt Salmon Associates GmbH	28.0	28.0	28.0	24.3	22.8
21	TMG Technologie Management Gruppe	28.0	25.0	-	-	-
22	Monitor Group	25.0	25.0	-	-	-
23	d-fine GmbH	21.0	20.0	-	-	-
24	RWE Systems Consulting GmbH	20.4	20.4	-	-	-
25	TellSell Consulting GmbH	18.7	17.2	-	-	-

Source: Lünendonk GmbH, 2005

Appendix III The Top 25 IT Consulting Firms in Germany, Ranked by Number of
Employees

Rank 2004	Name	2004	2003	2002	2001	2000
1	IBM Business Consulting Services	-	-	-	-	-
2	Lufthansa Systems Group GmbH	4,500	4,400	4,200	3,457	4,125
3	Accenture GmbH	3,603	3,600	3,606	3,450	2,506
4	CSC Ploenzke AG	4,900	4,911	4,823	5,070	4,783
5	gedas AG	4,930	4,751	4,814	5,211	3,808
6	CapGemini Deutschland Holding GmbH	3,256	3,085	3,124	3,555	3,279
7	BearingPoint GmbH	2,600	2,800	3,277	-	-
8	Atos Origin GmbH	3,500	2,400	2,200	2,300	1,800
9	SAP SI Systems Integration AG	2,200	1,859	1,819	1,536	1,136
10	IDS Scheer AG	2,132	1,955	1,379	1,400	1,032
11	Deutsche Post IT Solutions GmbH	1,300	1,300	-	-	-
12	Msg Systems AG	1,900	1,650	1,450	1,300	1,150
13	ESG Elektroniksystem- und Logistik-GmbH	1,030	1,003	990	845	816
14	Softlab GmbH	1,180	1,042	1,114	1,230	1,451
15	IT-Services and Solutions GmbH	1,200	1,300	1,300	1,450	1,400
16	LogicaCMG Deutschland GmbH & Co. KG	1,500	1,922	-	-	-
17	Intelligence AG	936	1,068	1,465	1,486	1,433
18	GFT Technologies AG	1,039	1,058	1,204	980	562
19	sd&m Software Design & Management	950	877	897	906	790
20	Unilog Holding GmbH	1,100	786	1,111	1,129	1,135
21	Materna GmbH	1,100	1,115	1,309	1,150	1,050
22	Unisys Deutschland GmbH	462	506	-	-	-
23	SerCon Service Consulting GmbH	950	1,066	1,276	1,649	1,650
24	C1Group GmbH	629	467	-	-	-
25	entory AG	485	485	-	-	-

Source: Lünendonk GmbH, 2005

Appendix IV The Top 25 IT Consulting Firms in Germany, Ranked by Sales

Rank 2004	Name	2004	2003	2002	2001	2000
1	IBM Business Consulting Services	966.0	966.0	-	-	-
2	Lufthansa Systems Group GmbH	628.0	628.0	557.4	478.1	-
3	Accenture GmbH	586.0	586.0	594.0	644.0	1,070.0
4	CSC Ploenzke AG	571.0	404.0	608.0	719.0	1,375.0
5	gedas AG	567.0	150.0	619.0	628.0	964.0
6	CapGemini Deutschland Holding GmbH	477.0	477.0	466.0	519.0	1,105.0
7	BearingPoint GmbH	400.0	400.0	488.9	578.3	-
8	Atos Origin GmbH	380.0	380.0	250.0	260.0	440.0
9	SAP SI Systems Integration AG	336.0	269.0	293.2	268.8	364.0
10	IDS Scheer AG	280.2	111.2	181.4	160.2	246.0
11	Deutsche Post IT Solutions GmbH	216.0	216.0	-	-	-
12	msg Systems AG	203.0	185.3	162.0	144.0	250.0
13	ESG Elektroniksystem- und Logistik-GmbH	175.0	185.3	143.0	166.0	233.0
14	Softlab GmbH	165.0	135.0	164.0	173.0	370.0
15	IT-Services and Solutions GmbH	151.0	151.0	143.6	166.0	310.0
16	LogicaCMG Deutsch- land GmbH & Co. KG	136.0	136.0	-	-	270.0
17	intelligence AG	131.0	64.9	168.5	182.9	290.0
18	GFT Technologies AG	125.5	84.3	155.7	147.9	-
19	sd&m Software Design & Management AG	125.0	125.0	129.0	138.0	245.0
20	Unilog Holding GmbH	125.0	125.0	113.0	126.0	-
21	Materna GmbH	120.0	108.0	153.0	181.0	349.0
22	Unisys Deutschland GmbH	106.0	106.0	-	-	-
23	SerCon Service Consulting GmbH	85.0	85.0	125.0	161.0	-
24	C1 Group GmbH	76.3	76.0	-	-	-
25	entory AG	67.4	61.5	72.5	96.5	-

Source: Lünendonk GmbH, 2005

2 The Consultant: A Clear Outsider's Inside View

Klaus Reiners

Bundesverband Deutscher Unternehmensberater

2.1 The Management Consultant in Germany: A Job Profile

Management consulting has developed remarkably in Germany and throughout Europe over the last decades and is now an indispensable business-related service. Thus the consulting industry is one of the most dynamic economic sectors. Business reengineering processes, company mergers, deregulation and privatization, the globalization of economic activities at large, as well as the short-lived developments in information and communication technologies provide for always new consulting projects.

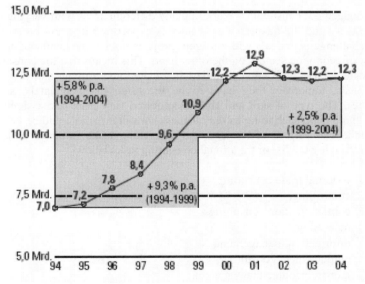

Fig. 2.1. Development of the Consulting Industry in Germany

As is also the case in most other countries the job title "management consultant" [Unternehmensberater] is not protected in Germany. Anybody may – irrespective of his/her vocational aptitude, qualifications and experience – call himself/herself "management consultant". This means that it is particularly easy for unqualified business consultants to establish themselves on the consulting market, thus damaging the reputation of the whole industry. The Federal Association Bundesverband Deutscher Unternehmensberater, which was founded in 1954, has implemented demanding quality criteria for the industry so as to counter this unsatisfactory situation. BDU members to come have to observe a strict admittance procedure, where they have to prove their ability as well as their job experience and they must submit verifiable customer references and they also undertake to abide by the comprehensive job principles as to which rules have to be observed when working as a management consultant, resp. executive search consultant. Pursuant to these principles professional management consultants are only offering their services if it is to be expected that their work is beneficial for their customers. This also means that they must be qualified and have sufficient staff and time to complete the mission within an adequate period. Moreover, it is being expected that they are basically acting as individually accountable persons and do not accept any limitations to their independence by third parties. Their consulting service is always non-partisan and objective. Expert opinions rendered out of complaisance or the will to please are a no-go. Fees must be proportionate to the type and volume of work to be carried out and should be agreed with the customer before the start of the assignment.

Management consultant's work in many different areas with varying degrees of complexity and the business community is expecting more and more from them. The challenge is to deals with different projects on the one hand and an enormous range of economic sectors on the other hand. This means that the consultants have to tackle a variety of demands, today they have to be brilliant analysts or cautious strategists, tomorrow they have to be the target-oriented catalysts or trusted coaches. The type of skill and abilities required vary from one assignment to the next, there is no such thing as *the* business consultant who could be described in a nutshell. The variety of management consulting tasks is better understandable when studying the list of traditional consulting tasks below:

- External trade consulting,
- controlling,
- communication consulting,
- marketing,
- information management,
- outplacement consulting,
- human resource management,
- management consulting,
- project management,
- quality management,

- business reengineering and insolvency management consulting,
- technology and logistics,
- company management and strategy consulting,
- business start-ups.

Management consultants support their customers by drafting and implementing solutions to their problems in all entrepreneurial, business economics and technological areas. One of the consultants' biggest assets is his/her unbiased inside view from the outside. Operations, processes and structures in the company are being subjected to a critical, objective analysis at the beginning of a consulting project. As a rule this comparison between the present situation and the wishes for the future is followed by a conceptual stage. Most projects include the implementation of the proposals drafted by the team and the customer's staff members. Today, consultants consider their task as "implementation consulting", where the consultant's knowledge is transferred to the customer company by means of the intensive project work and the results of the project which remains available to the company upon conclusion of the project.

The areas of activity of management consultants today probably count among the most interesting and challenging that can be found in the business community and industry. Changing projects and sectors reflect the whole range of economic activity. Traditionally consulting is subdivided into four main consulting areas: *Strategy Consulting* helps companies and organizations first and foremost with concepts serving to secure their further growth. This includes the development of new markets and far reaching decisions on company concentrations or mergers and acquisitions.

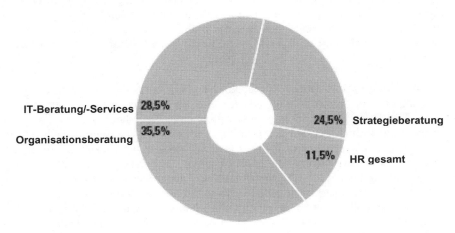

Fig. 2.2. Consulting 2004

Organization Consulting aims at optimizing operational processes and business process reengineering. For this purpose project and quality management or e.g. the technology, logistics or sales department are put to the test. *IT Consulting* focuses mainly on individual and standardized solutions of IT driven processes in the companies. These may include technical systems for customer relationship management or materials management, but also data linking in companies and organizations of any size. Projects to expand business activities via the Internet, so-called e-Business, play an increasingly important role. The fourth classic consulting area, *Human-Resource-Management* (HRM), is with a share of 11.5% of the total turnover in this industry in 2004 the smallest consulting area in Germany. The range of services within HRM included the search for and selection of leading technical experts and senior executives as well as the conception and implementation of human resource development measures and remuneration and outplacement consulting, as well as career coaching.

2.2 The Importance of Human-Resource-Management in a Knowledge-Based Sector

Above-average demands are placed on management consultants. Besides formal qualifications personal characteristics are important for a consulting job, because here, too, the ideal management consultant shall be able to learn, to solve problems under time pressure, must have team spirit, logical analytical thinking, excellent communication skills – and this not only in his/her mother tongue, negotiation skills and creativity. High professional competencies in a particular area and perhaps in a specific branch of the economy are considered further important preconditions for being accepted as an expert by the customer. Consultants must improve the customer's entrepreneurial success and in this context professional competencies but also leadership skills, team spirit, flexibility and communication skills are required.

Competition and the business reengineering as well as the increasing competitive situation in the consulting industry also lead to changes within consulting firms. The latter are considering above all whether they should expand their services or streamline their service portfolio and how they can optimize their customer relations management. There is a strong trend in the consulting companies to expand their own business by areas of activity like trade in companies, supply of venture capital and the takeover of customer departments (Outsourcing) and by offering interim management service. These developments are also constantly increasing the skill requirements of the consultants and thus their regular further training, as the customers pay close attention to expert knowledge, quality and experience as well as the consultant's personality. Today there is hardly any longer a demand for concepts only or standardized solutions. The companies are expecting that the consultants find individual answers to their questions and implement the necessary projects together with the customer's staff members by means of tailor-made measures.

Access to the occupation of a consultant, as mentioned above, is not regulated in Germany. However, as a rule, a university degree is the entry condition to becoming a consultant today. Consulting firms recruit university graduates who have acquired thorough commercial and economic know-how during their studies. But other academic studies are in the meantime also represented among management consultants. In the past natural scientists, physicians, lawyers or philologists were considered exotic in the consulting business, whereas nowadays university graduates from these faculties nowadays are regular members of project teams. Consulting firms are also pleased if they can recruit consultants with good to very good PhD or MBA degrees. This outstanding evidence of academic performance is often a good career catalyst. Special university degrees in consulting are still the exception from the rule in Germany, even though a positive development has taken place in recent years.

Consulting firms have a lot to offer to applicants and future staff members with regard to their professional and personal development. Comprehensive methodological and sector-related experiences that can be acquired by having worked in a number of different consulting projects improve the career opportunities and thus open many a door for consultants. Numerous top managers of German companies have proven their maker and problem solution skills in the past - as management consultants before they changed to a former customer enterprise, often directly after the end of the consulting project. Moreover, most consulting firms offer sophisticated training and further training opportunities as in no other sector of the economy. In addition, medium-sized and top consulting firms have a transparent and rapid promotion career system where a very good and ambitious performance is rewarded by speedy advancement. It is not unusual for consulting firms to make 7 to 10 % of the annual turnover available for training and qualification measures and thus invest not only in the added value for the customer but also in the knowledge capital of their own consulting firm. The described requirements to be fulfilled by a management consultant to perform well in his projects, illustrate what importance a targeted human resource management plays in a consulting firm: All the efforts undertaken in this field serve not only the personal qualification and motivation of the staff members, but secure the professional implementation of the consulting projects and thus the entrepreneurial future of the consulting firms.

2.3 Further Education in the BDU

It is against this backdrop that the BDU, as a sectoral association, offers all management consultants in Germany – irrespective of whether they are BDU members or not – tailor-made further training in the form of congresses and seminars. In its seminars and workshops the BDU provides for basic training as well as further training courses. Both offers are interesting in particular for self-employed management consultants or consultants employed as project leaders by management consulting firms.

Since 2001 the BDU cooperates closely with Prof. Dr. Christel Niedereichholz, academic director of the Heidelberger Akademie für Unternehmensberatung (HafU) [Heidelberg Management Consulting Academy] and founder of the MBA university course "International Management Consulting IMC" at the FH für Wirtschaft in Ludwigshafen [Ludwigshafen University of Applied Sciences].

The further training offers concentrate on working techniques, methodological questions, and the strategic orientation, but also the professional questions consulting firms are dealing with. All workshops are designed so as to be of great practical value and easy to implement. The "Basic Training Course for Management Consulting" includes i.a. subjects such as consulting marketing, how to get a consulting job, how to advertise for your services, professional drafting and calculation of an offer, analysis techniques and contents or consulting methods in the course of the implementation of the assignment. In the "Further Training Program" the latest research and practical findings on subjects such as "Innovative models for company financing", Lean Consulting with a "Balanced Scorecard", "Change Management Methods" or "Project Management for management consultants" are being taught. About 30 such seminars are organized by the BDU every year with changing focuses.

The BDU's further training offers are fully tuned to the basic and topical requirements of the management consulting sector. This is ensured by carrying out surveys among the market participants. With the help of direct mailings informing about 10,000 management consulting firms about the BDU seminar offers-people are being asked about ideas for further training seminars. From the replies and the frequency of mentioning certain subject a part of the new program will be developed.

The selection of the trainers is strictly done on the basis of professionalism. Our trainers all have long years of training and branch experience. This guarantees that the seminars are exclusively providing know how that has already proven relevant for the practical work of consultants. A huge majority of our further training teachers possesses the international renowned title "Certified Management Consultant CMC", which is proof of excellent quality and professionalism in the eyes of the consulting sector and the clients. The CMC title is awarded by the International Council of Management Consulting Institutes (ICMCI) that has its place of business in California. The ICMCI sees itself as a global association for quality assurance in management consulting. Upon conclusion of the seminars and workshops an anonymous written survey is carried out among all participants with regard to the organizational quality of the seminar as well as professional and methodological competence of the trainer. Only seminars that get excellent ratings will continue to be in the catalogue of BDU further training offers.

Two renowned sectoral congresses which are organized by the BDU – the "Beratertag" [Consultants' Convention] and the "Deutscher Personalberatertag" [German Management Consultants Convention] – add to the further training offer for the consulting industry in Germany. While the former rather addresses management and IT consultants, the latter is explicitly a platform for further training and for an exchange of experiences for management consultants and human resource managers. The 1 ½ day events are always addressing topical trends and developments of the market segments and the related requirements and challenges for the market players and provide for an intensive discussion of the substantive issues by means of lectures, panel discussions as well as workshop fora. The aim of both types of event is to give the participants new ideas as well as practical solutions which can also be used by management consulting firms in their day-to-day business. Against the background of weak market demand the last two *'Personalberatertage'* in 2003 and 2004 e.g. dealt with the search and selection of professional and management staff in particular with a view to alternative or supplementary consulting services. Information and discussions about subjects like outsourcing of human resources services, interim management, coaching or management audits were central issues. On the basis of 6 trend theories and associated future scenarios the *Beratertag* 2004 dealt intensively with the needs of and changes in society, the economy and politics and discussed what that meant for management consultants. The main questions raised were

- Which demands are the clients often formulating vis à vis the management consultants?
- How are the clients changing?
- How is society changing?
- The role of management consultants in the future;
- changes in the consulting market;
- organization and bionics;
- relationship innovation management and creativity.

The presence of highly renowned experts from the management consulting sector, from the business community, from science and research, politics and administration guarantees a high quality level at our sectoral congresses.

Management consulting companies that are members of the BDU, moreover benefit from the ongoing exchange of information and experience which takes place in the framework of 15 professional groups (e.g. for controlling, marketing, human resources management or restoration management) within the BDU in which all members can actively participate. Consultants from the members' associations are working on the further development of the areas of activity of the present management consulting market and thus ensure an ongoing improvement process for the business community, industry and the public sector.

The members of the BDU's professional groups are normally meeting three times per year for one to two-day working meetings, mostly at four months' intervals, i.e. in spring, summer and autumn of any year. These meetings are prepared in organizational and professional terms by the BDU main office. The agenda includes topical subjects from the various consulting specialists. The collection of topics to be included in the agenda is done by the professional groups at the beginning of the year and is supplemented and adjusted throughout the year, where necessary. The exchange with external experts from the economic and science community at the working meetings guarantees the necessary critical consideration of permanently changing challenges which are encountered in daily consulting activities. This close cooperation often leads to the publication of books or studies, some professional associations draft and publish their own publications including interesting papers for consultants. The *Handbuch Personalberatung (BDU-Fachverband Personalberatung)* and the *Handbuch Controlling (BDU-Fachverband Unternehmensführung und Controlling)* are considered as mandatory reading for consultants.

The members of the BDU's professional group 'personnel management' are dealing with topical questions concerning human resources twice a year in their half-yearly publication *„Bausteine zur Personalentwicklung"* ["Building stones of HR development"].

The BDU's professional group 'Public sector clients' is also publishing a half-yearly magazine called *„Für den Dienstgebrauch"* ["For official use only"], a collection of consulting projects in the public sector. Both publications have an edition of approx. 5,000 copies and are distributed free of charge to decision makers in HR departments and/or administrative departments.

Part I:

HRM as Strategic Partner and Change Agent

3 Demands and Challenges: Values and Value-oriented Corporate Culture

Walter Jochmann

Kienbaum Management Consultants GmbH

3.1 Kienbaum Consulting Group

Founded as a organizational consulting company by Gerhard Kienbaum, today Kienbaum looks back on more than 50 years of history. During the 1950s and 60s, the consultants' work was characterized mainly by all-embracing restructuring projects in the engineering, plant and construction industries thus, in the producing industries. Kienbaum's core competencies then were consulting services concerning the clients' ordering/purchasing systems, process and production optimization as well as the implementation of efficient R&D processes. In the 1970s the recruitment of top-specialists and, in particular, top-executives became a second main pillar of Kienbaum's business. Until today, Kienbaum is one of the leading search companies in the German-speaking markets, applying both methods, – executive-search/ headhunting and advertisement-based personnel marketing. In the 1980s the consulting business started to focus more and more on services for the public sector, referring to questions of the potential increase of internal efficiency, and on surveys stating the quality and benchmarks of classification systems (clients then were e.g. schools, universities, public safety units). In the 1990s with the division 'human resource management' the field of personnel- and corporate-development consulting became the third main pillar of our business; here, we offer our clients consulting services referring to all relevant steps of the HR-value-added process. Recently, we have launched the division 'outsourcing' which offers small- and medium-sized service providers full-support in the field of accounting/controlling.

Kienbaum

China
Germany
France
Croatia
Luxembourg
Austria
Poland
Russia
Singapore
South Africa
The Czech Republic
Hungary
United Kingdom
Switzerland

Kienbaum
Partner Network

Denmark
Italy
The Netherlands
Norway
Sweden
Spain
USA

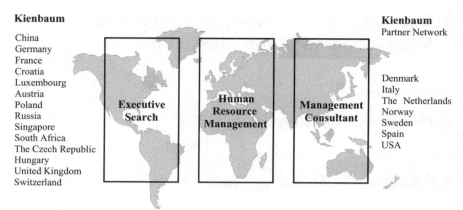

Executive
Search

Human
Resource
Management

Management
Consultant

Fig. 3.1. Kienbaum Consulting

Kienbaum Consultants employs 500 people (300 consultants, 200 employees within the service and outsourcing unit). The company's key markets are within the German-speaking region of Europe, most of the subsidiaries are located in Germany, Austria and Switzerland. The individual locations are structured and staffed according to the particular requirements of the region they are in and offer recruitment services; the subsidiaries in Gummersbach, Cologne, Dusseldorf, and Berlin, however, offer our clients a wide range of 'traditional' consulting services. As Europe is the company's core market, Kienbaum has many subsidiaries and strategic partners at all relevant European business locations and cities. After in the first years, Kienbaum's clients had been mostly major companies, between 1970 and 1990 we also started to put a rather strong focus on middle-sized businesses. Today, we have integrated three categories of business in our client portfolio and thus, our strategic alignment concentrates on

- the top 100 businesses in German-speaking and other European regions;
- the larger medium-sized businesses with an interest in global markets;
- institutions of the public sector (ministries, authorities, cities, further public and semi-public institution).

We understand ourselves to be a partner to the client and change agent. This credo calls for

- competence teams that we staff according to the individual industries' needs to guarantee that our consultants "speak our clients language", have the expertise for the special field our client is working in, and can develop appropriate concepts and solutions together with the client;
- the consequent expansion of expertise in the core competence fields/ key industries we cover (data bases, benchmarking);
- the implementation of the developed consulting concepts in close cooperation with our clients which is accomplished by experienced consultants.

Our company's vision is to establish Kienbaum steadily as one of the most significant and market-leading consulting enterprises in all relevant European business regions. In particular, for questions concerning personnel management Kienbaum shall be recognized as a market-leader and trendsetter that communicates openly, has an influence on the development of the society, and always offers innovative solutions to problems as well as instruments for personnel management. Our mission is to enhance our clients success effectively through efficiency-increasing solutions in the fields of human resources, organization and corporate management.

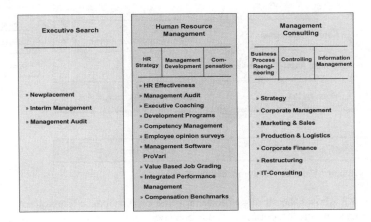

Fig. 3.2. Core Competencies & Top Products

3.1.2 Instruments for Quantitative and Qualitative Personnel Planning

All goals and performance-indicators of the personnel planning (and thus, of the human resources management which is central to consulting companies) are geared towards the company's overall strategy and the sub-strategies of the company's divisions. Within the scope of a medium- or long-term business planning (3 years and of course, annual planning) the following questions have to be defined/faced:

- Our positioning targeted with the help of the consultants' core competencies and critical factors for success, compared to the ones of the competitors;
- concrete financial goals of the company (company's development, growth and profit);
- strategic initiatives (projects relevant to the development of product innovations/ innovative consulting services and new markets);
- fields of optimization identified within the scope of regular SWOT analyses;

- results of the annual personnel-portfolio-discussion;
- the evaluation of customer surveys;
- strategic co-operations (with focus on the markets in the U.S. and Asia).

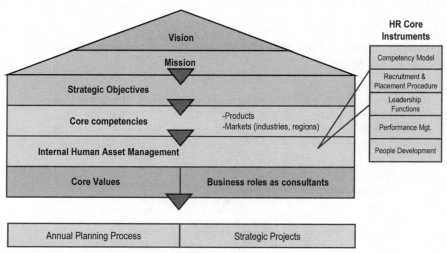

Fig. 3.3. Strategy Model & HR-Implications

Figure 3.3. shows the strategy model applied by Kienbaum Consultants with its consequences on the essential hr-functions: personnel recruitment, support, personnel development, performance management and career planning/development. Referring to quantitative and qualitative personnel planning, we use the following instruments:

- Requirement profiles for various consulting services and immediate functions, which result from a unique model of competency that is deducted from the company's corporate strategy;
- headcount-planning with recourse to performance-indicators (consultants' per capita sales, necessary capacity of leaders, service quotas of the service division);
- consequently, budgeting of the personnel costs and recruitment requirements/ recruitment costs;
- personnel portfolio (annual update);
- succession planning for all top- and key positions, – with special respect to our career model, the individual career expectations, and a retention-risk-analysis;
- annual planning of personnel development on the basis of annual feedback conversations with the employees/performance reviews, and an overarching portfolio discussion that the top-level executives are to hold.

3.1.3 Strategic Competency Management

A basic principle of our personnel management is the realization of our intensive human resources management know-how. Besides image, branding, international presence and financial strength, most likely, human resources management is the essential strategic success factor for success for consulting companies. Aspects of these overarching hr-factors for success are:

- Expertise;
- non-professional competencies;
- employer's attractiveness for top-talents;
- long-term retention of high performers;
- career expectations of a consultant for the individual period of life get indicated in an appropriate career model for the respective consultant.

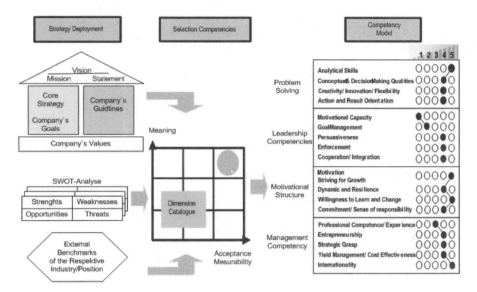

Fig. 3.4. Developing the Kienbaum Competency Model

Figure 3.4. demonstrates the development process of a tailor-made, overarching competency model that covers the needs of 3 divisions of a company and, in the next step, results in specific requirement profiles, e.g. for consulting or executive positions. It is crucial to deduct directly and indirectly professional and, in particular, non-professional/social requirements that result from the strategic factors for success and also from the specific business situation. Here, external benchmarks have to be linked; business models and the philosophies of consulting companies on a regular basis have to be checked against the feasibility of their contents. Figure 3.5. shows the present competency model of Kienbaum Consultants International, which is definitely based on non-professional competencies (behavior, opinion/personality) and general consulting competencies (ability to manage and be in charge of projects, sales and marketing skills, ability to develop products). The indicated requirement profile refers to our leaders'/executives' section; further profiles –based on identical rating scales– are available for

- Senior consultants;
- junior consultants/post-graduates (high relevance for the recruitment process);
- internal specialists for Service/Administration;
- positions in the field of service/support (for instance, project assistance, processing).

		1	2	3	4	5
Problem-Solving	Analytical Skills	o	o	o	o	●
	Conceptual- & Decision-Making Qualities	o	o	o	●	o
	Creativity / Innovation / Flexibility	o	o	o	●	o
	Action and Result Orientation	o	o	o	●	o
Leadership Competencies	Motivational Capacity / Leading by Example	o	●	o	o	o
	Goal-Management	o	●	o	o	o
	Persuasiveness	o	o	o	●	o
	Enforcement	o	o	o	●	o
	Cooperation / Integration	o	o	o	●	o
Motivational-Structure	Motivation / Striving for Growth	o	o	o	●	o
	Dynamic and Resilience	o	o	o	●	o
	Willingness to Learn and Change	o	o	o	o	●
	Commitment / Sense of responsibility	o	o	o	●	o
Management-Competency	Professional Competence / Experience	o	o	●	o	o
	Entrepreneurship	o	o	o	●	o
	Strategic Grasp	o	o	o	●	o
	Yield Management / Cost Effectiveness	o	o	o	●	o
	Internationality	o	o	o	o	●

Fig. 3.5. Present Competency Model of Kienbaum Consultants and Target Profile Manager (entry level)

In particular, we apply our competency model in recruitment processes (for avoiding wrong decisions and identifying potential in personnel), in the annual feedback processes (note the key instrument "employee discussion") and in the resulting planning of professional and non-professional personnel development measures. Which qualifying measures to be chosen for the individual employee mainly results from the previous professional career/ biography (the time, the person has worked in a certain position and the experience) and from the feedback given by project managers and supervisors. Our competency model considers professional competencies relevant for consulting and consulting instruments as well as certain fields of business/industries with the most important business processes; accordingly, each division has developed additional professional competency profiles for each field of competency. In the field of non-professional skills/competencies, the analysis of the employee's status quo and the actually required status quo results in budgeted qualification measures such as

- Behavior trainings;
- coaching;
- exchanging professional experiences in job-related work groups;
- mentoring performed by experienced consultants/executives (excluding mentoring by somebody's direct supervisor);
- national and international conferences;
- job-rotation.

From the range of well-established personnel development processes and instruments those ones that are of particular importance to Kienbaum and thus, are based on specifically designed and tested tools and application processes are marked in figure 3.6.

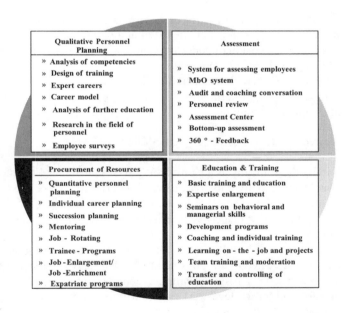

Fig. 3.6. Instruments Relevant for Personnel Development

As in the field of consulting there are many individualists and ambitious people working, referring to the internal human resources management, an essential part is the continuous and consistent career planning. Within this context, the employee discussion is a key tool which consists at Kienbaum of the following modules:

- Management by objectives (the objectives of the previous year are assessed on, objectives for the following year are agreed on);
- feedback on the behavior (GAP-analysis based on the strategic competency model and the requirement profile for the respective job-group);
- deduction of qualifying measures/training;
- analysis of potential for further fields of responsibility which of course, get checked against the employee's personal career expectations.

The results are based on appropriate instruments (noted-down agreement on objectives, personnel development plan, career plan) and are processed further in strategy meetings, in particular for the human resource management/planning. Here, the set-up of a personnel portfolio for all divisions of our company is especially important (see Figure 3.7.). Individual career expectations as well as an employee's obvious weaknesses in performance result in a development plan which focuses on

- Accelerated improvement, or otherwise, in a limitation of responsibilities or even in an outplacement on the external job market;
- systematic extension of consulting and general responsibilities (e.g. in form of being in charge of a project);
- internal and external responsibility for projects;
- short- and medium-term promotion planning, based on respective objectives and supportive training.

Our career model concentrates on the following levels:

- Joining the company as a Consultant's Assistant/Junior Consultant;
- Consultant (usually 2 to 4 years experience);
- Senior Consultant;
- Senior Project Manager (within the career model for extended operational careers);
- leadership level 2 (full responsibility for the results of the profit center and the team allocated to the Consultant's certain field of competency);
- leadership level 1 (usually Partners, complex responsibility for a consulting division and for the level 2 Managers within this division);
- Executive – full responsibility for all individual divisions of the company; together with other Executives responsible for the group's strategy.

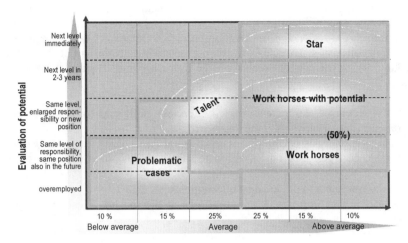

Fig. 3.7. Personnel Portfolio

The single career steps are based on clearly defined entry criteria/requirements which refer to objectives concerning the consultant's performance as well as the behavior. If these criteria have not been met for two years, the job position is adjusted to the consultant's performance/ behavior and thus, his/her responsibility is reduced, accordingly. This way, we develop towards a targeted model of 'inner mobility' that we prefer to the up-or-out principle which in our opinion, does not offer any perspective with respect to the narrow job market and increasing expectations about a consultant's experience.

The qualifying/ training measures are realized by an internal hr-team that organizes in-house training programs and analyzes the external market of training providers; if necessary, they make first contacts with external trainers/ experts. Our in-house training program, offered by the Kienbaum Academy, provides our employees with the following services:

- Welcome @ Kienbaum event for employees new to the company;
- organization of in-house trainings (some of them are performed by; Kienbaum-trainers, others by selected external trainers);
- transparent information on the recognizable external training providers and renowned topics/speakers;
- support in the chose of seminars and external seminar providers;
- purchase of external coaches for single training and consulting.

The creation of value regarding an excellent personnel selection, which guarantees that potential is identified and wrong hiring decisions are avoided, is likely to be higher than the outcome of a permanent investment in qualifying measures for the employees. This holds true especially for the highest requirements like problem solving, stress-resistance, motivation, social competence, and flexibility in behavior are concerned. Therefore, the recruitment and selection processes are one of the key tasks of managers/executives; the following tools support these crucial processes:

- Partly-structured, competency-based interview guidelines for at least 2 comprehensive interviews with the applicant;
- systematic analysis of the professional biography, based on our experience (grades, colleges/universities graduated from, milestones in the biography etc.);
- self-assessment and personality-questionnaire;
- partly-dynamic single-assessment tailored to the job level of consulting the person has applied for.

In the assessments, we apply the four-eyes-principle (meaning that always two observers assess the applicant) and simulate typical situations a consultant is confronted with in his/her every day's work, for instance, analyzing a problem, having a conflict discussion with another consultant or a client, planning a project, performing in acquisition/ presentations and (for managerial or executive level) leadership tasks. Our good reputation as a consulting company that provides its clients with excellent assessment centers and management audits reflects our profound knowledge in the field of hr-consulting, and in particular, in the selection and assessment of personnel. Thus, we consequently use our expertise for our company's internal recruitment processes. Having concentrated on graduates for our company's recruitment division in the past, today, our main target group are experienced consultants that are presently working for competitors and senior managers working in fields of business/ industries that are interesting to us. While the recruitment division's focus is on experienced consultants, hr-managers, and sales managers, our two divisions offering consulting services in the "traditional" sense (i.e. human resources management and Business Efficiency division) concentrate on three different kinds of candidates. One-third of the employees we take in here, are graduates that enter our company as assistants/ junior consultants, the second group consists of experienced specialists, and the third one of top-leaders/ managers from competitors and target companies.

3.1.4 Performance Management

The costs for personnel are, by far, the highest cost factor in a consulting company. They are, however, also an investment in the human resources, a retention factor for the human capital and a key factor guaranteeing that the potential in the employees will be used by the present employer. In the hr-process, the performance management is the second important pillar (besides competency management) on which our company's personnel management is based. We make sure that our company's business planning, the score-card based fine-tuning, and development of objective categories and clear objectives for the individual job groups/ consulting levels are linked in an optimal way (see Figure 3.8.).

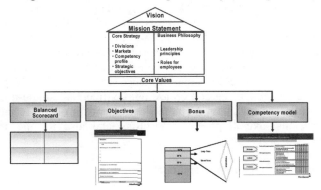

Fig. 3.8. Performance Management

Hence, our key instrument, the "employee discussion", is not primarily based on an exchange between the leaders/managers and their employees on the individual expectations and suggested objectives. Within the scope of the annual planning/ budgeting of the previous year and a two-day strategy meeting for our company's single divisions and sub-divisions, financial as well as non-financial objectives (the latter ones being e.g. projects and further relevant objectives referring to the company's positioning/ development of competencies/ product innovations) are agreed on and outlined. Kienbaum's management by objectives consists of 3 to 5 objectives agreed on, according to the following objective categories:

- All-embracing overarching financial objectives (obligatory for all divisions);
- financial objectives (here, results are given preference to growth) for a level one manager's field of responsibility (division), referring to the consultants' results this concerns the consultants' fees generated and their profitability;
- successful acquisition with reference to the explicit utilization of Kienbaum clients and the acquisition of new clients (according to our recently restructured sales processes, usually in close cooperation with manager/executives);
- quality of consulting, measured by the feedback of project manager/s, colleagues, and external customer survey;
- successful performance of projects, – in particular referring to product development and the optimization of internal processes;
- objectives concerning the personal development/further qualification, based on our competency model.

The remuneration system for the consultants is based on compensation layers according to the different levels of responsibility they are working on; between 15 and 40% of their compensation however, consists of a variable component which is controlled via the management by objectives. The weighting of the objective categories is checked once a year in the strategy meeting; anyway, a minimum of 60% of the weighting is put on the two binding financial objectives. Applying this flexible weighting system, we gear towards key goals and strategic key initiatives (e.g. the set-up of new co-operations or the development of new fields of business). We assure that objectives are cascaded systematically and comparable parameters for assessing the objectives are complied with via a computer-based controlling tool which we have developed in-house (see Figure 3.9). Thus, the forms for filling in the objectives agreed on are not confidential, single-use documents (at the latest, after 1 year...) but a control instrument for quarterly feedback/ employee discussions, overall project controlling and also for the activity-plan-management.

Further, our total compensation approach includes:

- The use of dynamic scales for the assessment of the financial objectives;
- the possibility to obtain a company car (with the possibility to chose from several options);
- a pension system with an attractive co-payment rate for our employees.

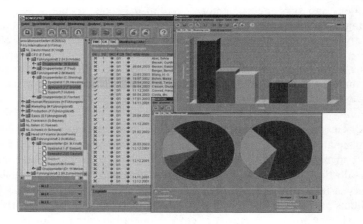

Fig. 3.9. Management Software ProVari

3.1.5 Corporate Culture and Change Management

Referring to the employees' motivation and retention, consulting companies face high requirements as they have to deal with their high demands on their employees' individual performance and, accordingly, possible high negative deviations of these individual objectives; furthermore, with the requirements determined directly by the clients and the competitors, and the dynamic changes of the markets consulting businesses have been confronted with during the last years. In particular, the demands for qualified consultants who have several years of experience requires long-term work-life-balance concepts that are linked to an attractive corporate culture. The forecasted, increasingly narrow job markets and thus, an at least medium-sized "war for talents" preserve our outlined attractiveness as an employer due to the described essential aspects as image, career chances, variety of tasks, compensation etc. To us, the internal corporate culture and the external image as an employer are 'two sides of the coin'. These aspects have to be underpinned by long-term instruments for leading employees and for designing our corporate culture (see Figure 3.10.).

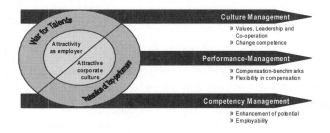

Fig. 3.10. Management of Culture and Change

Our understanding and model of leadership is expressed in the competency model. On the one hand, it is based on the two pillars 'motivation' and 'team integration', and on the other hand, on 'management by objectives' and the 'optimal use of potential'. The support and challenge of our outstanding employees is a definite factor for success which we underline with leadership key performance indicators (number of identified talents, internal placement and key positions, competency-fit and retention rates) within the scope of our balanced score card. While the quality of leadership can immediately be optimized through feedback and qualifying measures, changing the corporate culture is a medium-term process. On a regular basis, we accomplish 360-degree-feedbacks and comprehensive employee surveys in our company to document improvements made as well as potential short- and long-term threats with respect to the employees' motivation and retention (see Figure 3.11.). In these processes, we are in particular eager to match with our company's values that have been binding for us for almost 20 years now; thus, our goal is to be:

Competent

- Top-know how in all fields of hr-management;
- be convincing as far as the consultant's personality and the service's contents are concerned;
- convey to the client our experience regarding the realization and application of solutions in a plausible way.

A Partner to the Client

- Avoid giving the client the impression of arrogance/elitism;
- develop important contents of the project together with the client's managers in charge;
- be a creditable partner, not only to the client's top-management but for all employees, and groups of people that will apply the developed strategies and systems.

Innovative

- Up-to-date knowledge and clear assessment on international hr-trends;
- be a stimulator for creative and innovative solutions;
- be sensible for changes regarding business and society.

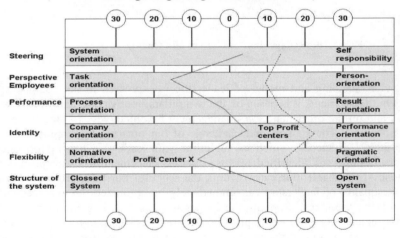

Fig. 3.11. Kienbaum Employee Survey

Moreover, Kienbaum executives and senior managers have developed a leadership and co-operation model that, for instance, defines the following self-demands and objectives:

- Our competence and strength, – is our team. We assure that all employees are familiarized in their jobs systematically, support them in their permanent further development, and assure the establishment of a long-term relationship with our company.
- Our executives and senior managers, – concentrate on their key tasks which are leadership and acquisition.
- We set trends, – we develop new, innovative products and improve our existing portfolio.
- We lay all workforce in the projects, – continuously, we gear our organizational structure towards the profit of our clients and guarantee them optimal consulting services.
- We are reliable, – we are goal-oriented and keep our promises.
- We support the personal work-life-balance, – we support our employees in balancing their profession against their personal needs for well-being, free time, and their family.

Each of the 11 guidelines is underlined by activities and set by measurement categories (see Figure 3.12.) for the determination of work-life-balancing.

"We support the personal work-life balance, - we support our employees in balancing their profession against their personal needs for well-being, free time, and their family."

Our Way:

We

»enable and foster a flexible working-hours model.
»have developed a sabbatical concept.
»give our employees sufficient free time to spend with their family or on their hobbies.
»accept that our consultants realize different monetary results, - according to their individual ambition and situation of life (with respect to the employee discussion, the budget, and our flexible salary system)
»reduce inconvenient travelling through staffing projects with consultants closest to the clients

Results:

»Lower absenteeism ratio
» realization of the sabbatical concept
» wellness is defined as an aspect of leadership qualities
» technical support and acceptance of home offices (also for project assistants)
» reduction of time consultants spend on travelling
» health-seminars offered by the Kienbaum-academy
» employees receive a reduction on membership-cards for fitness clubs

Fig. 3.12. Guideline Work-Life Balance

The external image as an employer has been established on a long-term basis as one of our company's eight goals and gets measured with the help of company rankings. The preservation and optimization of our company's internal culture is a permanent process in which

- Established and potential executives have to be supported and qualified.
- Successful teams have to be "welded together" (in particular when restructuring processes take place and with the help of external coaches).
- The results of employee surveys and 360-degree-feedbacks have to be documented in generally binding, division-specific activity plans.
- Symbolic experiences/ symbolic violations that have a negative impact have to be cleared.
- Transparency, regarding the situation of the company and the market has to be guaranteed through the continuous use of communication instruments.
- On a regular (cascaded) basis in monthly meetings of the single divisions, reviews and activity planning are discussed and organized.
- The communicated values and beliefs of our company become plausible and reliable by the exemplary behavior of our top-management.

Part II:

HRM as Administrative Expert

4 Human Resources Management in International Consulting Firms: Distinguishing Second and Third Wave Company Patterns

Michael Dickmann[1], Michael Graubner[2], and Ansgar Richter[2]

[1] Cranfield University, School of Management, UK
[2] European Business School, Schloss Reichartshausen, Germany

4.1 Introduction

The consulting industry is rapidly becoming a large and mature sector. Between 1995 and 2000 alone, the size of the global consulting market, measured by total revenues, has more than doubled, growing from $51 billion in 1995 to more than $110 billion in 2000 (Kennedy Information 2001: 35). Only in recent years has this development, at least temporarily, tapered off. With the growth of the industry, its importance from an economic point of view has increased, too. According to the European Federation of Management Consulting Associations (FEACO), management consulting revenues have risen as a percentage of European GDP on a yearly basis from 0.12% in 1994 to 0.48% in 2002 (FEACO 2002: 9). The fact that the comparable figure for the United States is around 0.70% suggests that there may be scope for further growth of the industry in Europe.

A second aspect of the economic relevance of the consulting sector lies in its function as an employment market. Focusing on Europe, the number of management consultants has grown from less than 100.000 in 1994 to approximately 300,000 in 2001/2002 (FEACO 2002: 8). Although the consulting market is fragmented in that there are a large number of small consulting firms, the large and medium-sized consulting firms dominate the market with a market share of more than 90% of revenues. These firms – the top 20 and the larger mid-sized firms – are almost exclusively international players in the full sense of the word: Not only do they export their services from one country to another, but they also have offices with local employees in several countries. It is on the employment and, therefore, the human resource management (HRM) practices of these international companies that we focus in this chapter. Whilst understanding the changing dynamics of the employment relationship in the consulting sector and drawing consequences for HR policies in consulting firms is of importance in its own right, it is equally relevant from the perspective of students and other groups of potential candidates and of non-consulting companies in the economy. Consulting firms serve as an increasingly important entrance point into formal employment relationships for high-calibre candidates from a variety of academic subjects and experience backgrounds (Ruef 2002). Therefore, consultancies shape the perspectives, expectations and skills of young professionals at a critical phase in their lives. In many cases, these people move on to form the managerial elites in business and public life. In addition, consulting firms often serve as trendsetters for other organizations in the economy. Therefore, the HR practices prevalent in the consulting industry exert an influence extending beyond the scope of consulting firms.

The structure of this chapter is as follows. In section two, we investigate the development of the consulting industry, and in particular the changing dynamics of the employment relationship in the leading players in the industry. We also take a look at the internationalization of the sector, which is one of the key factors that have affected employment relationships in the industry. Thereafter, in section three, we draw the implications from our earlier observations on the HR policies and practices in consulting organizations. We also compare the practices prevalent in consulting firms with those of multinational organizations in other industries. In the fourth section, we provide empirical evidence for our theses, using the results of an interview series we conducted with over 30 consulting firms, and casual evidence from public sources and own experience. Finally, we summarize our findings and provide hypotheses with regard to the further development of HR management in consulting firms.

4.2 The Development of the Consulting Industry: Dynamics of the Employment Relationship in Consulting and the Internationalization of the Industry

Consulting as a profession is a young industry. While managers of large-scale industrial companies have asked for the advice of outsiders such as accountants, financiers and engineers since the beginning of the industrialization in Great Britain in the late 18th century (Ferguson 2002) and during the 19th century in other countries, the emergence of management consulting as a distinct activity can only be dated back to the first two decades of the 20th century (for a brief overview see Wilkinson 1995). Broadly speaking, since then there have been three overlapping waves of consulting, distinguished by the type of services provided and the organizational features of the firms rendering these services (Kipping 2002; see Figure 4.1.).

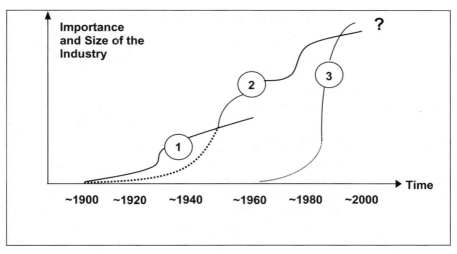

Fig. 4.1. The Three Waves of Management Consulting

The first wave of consulting began to emerge during the second decade of the 20th century. It was closely linked to the scientific management movement spearheaded by Frederick Taylor and others in the United States. The overall objective of these consulting services was to enhance the operational efficiency of clients. The consulting firms that emerged during this period and came to dominate the industry from the 1930s to the 1950s include the Bedaux consultancy and Harrington Emerson in the US, and the British Bedaux company, Urwick Orr, Production Engineering and Personnel Administration (PA Consulting) in the UK (Ferguson 2002). Although these companies carried out some projects in foreign countries, they did not set up international offices during that period. They were comparatively small organizations and their structures remained relatively undifferentiated during their heyday. The people working in these firms came mostly from a technical background, apart from a few trained in accountancy and administrative areas. Of importance to our chapter is the fact that training in many of these firms took place through the apprenticeship model, i.e. with junior consultants working alongside more senior consultants in order to learn from direct experience.

The second wave of consulting firms can be dated back to the 1950s. It is related to the rise in demand for a broader range of management consulting services (beyond efficiency-enhancing concepts) from American firms, many of which had been founded during earlier decades: Arthur D. Little, founded in 1886 as a provider of technical services such as chemical testing (see Kahn 1984), Booz Allen & Hamilton, set up in 1914 as a business survey firm, McKinsey & Company (founded in 1926), and others that emerged in their wake (e.g. A.T. Kearney, which split from McKinsey in 1946, the Boston Consulting Group founded by former ADL consultant Bruce Henderson, and so on). During the second wave, consulting firms are characterized by two features that are of particular importance for the present chapter: First, they internationalized rapidly to develop multinational, and even global organizations. For example, in addition to its manifold project-based operations in developing countries ADL set up its first European Office in Zurich in 1957. McKinsey opened its first office outside the US in London in 1959 (see Kipping 1999). Second, despite many differences, these rapidly growing firms developed common organizational features often classified as the professional partnership (P^2) model (Rose and Hinings 1999). These features include, among others, an ownership and governance structure distinctively different from other established international firms. The partners, as co-owners were both the key 'production personnel' and at the same time the managers of their firms (Greenwood, Hinings and Brown 1990). This means, as will be detailed below, that many aspects of human resource management are embedded into the structure of the firms belonging to this class, rather than being organized as a functionally separate human resource management unit (see Graubner and Richter 2003). The professional partnerships that emerged during the second wave of the development of the consulting industry embodied a particular model of human resource management, which spread rapidly across the globe as these firms expanded and set up international offices.

The third wave of consulting firms can be traced back to the beginning of the 1980s. It is characterized by new types of consulting firms with service offerings, organizational and economic models that differ markedly from the classical P^2 firms, many of which continued to exist in parallel. Attracted by the substantial margins in consulting and the prospect of cross-selling along the different stages of the value chain, combined with the fact the entry barriers in consulting are low, many companies in related professional service industries (accountancies, auditors, actuaries), as well as hard- and software providers in the IT industry, began to offer consulting services. In addition, an increasing number of small, specialized consulting service providers established themselves in particular functional niches of the consulting market (e.g. economic advisory services, pricing, M&A advice, industry-specific consulting services, corporate finance advisory, risk management, etc.). As a result, the third wave of consulting is fairly heterogeneous. The new consulting providers that emerged from the established accounting and IT firms, however, differ substantially in organizational structure and governance from the P^2 model. Powell, Brock and Hinings (1999) have characterized these as managed professional businesses (MPBs). The accounting and IT firms from which the new consultancies emerged were already internationally active (Aharoni 1999) and had established administrative structures. In addition, the scale of their operations was significantly larger than even the biggest P^2 firms. Therefore, these new consultancy arms of the old accountancy and IT firms were internationally active almost from their inception, not needing to build international networks from scratch. The historical development sketched above implies that this industry is characterized by a significant proportion of global firms, which not only export their services but also operate local offices in several countries. This situation is the result of an internationalization process that took place over a relatively short period of time, beginning roughly half a century ago. It was kick-started by 'second wave' consultancies during the 1950s. These firms developed into global organizations mainly through organic growth by setting up offices in new locations with experienced consultants from other locations, complemented over time by local staff. However, on a number of occasions the acquisition of a local consultancy has been used as an entry mode into new markets. For example, in 1991 Roland Berger & Partners acquired the Japanese consulting firm Vaubel & Partners in order to enter the Japanese market (Richter 2003). Similarly, in 2000 Mercer merged with the Mexican company Análisis y Desarrollo de Proyectos (ADP). During the 1980s, 'third wave' consultancies joined the competition. These firms, however, started from different base conditions than their older 'second wave' peers. In many cases they were able to use existing office locations to start local consulting businesses as an extension to their original service lines in accounting, legal or IT. Examples of this trend include Andersen Consulting (now Accenture) from its parent Arthur Andersen, IBM, KPMG, Oracle, Price Waterhouse and Coopers & Lybrand (later merged into PricewaterhouseCoopers whose consulting arm was recently acquired by IBM).

The geographic expansion of consulting services is characterized by distinct periods. In the late 1950s and early 1960s, the first American consulting firms began to enter Western Europe as the initial step on their way abroad. Central and South America as well as Japan became the focus of activities during the 1970s. Following the fall of the socialist system, offices in Eastern Europe were established, often as preliminary satellites from Western Europe. The last decade of the 20th century also witnessed an enormous expansion of consulting activities into South-East Asia. As a result, with the exception of Africa, few regions in the world have been left untouched by the internationalization of the consulting industry. The following table shows which country offices some leading consultancies established during the periods discussed. Needless to say, all of these firms have continued to open further offices in these areas in the following decades. Three main driving forces behind the internationalization of second wave consulting firms can be identified: First and foremost, the existence of promising business opportunities abroad. Consulting basically followed general economic and political developments. While during the 1950s numerous well-established consulting firms including Arthur D. Little, A.T. Kearney, Booz Allen Hamilton and McKinsey had to compete for business in the U.S., the consulting markets outside North America were virtually untapped. With the general economic development of Western Europe after World War II, the development of South America during the 1970s and 1980s, the adoption of capitalist market systems in Eastern Europe following the collapse of the socialist system and the "Asian decade" of the 1990s, demand for consulting services began to rise. At the same time, clients were economically able to afford consultants' fees and to exploit the value generated by their work across large enough output runs. A second reason, closely related to the first one, consists of the limits to further growth in established markets, which forced consulting firms to look for opportunities abroad. As local or regional consulting markets mature, competition among different players becomes more intense. As a result, in order to gain market share firms need to differentiate themselves from their competitors either on the basis of quality, which is hard as plenty of high-quality providers exist, or on the basis of price, therefore accepting lower margins.

In foreign markets characterized by fewer players and lower competition, the need for heads-on competition with other players is more limited.

Table 4.1. Geographic Expansion of Leading 'Second Wave' Consulting Firms

Consulting Firm (year of foundation)	Geographic Expansion			
	Western Europe (1960s)	Central and South America, Japan (1970s)	Eastern Europe (1990s)	East Asia (1990s)
A.T. Kearney (1946)	1964 Duesseldorf 1967 London 1967 Paris 1968 Milan	1972 Tokyo	1992 Prague 1995 Warsaw 1996 Moscow 1998 Istanbul 1999 Budapest	1988 Singapore 1992 Hong Kong 1995 Beijing, Seoul 1996 Kuala Lumpur 1997 New Delhi 1997 Jakarta 1999 Bangkok
Boston Consulting Group (1963)	1970 London	1966 Tokyo	1994 Moscow 1997 Warsaw 1997 Budapest	1991 Hong Kong 1992 Kuala Lumpur 1993 Shanghai 1994 Bangkok, Seoul 1995 Jakarta 1995 Singapore 1996 Mumbai
McKinsey (1926)	1959 London 1964 Duesseldorf 1964 Amsterdam 1964 Paris 1966 Zurich	1970 Mexico City 1971 Tokyo 1974 Caracas 1975 Sao Paulo	1993 Prague 1993 Warsaw 1995 Moscow 1997 Budapest	1991 Seoul 1993 Delhi 1995 Jakarta, Beijing 1997 Bangkok 1997 Kuala Lumpur 1997 Singapore
Roland Berger (1967)	1967 Munich 1969 Milan	1976 Sao Paulo	1991 Moscow 1992 Bucarest 1993 Prague 1993 Riga 1994 Kiev 1997 Budapest 2000 Warsaw	1995 Beijing

Roland Berger – today, Germany's second biggest management consulting firm with an estimated 4.3% market share after McKinsey with 8.4% (Lünendonk 2002) – quickly turned abroad after having established itself in its home market. The firm opened an office in Sao Paulo in 1976, long before many other players discovered the potential of the South American market. Similarly, it moved strongly into the Eastern European market immediately following the opening of the borders and the removal of institutional restrictions at the beginning of the 1990s (Richter 2003). The third force behind the internationalization trends described above are the differences in factor prices. Cost pressures in the industry have caused firms to move not directly client-related activities such as support functions, to low-cost regions such as India. 'Third wave' consulting firms in particular, with their large overhead staffs, participated in this trend. For example, Sapient today employs more than half of its staff in India (King 2003). Similarly, Accenture runs large parts of its back-office operations, including programming activities, from India. 'Second wave' consultancies also followed suit. McKinsey and A.T. Kearney have moved services like graphics production, publishing, and information research to places such as Madras and New Delhi. As a result of these developments, many large consulting firms obtain the majority of their revenues from 'foreign' operations and count more 'foreigners' among their consulting staff than people from those countries in which the firms were originally founded. Similarly, their leadership has become highly international (see Table 4.2.).

However, it is not just the importance of foreign operations and the national diversity of consulting staff that have shaped approaches to international personnel management within P^2 and MPB firms. Compared to other large multinational firms, the organizational structure and governance characteristics of 'second wave' professional partnerships have a distinct effect on their human resource management practices. Some key elements include:

- Professional training and internal socialization of members through the 'apprenticeship model', with younger firm members working alongside more senior members in order to learn their trade.
- Promotion and advancement on the basis of professional merit (which, as Perkin 2002 shows with respect to the UK, was rooted in the 'professional ideal' that emerged during the late 19th and early 20th and favored individual contribution rather than inherited status as the basis for one's position in society; see also Perkin 1996, pp. xi-xviii).
- Frequent performance evaluation on a continuous basis, combined with repeated feedback and mentoring.

Table 4.2. Degree of Internationalization of Leading Consulting Firms

Consulting Firm	Country of Origin	Name and Nationality of Global Leader	Total Number of Consultants	Share of Foreign Consultants	Total Revenues	Share of Foreign Revenues
Accenture	USA	Joe Forehand (American)	ca. 63.000	> 50%	11.500m USD	> 50%
Arthur D. Little (1999 figures)	USA	Lorenzo Lamadrid (American with Cuban family origins)	2.200	70%	690m USD	> 60%
A.T. Kearney	USA	Dietmar Ostermann (German)	2.600	> 60%	1.100m USD	ca. 55%
Boston Consulting Group	USA	Hans-Paul Bürkner (German)	2.700	77%	1.050m USD	ca. 65%
Booz Allen Hamilton	USA	Ralph Shrader (American)	10.500	ca. 25%	2.300m USD	ca. 25%
McKinsey	USA	Ian Davis (British)	7.200	ca. 75%	3.300m USD	ca. 70%
Roland Berger	Germany	Burkhard Schwenker (German)	1.200	59%	511m EUR	ca. 40%

Sources: Alpha Publications (2002); Firm websites; Kennedy Information (2001); Landriscina (2002); Vault (2003)

As this list indicates, in firms that conformed – or continue to conform – to a greater or lesser degree to the P^2 model, many aspects of human resource management differ from those of multinational companies in other sectors. Consultancies that use the P^2 model tend to have more fluid and frequent interaction between professionals and their superiors. As many human resource development, appraisal and promotion processes are anchored to project work, HRM is more deeply embedded into the structure and the core (value adding) functions of the firms (Graubner and Richter 2003). Therefore, the HR departments of professional partnerships tend to be relatively small. In sum, the professional partnerships that emerged during the second wave of the development of the consulting industry embodied a particular model of human resource management, which differed strongly from that of established MNCs. In comparison, employment in the predominantly third wave MPB consulting firms also followed rather different rules than was the case in P^2 firms: With larger numbers of employees, more extensive hierarchies and significantly higher leverage ratios (Maister 1993), training through direct observation and experience as in the apprenticeship model needed to be replaced by more formal mechanisms. The partnership model with its incentive mechanisms for advancement and promotion was replaced, in many cases, by external share ownership. Overall, MPB firms were, and continue to be, characterized by more standard employment relationships than can be found in other service industries such as banking and insurance. As a function, human resource management in these organizations tends to be the prerogative of specialized HR staff, rather than the professional duty of consultants.

Which of these models will prevail in the long run will not be discussed in the present chapter. It is important to note, however, that as a result of the historical development of the consulting industry, different employment models co-exist in the market today. This heterogeneity in employment models results in a wide variety of human resource management practices and policies across different consulting firms, as will be evident from sections three and four below.

4.3 Implications for Human Resource Management in Consulting Firms

The first two sections of this chapter have provided an overview of the historical development and internationalization of consulting firms. It was argued that the largest and most global players in the industry belonged to second and third wave firms. These consultancies display two key organizational forms and government approaches. The P^2 model is associated with organic human resource management practices embedded in the structure of the organization. In contrast, the approach to human resource management in the MPB model is seen to conform more to that of multinational corporations (MNCs) operating in other service industries. The question arises, therefore, as to how these differences manifest themselves in individual HRM strategies, policies and practices. Since other chapters in this book cover a range of personnel management aspects in consulting firms, we will focus in particular on issues associated with *international* HRM (IHRM). This section outlines the different human resource approaches of typical 'second wave' and 'third wave' consultancies and compares them with those of multinational organizations.

Identifying a "typical" MNC for purposes of comparison is not an easy task since international HR strategies, structures and processes vary significantly across globally operating firms. In their seminal contribution, Bartlett and Ghoshal (1989) suggest that four international configurations of MNCs exist: the multidomestic, global, international and transnational firm. Bartlett and Ghoshal maintain that the competitive advantage of the multidomestic firm lies in its local responsiveness. The global company's strength is seen as efficiency, while the hallmark of an international firm is innovation. Only the transnational firm is able to overcome the "global – local" dilemma of tensions between local differentiation (the need to respond to local interests) and integration (the desire to achieve global efficiency). At the same time, the transnational organization is seen to be highly innovative. The key to gaining competitive advantage among multinational firms is increasingly seen in the quality of human resource management (Tregaskis et al 2001; Bartlett and Ghoshal 1989:71). Given this 'transnational ideal type', it is useful to outline transnational HRM in MNCs. We will use the results of a range of studies on Bartlett and Ghoshal's typology (Harzing 2000 for a review). In terms of international HRM, only MNCs that pursue moderately transnational approaches have been identified (Dickmann 2003 1999). These HRM configurations will be assessed and contrasted with the HRM structures, strategies and processes consultancy firms have created.

One key influence shaping the international HR configuration of consultancies is that many of these firms are organized as partnerships. The discussion above showed that the organizational form and governance type would typically be replicated in the international expansion drive of consultancies due to perceived advantages of entrepreneurship and local knowledge. One of the effects in consulting partnerships is a strong national centre of power and profit responsibility, combined with large degrees of managerial autonomy, which may contribute to distinct national approaches to personnel management. Brewster (1995) identifies distinctive forms of national HRM approaches by the degree of centralization and strategic orientation. He argues that some countries employ centralized mechanistic - legalistic HRM, concentrating on operative tasks (e.g. Italy, Belgium, Germany). In other national environments, HR managers are more likely to pursue a political approach where HR strategies are important and much of the HR development and day-to-day work is centralized (e.g. UK, Ireland, Spain). Other countries use integrated HRM where the function is strategically oriented and much of the HR delivery work is decentralized (Sweden, Switzerland, Norway). Lastly, he identifies regions where there is a tendency to have little strategic orientation and a high degree of decentralization (Netherlands, Denmark). Thus for consulting firms with large local degrees of freedom and a range of nationally diverse HR approaches an international coordination of HR strategies and instruments is difficult.

Table 4.3. Comparison of IHRM Principles and Practices between Moderately Transnational MNCs, Typical 'Second Wave', and 'Third Wave' Consultancies

Moderately Transnational MNCs	Typical 'Second Wave' Consultancies	Typical 'Third Wave' Consultancies
1. General International HRM Principles and Objectives		
Overall objectives, guidelines and competencies. Explicit and detailed; e.g. differentiated targets and rules for various management levels and sub-functions such as expatriation, remuneration, pensions, health & safety, etc.	Only a few but fundamental 'professional principles' linked to an overarching vision/mission. Low degree of differentiation between different seniority levels except for the partner – non-partner distinction; few explicit HRM policies	Overarching principles and competencies. Some explicit and detailed objectives in particular for different functional specialties/job categories (e.g. different policies for programmers and strategy consultants)
Medium to high degree of heterogeneity in HRM principles across different countries/regions	Similar/identical principles apply across countries/regions, often rooted in 'one firm concepts'	Medium to high degree of heterogeneity in HRM principles across different countries/regions
2. Individual HRM Policies and Practices		
2a. Recruitment and Selection		
Hiring from a broad range of good schools	Hiring from a select few 'top schools'	Hiring from a medium range of very good and top schools
Focus on well-defined, often technical or commercial skills	Focus on a broad range of general skills, ideally combined with some business training (e.g. MBA)	Preference for strong commercial or technological over general skills
Focus on a broad range of candidates from college graduates to experienced hires	Preference for candidates with postgraduate qualifications	Focus on graduate and some postgraduate candidates
Use of both personal interviews and standardized assessment centers, but with greater emphasis on the latter	Recruitment and selection largely based on personal interaction (case interviews, presentations, etc.), potentially complemented by some formal tests	Recruitment and selection based on both personal interviews and assessment center techniques
Process run primarily by internal or external HR specialists	Process run primarily by consultants, with support from HR staff	Process jointly run by professionals and specialized HR staff
International recruitment concentrates on few high potentials	International recruitment may include many professional staff	International recruitment may include many professional staff
2b. Training and Development		
Acquisition of specific knowledge important objective of formal training courses	Training primarily through direct observation and experience	Training through both on-the-job experience and formal coursework
Emphasis in formal training courses on relatively technical/ specialized skills, complemented by general managerial skills	Emphasis in formal courses strongly on professional and interpersonal skills, complemented by analytical skills	Emphasis in formal courses on analytical, managerial and technical skills (e.g. programming languages), depending on job specification
Often relatively structured training programs at junior levels, becoming less structured at progressively more senior levels	Highly structured training programmers at all career levels	Highly structured training programmers in particular up to project manager level; slightly less so at more senior levels

Table 4.3. (cont.)

Moderately Transnational MNCs	Typical 'Second Wave' Consultancies	Typical 'Third Wave' Consultancies
2c. Performance Management		
Based primarily on a combination of global competencies and achievement of predominantly person-specific targets	Based primarily on global competencies and the achievement of general project-oriented targets	Based on global competencies and the achievement of a mix of person-specific and project-oriented targets
Similar processes used globally across managers at any particular level	Same processes used globally across consultants at any particular level	Same processes used globally across consultants at any particular level
Medium frequency of feedback	High frequency of feedback; 360 degree feedback schemes often used; strong emphasis on behavioral aspects	Medium to high frequency of feedback; higher importance of specific skills over personality/behavioral aspects in feedback schemes
Upward feedback by juniors desired, but often with little importance in terms of promotion/advancement decisions	Upward feedback and evaluation by juniors important part of performance metrics for seniors	International staffing opportunities available for high performers, but handled restrictively. Upward feedback by juniors often part of performance metrics for seniors, but with limited weight as compared to other performance indicators
2d. Career Management		
Elaborate long-term career plans and programmers. Normally choice of different career paths possible (top management, middle management, specialists). Progression often underpinned by formal HR instruments such as internal assessment centers (ACs)	Long-term career possible (but no long-term commitment from career starters expected). Little choice of different career paths: "Up-or-out" principle. Progression depends on 360 degree assessments – few formal HR instruments used	Elaborate long-term career plans and programs. Some choice of different career paths possible – sometimes "grow-or-go" principle. Progression sometimes underpinned by formal HR instruments such as internal ACs
Sophisticated international assignment/rotation programs, often early in career; opportunities for international assignments also for senior management	International staffing upon individual demand, primarily on short-term project basis or for temporary office transfers; opportunities available at all levels	International staffing opportunities upon individual demand available for most positions (but may be subject to local interests overruling global perspective)
International assignments actively supported by specialized HR staff	International assignments supported by HR staff on a case-by-case basis (if go-ahead is given by senior decision-making level)	International assignments supported by HR staff on a case-by-case basis (often depending on target country and relationship with local management)
2e. Reward Systems		
Primarily on a local (country-by-country) basis; some degree of international standardization for senior management and expats	Common point of reference for reward levels in those firms that operate a global profit pool, although salary levels in particular at junior levels are adjusted by differences in living costs and income/earnings levels in different countries; some commonalties but also some variance in benefit levels across countries (e.g. car policies)	Primarily on a local (country-by-country) basis; some degree of international standardization for senior consultants

Table 4.3. (cont.)

Moderately Transnational MNCs	Typical 'Second Wave' Consultancies	Typical 'Third Wave' Consultancies
3. International HR Communication and Coordination		
3a. HR Communication: Direction, Intensity, and Content		
Multidirectional and high intensity: Cross-national exchange of plans, ideas, information on instruments, implementation experience and results relating to new projects and ongoing HR work	Multidirectional and high intensity: Intensive communication: international exchange of plans, ideas, concerns, experiences, etc.; predominantly restricted to new, overarching HR projects (global meetings/task forces on "war for talent")	Multidirectional and moderate intensity: Intensive communication: international exchange of plans, ideas, concerns, experiences, etc.; predominantly restricted to new, overarching HR projects
3b. HR Coordination: Administrative, Personal and Social		
Administrative: Some worldwide HR planning and reporting; to some extent publicly communicated (e.g. through annual reports, etc.)	Administrative: Relatively little worldwide HR planning and reporting; key figures reported at partner meetings	Administrative: Relatively little worldwide HR planning and reporting; key figures reported publicly as legally required
Personal and social: Frequent contacts incl. occasional direct meetings among international HR staff	Personal and social: Some contact among international HR staff to the extent that differentiated HR functions exist; interactions relatively informal	Personal and social: Contact among international HR staff on an as-needed basis

We shall discuss these issues in more depth below. First, we focus on the international integration of general HR strategies, principles and objectives. Going beyond the traditional strategy and structure assessments (Harzing 2000) we will then concentrate on tangible practices of international HRM, including recruitment and selection, training and development, career management, performance management and rewards. Third, since innovation is of key importance in knowledge intensive firms we will focus on communication patterns (Wolf 1997) and coordination mechanisms (Ferner 2000) in IHRM. Table 4.3. contrasts the typical IHRM approach of a moderately transnational MNC, albeit simplified, with those of typical 'second' and 'third wave' consulting companies. This will allow us to assess and interpret the differences between the two waves of professional service firms.

The degree of international integration of *General HRM Principles and Objectives* gives a first indication of the nature of international HRM and points to the power distribution between the worldwide head office and local operations. Dickmann (1999) outlines that many German MNCs standardize some principles and objectives governing their IHRM. They have leadership guidelines, key management competencies and expatriation policies that are integrated on a worldwide basis. Some of these firms even have policies regarding the 'comparability of upper management rewards'. Moreover, it is interesting to note that many companies have international social or health objectives. These include striving for worldwide employment security, good working conditions, company pensions and health insurance. Amongst the more unusual elements are the "introduction of a

German cultural element" (Commerzbank) or the "cooperation with employee representatives" (Siemens). Overall, in transnational MNCs there is an extensive range of explicit IHRM principles and objectives. Nevertheless, certain practices such as remuneration or pensions may vary noticeably. There are some parallels to 'third wave' consulting firms in that leadership principles, mission statements and key competencies tend to be internationally integrated and that relatively explicit and detailed rules – in particular for different functions and job categories – exist. However, the extent of this integration may be moderated by the strong power position of local partners. For example, Baer and Stoll (1999: 200) outline the 'federal' structure of KPMG, which provides 'space for setting particular strategic focal points'. As with the transnational firms outside the professional service sector, the HR objectives and actual practices tend to be adapted to local or regional context factors and pressures. Typical 'second wave' consultancies, in contrast, differ significantly from the other two types of organizations discussed here. They have only few overarching professional principles which apply globally. Because there are fewer and less detailed HR objectives and rules, there is less need for local adaptation. Apart from the partner / non-partner distinction, all professional staff are essentially treated according to these global principles. These principles also tend to be anchored in the professional structure of the organization concerned. In contrast, 'third wave' consultancies and transnational corporations have not only globally integrated principles, but also more explicit and detailed objectives and rules. This more specific and less organic form of HRM requires a greater frequency of exceptions to rules and a higher degree of local adaptation. The origin of global HR principles and objectives (e.g. 'war for talent' activities) can generally be traced back to head office initiatives, although the actual formulation of leadership principles, for example, is more likely to be carried out by the (international) partners in both types of consulting firms. This may be an indication of the higher autonomy and greater power of local operations. The litmus test for global coordination, however, does not consist of the espoused principles, but of the international HRM instruments and processes used in the actual day-to-day operations.

For transnational organizations, *International Recruitment and Selection* implies standardization across borders of hiring criteria (focusing on well-defined, often technical and commercial competencies) for senior management and high potentials. Typically, graduates from good business schools and universities' accountancy and engineering departments constitute the key target group, and their selection is based on both a series of interviews and the results of a formal assessment center led by internal and external HR specialists. Overall, relatively few candidates – primarily those earmarked for an accelerated career – are selected in this way. In contrast, consulting firms seek many entry-level candidates from a relatively small set of leading business schools and universities. As application numbers in the sector can be very high, they also often rely on personal recommendations. For example, Accenture (then Andersen Consulting) had three million applications worldwide in 1998 (Gordon 1999). In that year, the firm recruited 15,000 new consultants based on the worldwide qualities of diligence, drive, 'brains' and teamwork. Within the consulting sector, 'third wave' firms and large transnational corporations show the most similarities. Both have a preference for strong commercial or technological skill sets, use similar selection techniques (interviews and formal assessment center methods) and, subsequently, have established recruitment processes in which HR specialists play an important role. In contrast, 'second wave' consultancies differ significantly from both MNCs and 'third wave' firms. Their recruitment drives concentrate on a few select 'top' schools, and emphasize general skills. Moreover, the selection methods that they use emphasize the importance of informal processes and behavioral aspects. Casse (1994) argues that traditional models of matching people to jobs do not apply in the context of knowledge-intensive firms. The propensity to use consulting staff rather than HR specialists, the widespread practice that all interviewers must agree on making a job offer to a particular candidate, and the moderate use of assessment centers all reflect a strong desire for person-organization fit. A side effect of large application numbers and the informal selection process might be that recruitment in 'second wave' consultancies is dominated by subjectivity and rejection (Robertson and O'Malley Hammersley 2000). The recruitment and selection methods employed by 'second wave' consultancies are, again, deeply embedded in the structure and the fabric of the 'classical' professional partnership model. Firms of this type emphasize the development of strong and shared organizational cultures that allow people to think and act within particular parameters (Handy 1995). The networking and training activities of 'second wave' consultancies also reflect these aspects.

Major consultancies tend to have extensive, internal *Training Programs* some of which are mandatory, whereas others can be booked by individual consultants as time permits. A Norwegian study showed the effects of training in consultancies to be significant (Sjøholt 1999). Effective knowledge management and individual, group and organizational learning are critical to the commercial success of consultancies. Ideally, consulting firms are "organization(s) peopled by self-developers" (Stewart 1999: 177). In most 'second wave' consulting firms training programs are largely standardized internationally and delivered by professional staff, i.e. consultants. The emphasis in formal courses is on professional and interpersonal skills, which are complemented by analytical skills. Most development takes place on projects and through the interaction with senior professionals, internal mentors and coaches. There is also a high degree of international standardization of training in most 'third wave' consultancies. These firms stress technical, analytical and managerial content in their training programs. The seminars are often delivered not only by internal experts but also by external specialists. Many companies have also developed international training and support mechanisms for global assignees. These policies and practices place the 'third wave' consulting firms in the vicinity of the training approaches prevalent in transnational firms. Multinational corporations also emphasize relatively technical and managerial skills in their formal training courses, which are delivered by teams of internal and external experts. Their international management training, however, is far more extensive and covers a large range of technical, managerial and cross-cultural training (Dickmann 1997). These MNCs have created systems to support the international development of their 'high potentials'. An example is the widespread use of cross-national project work – sometimes embedded in international management programs – aimed at raising cultural awareness. International development initiatives also serve another function of building networks across borders, given that other opportunities for international activities outside regular rotation programs and the like are rare. The key differences in training and development relate to the target groups, to the content and the international dimension. In both 'second' and 'third wave' consultancies, the target group for training programs comprises all professional staff, while MNCs distinguish more clearly between management and general staff. Specific knowledge transmission is more important in MNCs and 'third wave' consulting firms, while 'second wave' consultancies stress more generic skills. In essence, however, very little training that is specifically tailored to international assignments is available. Part of the reason might be the belief that the most valuable learning opportunities arise in the context of active project work and from one's own team members and superiors. This contrasts with the more formal and long-term system of international development found in many multinational enterprises. However, the formality of development programs in MNCs does not necessarily imply a lack of pragmatism or applicability. Participants in such training programs may often present the results of their projects to board members and other senior staff, thereby raising the participants' exposure and even their career prospects.

Career Management in MNCs can be highly sophisticated. Many transnational corporations have elaborate long-term career plans and programs. Progression takes place in relation to appraisals and is often underpinned by formal HR instruments (such as capability analyses and assessment centers). Normally, a full range of different career paths is available. For example, the outcome of the 'AC Management' at Volkswagen entails recommendations for careers at top management level, middle management level or in specialist functions. This procedure contrasts substantially with many 'second wave' consultancies. In these firms, career progression means rising through the internal hierarchy to become a partner. While progression is strongly related to so-called 360-degree appraisals, additional, formal HR instruments do not underpin these. In effect, little long-term career planning for individuals is conducted, as only one dominant career path is available. The effect is an "up or out" principle that applies to most consultants (with a few exceptions for knowledge specialists). 'Third wave' consulting firms' approaches to career management fall between the two poles of the other two types of organizations discussed here. In 'third wave' consultancies there is more long-term career planning. Promotion decisions are sometimes underpinned by the use of formal HR instruments. In essence, a principle of "grow or go" is operated which provides greater scope for specialist, non-leadership careers than is the case in 'second wave' consultancies. Of particular interest for this chapter are the international dimensions of career management. MNCs employ a large range of international assignment forms: So-called 'frequent flyers', short and long-term assignees, international commuters and traditional career expatriates. In many instances, these international assignments, regardless of their specific length or form, serve developmental or head office - subsidiary coordination purposes. Moreover, international assignees usually benefit from highly developed support structures. These may range from pre-departure preparation for assignees and spouses to repatriation help and the guarantee of an "adequate" position upon return. In comparison, most projects in 'second' and 'third wave' consultancies – even though they may have an international scope – are carried out by the local offices that tend to prefer local staffing if the specific competencies are available. Thus, the majority of international staffing that occurs is needs-driven and takes place through international commuting or short-term assignments for a specific project. In addition, there are opportunities for becoming a medium-term expatriate in consultancies. However, as consulting is a fast-paced business with a high turnover of staff due to the principles of 'up or out' respectively 'grow or go' discussed above, long-term expatriation often makes little sense beyond the development or motivation of individual high performers; the preferred arrangement in these instances is the permanent office transfer. In any case, arrangements such as these require support by senior decision-makers. In summary, both the objective and the mechanisms of international career management differ substantially between MNCs and consulting firms. MNCs use international assignments and other forms of global work to develop future 'leaders' or as means for social control and coordination of subsidiaries. Consultancies, which emphasize a strong common culture and entrepreneurship, use international assignments in a more ad-hoc, client needs-driven way.

The *Performance Management Processes* of 'second wave' consulting firms tend to emphasize project-related targets, paired with a focus on global competencies (such as general client management skills). These firms use highly standardized appraisal processes that encompass all their consultants, including both senior and junior professionals. Often, similar appraisal systems are also applied to the support staff. So-called '360 degree feedback systems' with a strong emphasis on behavioral aspects are widely employed and appraisals are generally carried out after each project. Paramount in these feedback systems is the quality of the relationships with peers, partners, and clients. This contrasts sharply with the performance management systems prevalent in many transnational corporations. Appraisals in these organizations predominantly centre on person-specific targets, which may differ widely according to the function and context of the job concerned. Moreover, the frequency of feedback is generally lower and performance management is less standardized across countries. The performance systems in place embrace a lower proportion of employees, and the use of '360 degree feedback' systems is often restricted to particular management levels. 'Third wave' consultancies occupy a hybrid position between the other two organizational types. They have a greater mix of person-specific and project-oriented targets than either of them. Furthermore, they place a higher value on the acquisition of specific skills over personality/behavioral aspects as compared to their 'second wave' competitors. In comparison with MNCs they tend to have more frequent feedback rounds and use upward evaluations by juniors more often. The performance management approaches of the two types of consulting firms differ mainly in their core areas of interest. In 'second wave' consultancies, appraisals are geared to behavioral and personality aspects, which are of general use for a large range of projects. The attention of these appraisals is focused on generic competencies. 'Third wave' consulting firms, in contrast, seek to strike a more even balance between generic competencies and person-specific skills.

Both MNCs and consulting firms tend to have essentially localized *Reward Systems* and pay levels, sometimes based on a worldwide system of job evaluations. Commonly, only senior management (and in most MNCs, expatriates) may have some element of international reward standardization. The strongest international integration can be found at board level in MNCs and in those consulting firms that operate a global profit pool. This confirms that pay levels and other benefits are largely localized and that most firms are interested in maintaining their freedom to adjust pay levels to market conditions. No stringent link could, thus, be found between the different organizational forms and international compensation systems. However, the organizational structure and governance had strong implications for international HR coordination and communication.

The creation and diffusion of know-how, skills and new ideas is paramount for the survival of knowledge-intensive firms (Asakawa and Lehrer 2003). Innovation is positively related to the application of new human resource practices (Laursen and Mahnke 2001). Many factors that are influenced by HRM systems and practices, such as communication, visits and meetings, can facilitate international knowledge transfer (Bresman et al 1999). Innovation in international HRM, therefore, benefits from intensive *communication about new HR practices* as well as coordination to increase the likelihood of their acceptance and implementation. Gupta and Govindarajan (1991) have shown that reciprocal information flows dominate in multinational companies. Looking at the direction of formal and informal cross-national communication, the intensity of information exchange and the content of the interactions, it is likely that international HRM is characterized by multidirectional, highly intensive communication patterns. HR specialists in typical transnational corporations frequently exchange HR plans, ideas, details on personnel instruments, implementation experiences and results (Dickmann 1999). To promote the communication flow, they use international forums, work groups and other means to facilitate contact. In comparison, 'second wave' consulting firms rely far less on HR specialists for international communication. Many HR suggestions are developed by consultants themselves who are involved in certain HR initiatives such as staffing or personnel management (e.g. recruitment). While particular initiatives, such as 'war for talent' programs or attempts to raise the proportion of women in consulting can lead to intense communication among consultants and HR staff, these issues are the exception rather than the rule. International HR communication about HR topics that are not currently 'en vogue' or considered to be of strategic significance is infrequent and characterized by low intensity. In contrast, key international HR information exchanges in 'third wave' consultancies are the responsibility of specialized HR staff. This reflects the stronger role and higher importance of specialized HR departments than is the case in 'second wave' firms. Nevertheless, there are two important differences in communication type between 'third wave' consulting firms and transnational corporations. First, the range of HR areas to integrate and, therefore, to discuss on an international basis, is far more restricted due to the greater local autonomy of national operations. Second, the most important HR ideas, such as suggestions to modify key competencies or leadership principles, and results are communicated and discussed among partners. Contrasting 'second' and 'third wave' consulting firms, it emerges that while the direction, intensity and content of international HR communication may be similar, the methods employed are markedly different. 'Second wave' consulting firms define HRM essentially as the work of professional consultants and use HR staff mostly as administrative backup. These consultants concentrate on core issues in international HRM, interact closely and develop new approaches, e.g. in recruiting practices. 'Third wave' consultancies have more HR specialists who communicate globally in the context of important HR projects and develop proposals, which would then be championed, discussed and decided upon among the partners. Thus while HRM is effectively a strategic support function in 'third wave' consultancies, it may be seen as a set of routine, yet strategic tasks for professionals in 'second wave' firms.

The diffusion of new HR ideas is also dependent on formal and informal means of control and power. Ferner (2000) distinguishes between *Bureaucratic, Social* and *Personal Coordination.* Bureaucratic coordination, termed here 'administrative coordination', is based on a framework of formal roles and procedures that are monitored and sanctioned. The planning and reporting of key HR budgets and initiatives between the head office and the subsidiaries falls into the realm of administrative coordination. Direct close supervision determines personal control. In IHRM, this is expressed by the relationship between key international HR managers and their counterparts at subsidiary level. Raising the commitment to the values and goals of the firm, internationally exerts social coordination. Means to increase social coordination within the realm of HRM include international management development, cross-national teamwork as well as international rotation of HR specialists. Ferner outlines that all three coordination mechanisms are mutually supportive, although trade-offs among them may occur in particular situations. Today, most transnational corporations employ standard instruments for worldwide HR planning and reporting of key figures. However, rather than relying exclusively on administrative control, they also often have an interest in the social coordination that is promoted by international management development programs for HR specialists and multi-directional exchange of HR managers across borders. Social coordination is most likely underpinned by personal control in the form of visits and frequent contacts between HR 'line managers' and their local counterparts. Due to the regional structure of consulting firms organized as partnerships, in terms of administrative control there is little worldwide HR planning and reporting. Moreover, there is little personal and social coordination of HR management within most 'second wave' consultancies. Key visits and contacts across borders are conducted by consultants in HR project groups and there are few international management training or expatriation programs for HR specialists. This practice is consistent with the fact that most HR staff in these firms have an administrative focus. In this respect, they differ from their counterparts in many 'third wave' consulting firms where HR managers have more of a specialist role. In these firms, HR specialists may visit foreign operations or work in important functions on cross-national HR projects. Coordination activities are less pronounced within HR management in 'second' or 'third wave' consulting firms as compared to MNCs. However, while 'second wave' consultancies use consulting professionals to shape important HR projects, 'third wave' firms rely to a greater extent on functional HR experts.

Overall, the differences between the approaches to IHRM in transnational corporations and global consulting firms are considerable. Consultancies have less formalized international HR systems and instruments, the onus for an international career lies primarily with the individual, and there is less HR-internal international communication and coordination. On the other hand, those international HR approaches that do exist apply to a higher proportion of total staff. Moreover, international HR learning is not the exclusive domain of specialists. It may be done by non-HR specialists on assignments with global clients, who have a long history of HR management and large foreign operations. In 'second wave' consultancies, in particular, such learning may be converted into innovation.

Our discussion has also pointed to significant differences between 'second wave' consultancies organized along the 'classical' professional partnership model, and 'third wave' firms organized as managed professional businesses. The latter typically have more established, differentiated international HRM systems, and in that respect are similar to many MNCs. Their HR configurations are characterized by relatively explicit and detailed HRM principles and objectives, greater importance of HR specialists and formal instruments in recruitment, in selection and career management. In these firms the person-job fit also tends to be of greater importance than is the case in 'second wave' firms. This can be seen in their selection criteria, training contents and performance management systems. The organic HR approach of 'classical second wave' consultancies differs significantly from this pattern. Professional consultants, rather than HR specialists, typically carry out most HR activities. Human resource management in these firms is guided by a few, but overarching professional principles. Less formal instruments are used, which could lead to a higher degree of subjectivity in activities such as selection or career management. 'Second wave' firms tend to emphasize general behavioral skills, whereas other types of consulting firms place more emphasis on specific managerial or technical competencies. The focus of 'second wave' consultancies on behavior and personality is not only apparent in staffing, training and development, but also in the great importance placed on aspects of person-organization fit in the recruitment process. In effect, these consulting firms are looking for cultural fit and general capabilities that enable them to assign individuals flexibly. One of these flexible assignments might be an HR-related task! The organizational structures of 'second wave' consulting firms and their knowledge-intensive services rendered by highly educated professionals means that these firms need to take more organic approaches to human resource management. Laursen and Mahnke's (2001) work on HR practices indicates that knowledge-intensive firms which cannot rely on standardization of input, behavior, jobs and output, apply work practices associated with organic structures. Therefore, the HR functions of these firms are embedded into the fabric of their professional activities. The concentration of efforts to create a global „common culture" results in the high degree of focus, commitment and flexibility that consulting firms strive for.

In this section we have presented arguments about the pattern of national and international human resource management in 'second wave' and 'third wave' consulting firms. We have outlined important differences in HR strategies, policies and practices between these two types of firms and contrasted them with those of transnational firms. In this context we have drawn a number of inferences, principally related to the different organizational structures and corporate governance models of classical professional partnerships and managed professional businesses. The following section presents some findings from a large-scale qualitative study on consultancies which refine these insights.

3.4 HRM in International Consulting Firms: A Look at the Evidence

In the previous sections we have argued that, broadly speaking, two types of large and internationally active consulting firms exist. In distinguishing between these two types of firms, we have left aside smaller firms focused primarily on their domestic market. Our argument was that 'second wave' and 'third wave' consultancies tend to differ markedly from one another with respect to their international human resource management objectives, policies and practices. In addition, they also differ from typical transnational organizations outside the professional services sector. In our view, the hypothesized differences among the various aspects of human resource management that we have discussed are rooted in the overall structural and strategic features of the organizations concerned. This argument is most striking with respect to classical 'second wave' consultancies. These firms are oriented to a lesser or greater extent towards the 'professional partnership' (P^2) model, implying that the basic features of HR-related aspects such as incentive and reward structures, training and development, career paths and others are already embodied in their overall organizational set-up. In other words, such organizations have a lesser need for formalized HR policies, specialized HR staffs etc. than organizations that are substantially larger and more oriented towards the Managed Professional Business (MPB) model of consulting firms that entered the market in the context of the 'third wave' development of the consulting industry. Our argument so far has mainly been a theoretical one. In this section, we aim at supporting our hypotheses with empirical evidence, drawing primarily on a series of personal interviews in 30 large and medium-sized consulting firms with operations in German-speaking countries (Germany, Austria, and the German-speaking part of Switzerland). The interviews covered all of the top 11 players in the German management consulting market, as well as 14 of the top 20 players in the Lünendonk (2002) list.

In selecting our interview targets, we aimed at capturing a broad range of firms, including firms from both the "second" and "third wave" of consultancies. Similarly, we were interested in the commonalties and differences among consultancies with different service strategies. We distinguished full service providers versus functional specialists (e.g. Simon Kucher & Partners for pricing or Horvath & Partners for controlling), or industry specialists that focus on advising clients in particular industries (e.g. ZEB for banking and Kurt Salmon Associates for retail and healthcare). All of the consultancies we interviewed were established, renowned industry players. Consultancies with less than 30 employees were excluded from the interview series because they mostly lacked HRM systems, structures and practices. We also excluded consultancies that are subsidiaries of large industry firms and work mostly for their parent company such as Siemens Management Consulting or Lufthansa Systems Group. The interviews of about 60 minutes each were conducted in spring and summer 2003 as part of a larger research project of the Department of International Management and Consulting of the European Business School, International University in Schloss Reichartshausen, Germany. Our interviewees were experienced professionals with a minimum of three years consulting experience. They include senior consultants, project managers, associate partners, partners, and senior partners. For confidentiality reasons, only aggregated information can be given about interview contents. However, information from public sources other than our interviews will be cited. Overall, our arguments developed in section 3 with respect to the HRM objectives, policies and practices in international consulting firms are broadly supported by empirical evidence. Using the conceptual scheme in Table 4.3. as a guide, our material provides rich information on the following areas of interest:

General International HRM Policies and Practices*:* Our interviews provide a clear distinction between 'second wave' and 'third wave' consultancies. In 'second wave' firms, the mission statement and a small set of fundamental guiding principles provide the basis for HRM policies and practices that are valid globally. Mission statements as well as guiding principles are fairly general, enduring, and focused on professional values rather than on specific regulations. However, they explicitly mention people development through superior management methods as a major goal. For example, according to its mission statement The Boston Consulting Group seeks "to inspire enterprising and imaginative people – at our clients and on our staff – with unparalleled opportunities for professional and personal growth." McKinsey aims "to build a great firm that is able to attract, excite, and develop extraordinary people". "Second-wave" consultancies rarely vary their international HRM principles and practices to fit local conditions. Especially those firms that adopt "one-firm" concepts clearly apply uniform policies and rules across the globe. Firms like The Boston Consulting Group, McKinsey, A.T. Kearney and others are widely known to apply the same rules and procedures on a worldwide basis. In contrast, HRM policies and practices in "third wave" consultancies are more specific and more heterogeneous across countries or regions. For some "third wave" consultancies, general international HRM policies and practices are identical with the regulations of their parent organization. In this respect, they are identical to the HRM policies and practices prevalent in large MNCs. Another distinction between "second" and "third wave" consultancies relates to the general responsibility for HRM, including its international dimension. While "third wave" firms rely for the most part on formally established and sometimes large HR departments for tasks such as training and career management, in many "second wave" firms the consultants play a much more prominent role in these activities. Often, HR staff merely supports and administers the recruitment events, training programs and assumes a coordination function. One exception to this general observation, however, relates to the issue of project assignment. In all of the major "second wave" consultancies that we talked to, assignment is carried out on an office basis by specialized staff. All interviewees confirmed that two ways of staffing existed, namely formal and informal. The latter one comprises direct discussions and negotiations between partners (looking for consultants to staff their projects) and consultants (looking for their next assignment). Formal staffing takes place through a staffing function that collects and matches internal supply and demand for consultant capacity. Formal staffing is done by designated HR specialists, depending on the size of the office and the strengths of industry or functional practices in cooperation with responsible office managers or practice leaders.

International Recruitment and Selection: In most consultancies, recruitment and selection are carried out on an office-by-office[1] basis, and therefore is primarily of a local or regional character. New hires are admitted into the general pool of consulting staff (e.g. Boston Consulting Group, McKinsey, A.T. Kearney) or hired by and for a particular industry or functional practice (e.g. Accenture, Arthur D. Little, Axentiv, Roland Berger). With only few exceptions, there is little global hiring for all office locations worldwide. Exceptions include, for example, global practice specialists. However, many of these firms, in particular among the 'second wave' consultancies, are quite active in hiring abroad for the local office. As an example, virtually all of the bigger 'second wave' firms hold regular recruiting events for German and German-speaking graduates at American top-tier business schools. Many of the bigger 'third wave' consultancies are engaged in similar activities, but their choice of target schools tends to be more broadly spread. Without exception, the responsibility for making recruitment decisions rests in all consulting firms with consulting staff. Consultants tend to be heavily involved in the recruitment and selection process, from holding recruitment presentations and workshops to conducting job interviews. In 'second wave' firms, the involvement of 'professionals' (i.e. consultants) all but excludes the participation of specialized HR staff, except for the organizational and administrative aspects of such events. In many cases, applicants at these firms will not have met a member of the HR staff in person until well after a job offer has been made. In 'third wave' consultancies, too, consultants are heavily involved in the recruitment and selection process, although some specialized HR staff might play an active role in recruitment processes. The primary role of HR professionals in both types of consultancies is to review written applications, to make an initial selection on the basis of defined exclusion criteria, organize the interviewing process, and sometimes support first-round interviewing. Interviews tend to revolve around cases. Three to

---

[1]In particular in 'second wave' consultancies, the term 'office' relates to a collection of several physical offices in different cities that form a single administrative unit within the same country or region; e.g. the 'German Office'

five interview rounds are common before a job offer is made. Some 'third wave' firms partly substitute personal interviews with an assessment center. While the process for hiring junior consultants is generally fairly standardized, the process for senior hires tends to be more flexible and informal due to their rarity. Most consultancies focus on university graduates or young professionals with less than three years work experience as their major talent pool. Many 'second wave' consultancies welcome applications from a wide variety of academic disciplines, whereas 'third wave' consultancies and many specialized players express a clear preference for particular subjects and profiles. Some consulting firms rely entirely on hires with several years of experience in the industry or the financial sector (e.g. ICME).

Training and Development: All interviewees unanimously confirmed that the overwhelming majority of learning in consulting firms takes place on the job. Experienced colleagues, 'One or two levels above' a consultant at any particular point in his or her career, tend to be the main source for information and coaching everywhere. However, in some firms even seasoned senior consultants, including partners, take time to teach their younger peers. Generally speaking, due to the lower 'leverage ratios' – David Maister's (1993) terminology for the classical concept of control spans in organization theory –, there tends to be far greater interaction between junior and senior consultants in 'second wave' consultancies as compared to their 'third wave' competitors. In some classical firms, upward feedback from associates is part of the performance metrics for project managers and partners, thereby giving senior consultants a material incentive to engage in on-the-job training and development for younger consultants. In all established consultancies, off-the-job training programs and seminars support on-the-job learning. Off-the-job training programs tend to be fairly standardized globally, if not identical. Many of these programs are held with participants from different countries providing consultants with the opportunity to develop their international network of peers. In fact, the establishment of contact networks is often a primary, if tacit, objective of such training events. That is one reason why the first training for new consultants might be held before they even start their job, as is the case with The Boston Consulting Group's "boot camps". In many 'second wave' consultancies, the focus of these trainings is on the development of professional skills in a broad sense, including client management skills, analytical abilities, and project and team management skills. In these firms, courses with a more technical focus are sometimes available, too, but are often not mandatory. As an example, in his book "Perspective on McKinsey" (1979) which is given to new members of the firm but is not available to the general public, Marvin Bower, the charismatic Managing Director of the firm from 1950 to 1967 demanded that training for associates should cover five areas: problem solving, recommendation development, project management, adherence to professional standards and the development of outstanding consulting skills in general. Some 'third wave' consultancies, in particular the firms with a strong IT-focus, offer their new hires extensive training to learn details on software and IT they might not have learned at university. Accenture is known to operate a whole campus as a training facility in St. Charles just outside Chicago mainly for this purpose. These initial trainings may extend over several weeks. Typically, experienced consultants act as faculty for off-the-job trainings and seminars. Some firms also have an internal training department, which not only administers trainings and seminars but also delivers part of the content. For some technical or subject-specific coursework many consultancies contract with external commercial service providers and even with university professors. While the importance of training tends to decrease with higher seniority, some 'second wave' consultancies have mandatory trainings even for their most senior levels. In most cases, these events take place on an international basis.

Performance Management: In virtually all consultancies, performance management tends to be fairly homogenous across office locations worldwide. With few exceptions, similar or even identical performance evaluation criteria and formats are used within a particular consultancy. Performance evaluation takes place on an individual basis (rather than on a group/team basis), with the person's performance on a particular project being the main criterion. In 'second wave' consultancies, in particular, individuals' contributions in non project-related activities (e.g. involvement in recruitment activities, writing articles in in-house journals and other knowledge building activities) may also be taken into account. Generally speaking, 'third wave' consultancies tend to be more revenue-driven than 'second wave' firms, so that such aspects tend to play less of a role in performance evaluations. Performance reviews are conducted at a minimum after each project; in the case of longer projects, there may also be interim reviews. Average periods for performance reviews range from every three to every twelve months, with 'second wave' firms at the shorter end of the spectrum. In addition to performance evaluation by project managers, many consultancies also take subordinate and peer-to-peer feedback into account in assessment processes. Overall, performance management systems in consultancies reflect the fact that consulting is primarily a team-based activity. The cooperation of individuals in closely-knit teams provides opportunities for continuous and close interpersonal observation and monitoring. Since assessing the performance of junior consultants, in particular, on the basis of quantitative output criteria, e.g. the number of charts produced, is largely inappropriate, immediate supervision and mutual monitoring are used as important elements in the performance management processes. The reviewees' mentors who collect feedback from different projects conduct performance reviews. In firms with strong functional or industry practices, formal superiors like practice leaders typically conduct performance reviews for the members of their units (e.g. Arthur D. Little, Axentiv, Roland Berger).

Career Management: In virtually all consulting firms, consultants progress through the organizational hierarchy along clearly defined career paths. However, there are significant differences among firms regarding the flexibility with which such career systems are managed. Generally speaking, international staffing can be found in three forms: Short-term staffing for one particular project, medium-term staffing as expatriates for a period of about a year, and long-term international staffing in the form of permanent transfers to other office locations. While virtually all firms offer the first form of international assignments to their consultants, many are fairly restrictive with respect to more extended international assignments (medium- and long-term). Part of the reason for this is the fact that in many consulting firms the key managerial accounting and performance metrics are based on the unit of the local office, thereby providing disincentives for office management to release high performers into whom significant investments in the form of training, early career mentoring and the like have been made. Also, the nature of the consulting business is fast-paced with high turnover among staff, making long-term transfers difficult and only reasonable for tenured consultants. Our interviews indicated that the 'second wave' consultancies tend to be significantly more open to and flexible in the administration of international staff transfers than most 'third wave' consultancies. Many of the latter are organized essentially as different firms merely working under the same global brand, so that the barriers between different offices or country organizations are significantly greater than is the case with most of the classical 'second wave' consultancies. However, in some 'second wave' firms, too, great barriers exist between regions (e.g. Europe versus the U.S.) which make cross-regional staff transfers difficult. The new organization of Arthur D. Little (a federation of offices rather than a consolidated firm after its recovery from bankruptcy) provides an example. In order to support career management, almost all consulting firms operate some kind of mentoring program. Design and use of these programs, however, vary widely across firms. Some consultancies assign an individual mentor to new hires to ease their transition into the firm. Such mentors are typically junior consultants with one to two years of tenure. Relationships between these mentors and new hires are mostly informal and tend to cease after several months. Mentors in this model have few rights and obligations such as conducting performance reviews. Their primary role is to facilitate the socialization of young members in the firm. Hence, this model is found in consultancies with strong industry or functional practices where formal tasks are often the responsibility of the practice leader. Other consultancies use mentorship programs more formally. In these programs, mentors are typically project managers, associate partners, or even partners who guide and monitor 'their' candidates throughout their development. They also collect performance feedback from projects and conduct performance reviews. Some firms use both types of mentorship programs described above. Although general patterns are hard to establish, the impression from our interviews is that 'second wave' consultancies that place greater weight on internal socialization and the development of a professional orientation among junior consultants invest significantly more into mentoring programs than some of the larger 'third wave' firms.

Reward Systems: In all companies that participated in our interviews, financial rewards are allocated on the basis of individual performance (see the section on performance management systems above). For junior consultants, compensation consists of a fixed base salary and an individual bonus contingent on performance. With increasing seniority, the share of variable pay rises. In consultancies organized as partnerships, partners are allocated a share of the profit pool of the firm or the local office that reflects their contribution to the 'pie', often measured in terms of the revenues generated by selling consulting services. In addition, they receive a share of the surplus that reflects the relative size of their ownership stake in the firm. In stock market quoted companies, share ownership schemes are widespread, often extending to the level of junior consultants. While reward systems in most consulting firms are more or less standardized across countries and regions, reward levels are more heterogeneous, reflecting differences in local fee levels, average income levels and the costs of living. Also, additional benefits such as company cars, contributions to non-mandatory insurances and the like, are highly specific to each individual country. In those consultancies that operate a global profit pool, a common point of reference exists, at least at partner level, enabling partners to demand comparable levels of rewards across countries, so that some degree of homogeneity in reward levels has developed. In the case of short-term, project-related international transfers, consultants usually remain members of their local office, therefore retaining their reward schemes. Additional travel-related expenses are generally covered. In the case of medium-term transfers, consultants usually receive expatriate schemes that tend to be generous in level; however, as indicated above, such arrangements are not frequent, in particular not at junior level. In the case of permanent office transfers, the reward schemes of the new office apply to the transferring consultants.

HR Communication and HR Coordination: In 'second wave' consultancies, many important aspects of HRM, including many of its international aspects are the responsibility of the consultants. With the exception of project assignment/staffing, the primary role of the HR staff is to provide supportive and administrative assistance. Accordingly, international communication and coordination of HR staff does not take place on an extensive basis. HR communication and coordination is driven by consultants at senior level. Partners elect and participate in international committees that determine global policies and procedures, including HRM-related issues such salary and bonus levels, recruitment practices, performance reviews, international transfers, and promotion schemes. It is in these committees that overarching HR projects, e.g. strategies for the "war for talent" are initiated, discussed and approved. The central HR function in a firm might actively participate in these committees. However, local or regional HR departments would not regularly be involved. The committees mentioned above also communicate HR-related issues, e.g. new selection policies, to the consultants involved in such processes. The role of the local or regional HR functions is to support the process of putting committee decisions into practice. A similar, albeit less stringent picture can be gained from 'third wave' consultancies. HR departments play a more active role in these firms, e.g. in the case of international transfers. Accordingly, international communication among HR staff is common on an as-needed basis for concrete projects or cases. The same applies to international coordination in 'third wave' consultancies, e.g. for the preparation of key HR data.

Overall, the evidence gathered from our interviews supports the arguments put forward in sections two and three with respect to both the nature of HRM in international consulting firms, and the differences in HRM approaches and practices between the two types of consulting firms broadly classified as 'second wave' and 'third wave' consultancies. International consulting firms have particular organizational and strategic features, such as well-defined leverage ratios, career systems, office structures and the like. Their HRM systems and policies are reflective of these characteristics. This is particularly evident in the case of those firms that form part of the 'second wave' of consulting firms. 'Third wave' consultancies – at least the large and international ones focused on here – can be considered 'mid-range' organizations whose employment models and HRM practices reflect aspects of both the classical model of consulting firms that emerged during the 'second wave' of the industry's development, and transnational corporations outside the professional services sector.

4.5 Summary and Outlook

In this chapter, we have provided an overview of the approaches of large, international consulting firms to HRM. However, in order to do so it has been necessary to distinguish different types of consulting firms, namely those firms that follow strategic and organizational models that emerged during the 'second wave' of consulting, and those firms that diversified into consulting during the 'third wave' of consulting that began to unfold during the 1980s. Needless to say, this distinction provides the basis for a broad classification only that cannot meet the specific features of every single case. Nevertheless, we believe that distinguishing between these two different types of consulting firms is necessary in the context of a discussion of the human resource management practices in consulting, as fundamentally different employment models, incentive structures and managerial models appear to be at work in the two types of firms. Classical 'second wave' consultancies follow to a greater or lesser extent the professional partnership model that emphasizes the notion of *membership* (rather than employment) of individuals in a group tied together by extended socialization processes and adherence to professional values. As a result, many of the key processes, by which the human resources of these organizations are managed, are an integral part of the organizational structure of the firms, and are run in practice not by a separate group of specialized HR staff, but by senior professionals (i.e. consultants) themselves. Crucial with respect to the issue of international HRM is that, many classical professional partnerships in the consulting sector emphasize 'one firm' concepts, implying that although local offices may have great importance as administrative units, the professional orientation of the people working in these firms extends to the worldwide partnership. Therefore, international career moves such as project assignments and office transfers are relatively easy in these firms, even if they are not managed in a formal way. Metaphorically speaking, human resource management is an organic, integral element of the system of professional partnerships as such, rather than a specialized managerial function that would help to safeguard the smooth operations of these firms from outside. In contrast, the larger and internationally active 'third wave' consultancies can be characterized as 'managed professional businesses' with many more 'corporate' features than the classical professional partnerships. Managed professional businesses tend to be larger, have greater leverage ratios (spans of control), more administrative staff and put greater emphasis on differentiated functional units, including human resource management units. The employment models prevalent in these firms are, in many respects. akin to businesses outside the professional service sector. With respect to international human resource management practices, however, many of these firms are hampered by the fact that they represent relatively loose collections of local or regional offices, without an overarching 'one firm' culture. In this situation, specialized HR staff, whose intention is to foster international programs such as mid-career transfers and the like, often represent the interests of international career development versus the declared objectives of local management, thereby deepening the perceived rift between 'them' and 'us', between consultants and staff in these organizations. It is then a matter of the distribution of power as to whose interests prevail. In one of the firms in which we conducted a series of interviews with the HR department, the members of that unit acknowledged that they had to be "more diplomatic and very persisting" with local partners, when it came to representing the interests of employees. In comparison with themselves, they thought it was easier for HR managers in traditional multinational corporations to promote their interests, as they could appeal more easily to top management *fiat*, i.e. to the priorities set by the board or chief executive. Today, both types of consulting firms that we have described compete with each other in a market that, in terms of its general development, is characterized by slower growth and falling margins. Which type of firm under these tougher conditions will prevail is open for debate, or at least for speculation. We believe that this question cannot be answered yet. However, as competition grows stronger, the ways in which the most important productive resources of consulting firms by far – their people – are employed and managed should prove to be a key source of competitive advantage or disadvantage. During the next few years, the true strategic importance of HRM in consulting firms will become evident.

References

Adler NJ, Ghadar F (1990) Strategic Human Resource Management: A Global Perspective. In: Pieper R (eds) Human Resource Management: An International Comparison. De Gruyter, New York, pp 235-259

Aharoni Y (1999) Internationalization of Professional Services: Implications for Accounting Firms. In: Brock D, Powell M, Hinings CR (eds) Restructuring the Professional Organization. Routledge, London, New York, pp 20-40

Alpha Publications (2002) Management Consultancy Services in Europe. Bucks, Beaconsfield

Asakawa K, Lehrer M (2003) Managing Local Knowledge Assets Globally: The Role of Regional Innovation Relays. Journal of World Business 38(1), pp 31-42

Baer J, Stoll M (1999) Human Resources Management als Eckpfeiler der strategischen und operativen Geschäftsentwicklung. In: Müller-Stewens G, Drolshammer J, Kriegmeier J (eds) Professional Service Firms. Wie sich multinationale Dienstleister positionieren. Frankfurter Allgemeine Zeitung, Frankfurt am Main, pp 198-221

Brewster C (1995) Project on International Strategic Human Resource Management. International Executive Report, Cranfield University, School of Management

Bartlett C, Ghoshal S (1989) Managing Across Borders. Hutchinson Business Books, London

Bower M (1979) Perspective on McKinsey. McKinsey & Company, Inc., New York

Bresman H, Birkinshaw J, Nobel R (1999) Knowledge Transfer in International Acquisitions. Journal of International Business Studies 30(3), pp 439-462

Casse P (1994) People are not Resources. Journal of European Industrial Training 18(7):30-36

Dickmann M (2003) Implementing German HRM abroad: desired, feasible, successful?. International Journal of Human Resource Management 14(2), pp 265-283

Dickmann M (1999) Balancing Global, Parent and Local Influences: International Human Resource Management of German Multinational Companies. University of London, Department of Organizational Psychology, Birkbeck College, p 371

Dickmann M (1997) The IPD Guide on International Management Development. IPD, London

FEACO (2002): Survey of the European Consultancy Market. Feaco, Brussels

Ferguson M (2002) The Rise of Management Consulting in Britain. Ashgate, Aldershot

Ferner A (2000) The Underpinnings of 'Bureaucratic' Control Systems. Journal of Management Studies 37(4), pp 521-539

Gordon J (1999) Seeking 15,000 George Shaheens. Forbes 163(5):104

Graubner M, Richter A (2003) Human Resource Management in Tomorrow's Consulting Firms. Forthcoming in: Consulting to Management 14(3)

Gupta A, Govindarajan V (1991) Knowledge Flows and the Structure of Control within Multinational Corporations. Academy of Management Review 16(4), pp 768-792

Handy C (1995) Beyond Certainty: The Changing World of Organizations. Hutchinson Business Books, London

Harzing AW (2000) An Empirical Analysis and Extension of the Bartlett and Ghoshal Typology of Multinational Companies. Journal of International Business Studies 31(1), pp 101-120

Hill C (2003) International Business: Competing in the Global Marketplace, 4th edn. McGraw-Hill, Irwin

Kahn EJ (1984) The Problem Solvers. A History of Arthur D. Little, Inc. Little, Brown and Company, Boston, Toronto

Kennedy Information (2001) The Global Consulting Marketplace: Key Data, Forecasts & Trends. Fitzwilliam, New Hampshire

King B (2003, March 19) More influence than size: The brisk and bright whizz kids of the dotcom era have made a lasting impression. Financial Times Special Report: FT-IT Review, pp V

Kipping M (1999) American Management Consultancies in Western Europe. 1920 to 1990: Products, Reputation, and Relationships. Business History Review 73, pp 190-220

Kipping M (2002) Trapped in Their Wave: The Evolution of Management Consultancies. In: Clark T, Fincham R (eds) Critical Consulting. New Perspectives on the Management Advice Industry. Blackwell, Oxford, pp 28-49

Landriscina M (2002) The 10 best consulting firms to work for. Consulting Magazine, Special Issue, November 2002

Laursen K, Mahnke V (2001) Knowledge Strategies, Firm Types, and Complementarity in Human-Resource Practices. Journal of Management and Governance 5(1), pp 1-27

Lünendonk T (2002) Führende Managementberatungsunternehmen in Deutschland. Bad Wörishofen

Maister DH (1993) Managing the Professional Service Firm. Free Press, New York et al.

Perkin H (1996) The Third Revolution. Professional Elites in the Modern World. Routledge, London New York

Perkin H (2002) The Rise of the Professional Society. England Since 1880, 3rd edn. Routledge, London New York

Perlmutter H (1969) The Tortuous Evolution of the Multinational Corporation. Columbia Journal of World Business 4(1), pp 9-18

Porter ME (1985) Competitive Advantage. Free Press, New York

Powell MJ, Brock DM, Hinings CR (1999) The Changing Professional Organization. In: Brock D, Powell M, Hinings CR (eds) Restructuring the Professional Organization. Routledge, London New York, pp 1-19

Pucik V (1992) Globalization and Human Resource Management. Globalizing Management. In: Pucik V, Tichy NM, Barnett CK (eds) Globalizing Management: Creating and Leading the Competitive Organization. John Wiley & Sons, New York, pp 61-81

Richter A (2003) Strategic and Organizational Management of Rapid Growth: Roland Berger Strategy Consultants. European Business School Case Study (forthcoming)

Robertson M, Hammersley G O'Malley (2000) Knowledge Management Practices within a Knowledge-intensive Firm: The Significance of the People Management Dimension. Journal of European Industrial Training 24(2/3/4), pp 241-253

Rose T, Hinings CR (1999) Global Clients' Demands Driving Change in Global Business Advisory Firms. In: Brock D, Powell M, Hinings CR (eds) Restructuring the Professional Organization. Routledge, London New York, pp 41-67

Ruef M (2002) At the Interstices of Organizations: The Expansion of the Management Consulting Profession, 1933-1997. In: Sahlin-Andersson K, Engwall L (eds): The Expansion of Management Knowledge. Stanford University Press, Stanford, pp 74-95

Schuler RS, Jackson SE (1987) Linking Competitive Strategies with Human Resource Management Practices. Academy of Management Executive 1(3), pp 207-219

Sjøholt P (1999) Skills in Services. The Dynamics of Competence Requirement in Different Types of Advanced Producer Services. Some Evidence from Norway. The Service Industries Journal 19(1), pp 61-79

Stewart J (1999) Employee Development Practice. Financial Times Management. London.

Tregaskis O, Heraty N, Morley M (2001) HRD in Multinationals: The Global/Local Mix. Human Resource Management Journal 11(2), pp 34-56

Vault. Retrieved August 20, 2003, from the World Wide Web: www.vault.com

Wilkinson JW (1995) What Is Management Consulting?. In: Barcus SW, Wilkinson JW (eds): Handbook of Management Consulting Services, 2nd edn. McGraw-Hill, New York et al., pp 13-116

Wolf J (1997) "From "Starworks" to Networks and Heterarchies? Theoretical Rationale and Empirical Evidence of HRM Organization in Large Multinational Corporations. Management International Review, Special Issue 1997/1, pp 145-169

5 Wanted: Experts on Strategy

Rainer Bernnat and Angelika Sonnenschein

Booz Allen Hamilton

5.1 Booz Allen Hamilton: The Company

5.1.1 Facts and Figures

The name Booz Allen Hamilton stands for a long and successful tradition. It all started 90 years ago: In 1914 Edwin Booz realized a seminal idea. He believed that companies would be more successful if they could call on someone outside their own organization for expert, impartial advice. In doing so, he created a new profession – management consulting – and the firm that would bear his name. The joining of his partners James Allen (1929) and Carl Hamilton (1935) strengthened his vision.

With 90 years of experience in delivering results that endure, Booz Allen Hamilton ranks among the world's biggest international management and technology consultancies. Today, with more than 16,600 employees spread across six continents, Booz Allen Hamilton generates annual sales of 190 million Euros in Germany, Switzerland and Austria – 3.3 billion Dollars on a worldwide scale. Over 430 of these employees currently work in the German-speaking area, with offices located in Berlin, Düsseldorf, Frankfurt am Main, Munich, Vienna and Zurich. The number of employees throughout this region has increased steadily over the past few years.

As a global leader in management and technology consulting, Booz Allen Hamilton provides services to major international corporations and government institutions around the world. The company offers extensive experience in the fields of strategy, turnaround, restructuring, organization, operations, systems and technology. Strategic and operational entrepreneurial assignments are completed in close cooperation with the client. The organization comprises a commercial *(Worldwide Commercial Business/WCB)* and a technology division *(Worldwide Technology Business/WTB)*.

"The Power of Both" serves as the basic principle of the service portfolio: As a consulting approach it combines strategy with technology and industry or functional expertise with the appropriate implementation. Booz Allen Hamilton's consultant teams measure their own efforts against the success they achieve with their clients. Through its global presence the firm is able to focus sectoral knowledge and functional expertise in compressed form on each particular project task. As a result, the firm has long-term experience in strategic, operational and IT-related problems.

5.1.2 Booz Allen Hamilton's Philosophy

"Booz Allen Hamilton combines strategy with technology and insight with action – working with clients to deliver results today that endure tomorrow."

The combination of strategy and technology and of analysis with implementation, is based upon the *guiding principles* of Booz Allen Hamilton, the most important of which is its position as a "practical strategist": a successful consultancy which not only develops strategies but also provides the instruments necessary for their implementation.

The *shared values* principle is reflected in everyday work: Booz Allen Hamilton is attributed "higher-than-average" competence in terms of its consistent realization of respect, fairness and team spirit in the working environment. Mutual respect and fair cooperation are the firm's most fundamental corporate values. Client orientation, entrepreneurial spirit and the ability to work in a team add to this – *values based leadership* approach.

The firm's vision is to be the absolute best management and technology consultant, measuring its success by the value it delivers to its clients and by its strength and spirit as an institution. In order to transform this vision into reality, Booz Allen Hamilton tries to work and live by certain core values: professionalism, fairness, integrity, respect, trust, client service, diversity, entrepreneurship, excellence and teamwork. Its consultants bring these values into play on a day-to-day basis:

- Professional excellence regarding client work;
- employee-centric approach to corporate citizenship activities;
- diversity programs.

5.1.3 Booz Allen Hamilton's Clients

Booz Allen Hamilton's clients are the world's largest corporations, emerging growth companies, leading governments, agencies and institutions that want to change their organizations and the world for the better. Examples of Booz Allen Hamilton client work for government clients include the following: Within the scope of the federal e-government project "BundOnline 2005", Booz Allen Hamilton advised the Federal Ministry of the Interior on strategy development conception and implementation. For the Federal Ministry of Economics, the firm developed and implemented the "Digital Integration" program. Furthermore, Booz Allen consultants support several authorities regarding the development of security strategies. At Federal State level, the firm also supports the government of North-Rhine Westphalia.

Together with "Initiative D21", the biggest national public-private partnership within the information technology sector, Booz Allen Hamilton is developing new initiatives in partnership: be it for the advancement of the information society or for the expansion of Germany as an innovator in the field of IT.

5.2 Booz Allen Hamilton: Personnel Strategy

Booz Allen Hamilton recognizes that it takes talent and unique perspectives to solve today's most important and challenging problems. The firm believes that its success is enhanced by employees with a wide variety of educational backgrounds. It not only hires graduates, but also recruits numerous former executives from industrial companies.

5.2.1 Personnel Planning

Consulting is attractive to a wide range of applicants – interns, graduates, postgraduates and "young professionals". Job specifications are comparatively demanding: they include excellent analytical skills, practical and international work experience, as well as fluency in English. Furthermore, applicants should possess imagination and creativity, motivation, superior interpersonal skills, the ability to work in a team environment and good communication skills. Some professional areas also require extensive experience with functional work.

Capacity is planned at the beginning of each fiscal year and is directly driven by the expectations of business development. Career development is supported by the firm-wide *Career Development Service,* whereby an assigned Career Development Manager coordinates staffing on client projects, planning of training, regular performance appraisals.

The *selection process* starts with the written application. Candidates who meet the requirements are invited for interviews, so-called "Recruiting Marathon Days": between five and seven one-on-one interviews are conducted by experienced consultants and members of the senior management team. Interviews focus on the applicant's background and on how applicants apply their knowledge to solving case studies. The aim is to test how a candidate approaches a problem, how he or she structures it, deals with information provided by the interviewer and how he or she ultimately proceeds to solve the case. Based on the results of the interviews, the applicant's professional expertise and his or her soft skills, the recruiting team reaches a final decision.

Consultancies recruit the best graduates from almost every faculty across the board. Nevertheless, graduates of business studies represent the largest group among all employees in the German-speaking region (46%) compared to only 26% being engineering graduates, 12% natural scientists and a mere 5% of consultants, who are humanities graduates. This variety of disciplines ensures the consultancy's success: an interdisciplinary exchange of this kind enhances the creativity and collaboration of teams in their daily work.

It goes without saying that *lateral hires* can be found at higher levels as well: Most of these are executives who have had several years of experience in another consultancy and in industry. At present, a significant percentage of all Booz Allen Hamilton employees have prior industry experience.

5.2.2 Career Planning

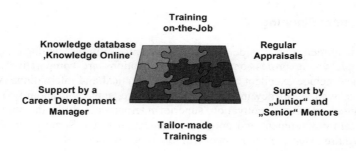

Booz Allen Hamilton's priority in HR is the individual development of each employee

Fig. 5.1. Employee Development

As a strategy consultant, Booz Allen Hamilton is committed to the continued development of its employees. Career planning and training are of major importance and have a direct impact on the speed of promotion in a performance-based organization.

New employees (consultants, researchers, etc.) start their career at Booz Allen Hamilton by attending the *New Hire Orientation (NHO)/Discover Booz Allen* workshop. This international introductory training week provides a broad overview of the firm and the way it operates. It offers an introduction to firm-specific approaches and concepts which support the work of a consultant – from the typical course of a project to basic information on captive research services. All graduates also participate in the *Consultant Program*. In addition to *Training on-the-job*, this program comprises several seminars on business-related topics and methods – elements that form a fundamental part of a consultant's education. Graduates who do not have a business background attend a complementary training course on business administration (strategy, economics and finance), based on MBA teaching methods.

Consultants with a business background take part in the *Industry Hire Jump Start* course. It ties in with the experience of the individual, linking it to Booz Allen-specific working methods in order to facilitate successful integration. In addition, the firm also offers workshops dealing with a variety of topics ranging from conflict management to presentation skills.

Continuous learning is another crucial factor of career development at Booz Allen Hamilton: In addition to their training on-the-job, consultants are given the opportunity to take part in various courses, designed to further enhance their skills. Trainings at all levels, as well as a regular exchange of experience with experts contribute to this. One of the company's main goals is to encourage consultants to find new approaches and innovative ideas, as this fundamentally contributes to their success. Irrespective of space and time every consultant has access to the firm's know-how pool: The firm-wide intranet-based system "Knowledge On-Line" includes knowledge and experience from a multitude of projects. Tools like these play a role in enabling consultants to meet the client's needs with maximum quality and competence.

The survey "Attractive Employers 2002" conducted by Hewitt Associates, a management consulting firm specializing in human resources solutions, ranked Booz Allen Hamilton amongst the top four of Germany's most attractive corporations. The major drivers for this result were a high level of individual responsibility and excellent professional development opportunities. The consultancy sector clearly dominates the group of top employers in terms of professional development opportunities.

The regular career path begins at Consultant or Senior Consultant level, moves on to Associate and Senior Associate level and then progresses to Principal and finally Partner level.

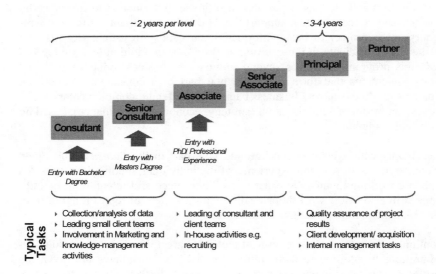

Fig. 5.2. A Consultant's Career Path at Booz Allen Hamilton

Each of the first four career steps take approximately two to three years. Within the first years, the work covers a broad range of projects, thus guaranteeing the acquisition of cross-industry expertise. Equipped with these „basics" of strategy consulting, the employee takes the next career step – that of a Senior Associate – in which he or she specializes in an industry or a functional area. Senior Associates already take on responsibility for a project, plan and structure analyses and support the client in implementing new strategies. The scope of duties of a Principal ("Partner in Training") again broadens: as an expert for strategic transformation, he or she is responsible for clients as well as business development.

After an average seven years of continual growth, consultants may reach the company's top management – Partner level. In addition to their continued excellent performance, Partners dispose of specific characteristics which ultimately lead to a consultant's success: the ability to support the development of employees, to define and develop clients and markets, as well as general leadership qualities.

- Example of a Booz Allen Career -

> Judith Mauel, 29, joined Booz Allen as a Senior Consultant in Spring 2001 and was promoted to Associate level after $2\frac{1}{2}$ years. Her first consulting project as a fully-qualified "Diplom-Engineer specializing in Waste Management" dealt with a topic which was completely new to her:
> E-Procurement in a mobile telecommunications company. A team of experienced colleagues helped her get to grips with the new matter. "The requirements necessary for the job – conceptual and analytical skills – were no problem for me as an engineer," says Judith. "My own strong interest and enthusiasm for new challenges were further basic requirements for the steep learning curve." Simultaneously, her affinity to engineering is not ignored. "After a couple of months working in different industries, I joined the "Operations Group" focusing on the manufacturing industry…
> I can't deny the fact that I'm an engineer! "

Assignments Abroad

Nearly all new consultants have previous international work experience and join Booz Allen with the expectation of working on a global level. Thanks to Booz Allen Hamilton's presence on 6 continents, the company is able to offer its employees opportunities abroad. Providing the employee has the appropriate experience and the market situation warrants it, such assignments will be either for the duration of a project or as a temporary deployment.

Compensation System

Booz Allen Hamilton's *compensation system* offers above-average salaries for entrants. These are complemented by the usual benefits such as a company car, life insurance and an additional pension fund. Consultants working at the same level receive the same basic salary – their cohort salary. The only differentiation is the performance-related cohort bonus, of which the amount is dependent upon the individual's overall business performance.

5.3 Booz Allen Hamilton: Human Resources "Best Practices"

The firm is committed to the individual career development of all employees. As a part of its corporate philosophy, outstanding performance is required and in turn rewarded. The "Professional Excellence Award" for instance, which honors the best teams, is a sign of this appreciation. Once a year, a committee of Partners from different countries grants this award to the project teams who obtained outstanding results in their client work: It is they who, by means of their excellent performance, not only help to advance the team but also the entire firm.

The *information culture* at all levels of hierarchy as well as within project teams boosts the overall success of the firm. Booz Allen Hamilton supports this in several ways: The literal "open door policy" for instance is decisive for a positive working environment. The so-called "Home Office Days" - days on which consultants spend their time working, meeting or participating in training courses at Booz Allen Hamilton offices - enhance open communication amongst the colleagues and establish local and international networks. Furthermore, a non-bureaucratic culture supports these activities: continuous exchange of information between employees and the executive board ensures active communication just as much as the publication of team and industry-related newsletters at national and international level. Amongst other things they contain a press review and the latest news on Booz Allen Hamilton both worldwide and "on-site". Last but not least, it is the communication between staff which greatly contributes to the high degree of cooperation within the project teams.

5.3.1 Mentoring Program

Being able to learn from as many colleagues as possible is an important element of an individual's career development. Booz Allen Hamilton has established an intensive mentoring program, whereby one junior and one senior mentor are nominated to support the professional development. Senior mentors guide their general career development and junior mentors serve as contact points in day-to-day working life through coaching and counseling.

5.3.2 Sponsorship Program

After 24 months of excellent performance, interested consultants can apply for sponsorship from the firm to complete their doctorate or participate in an MBA program. This is essentially an offer open to all young consultants who are highly qualified and have the potential to build a long-term career at the firm. The *MBA sponsorship* supports one or two year programs. During this period, Booz Allen Hamilton covers all tuition fees, provides a laptop and e-mail access, as well as the utilization of in-house resources. Upon completion of the course, reintegration into the firm is assured. Currently, 46% of all Booz Allen consultants in Germany, Austria and Switzerland hold a doctorate degree and 25% have an MBA.

Structured Performance Evaluation

Consultants must constantly generate excellent output for their clients. Careers depend on each individual's continuous performance development. A consultant's past performance and success and his or her potential for development and further growth are continually measured and evaluated through the systematic appraisal process. Performance evaluations at Booz Allen Hamilton support the career development of each employee – from Secretary to Consultant to Partner. This kind of „monitoring" has been conducted globally for over 40 years. Once a year, personal evaluation assessments are conducted via a „360 degree process" along a set of standardized competency criteria. The process starts with the employee writing a so-called „self assessment" and discussing it with his or her assigned appraiser. Based on this initial input, a senior member of staff who has not worked directly with the appraisee then conducts structured interviews with peers, supervisors and juniors, with whom the appraisee has worked during the appraisal period. Three main categories covering ten core competencies are assessed:

Delivering Value to Clients

- Using core consulting craft skills;
- demonstrating thought leadership;
- structuring and managing work;
- effecting lasting change.

Developing People and Relationships

- Managing and leading work teams;
- working effectively with others;
- cultivating career growth.

Building the Institution

- Developing intellectual capital;
- generating new business with both existing and new clients;
- contributing to firm development and initiating good will for the firm.

These competencies obviously vary from level to level. They demonstrate how staff should strengthen and broaden their portfolio of skills as they advance within the firm – a Principal should possess the competencies defined for a more junior member of staff and develop those specified for his or her current level. Promotion to the next level will only occur once the employee has demonstrated most of the competencies required for the next level. For example, an Associate must successfully manage teams and projects before he or she will be promoted to Senior Associate level, i.e. to Project Manager level.

The appraisal is then presented to an Appraisal Committee - made up of Partners and Principals – which reviews each appraisal for completeness and consistency. Special emphasis is given to development actions and steps which will help staff to address their development needs and realize their full potential. All decisions relating to the future career of staff are taken by the Appraisal Committee. The appraisal process also applies to Partners.

The process is designed to give each Booz Allen employee a sense of his or her own potential, direction and ownership in terms of the advancement of their careers. The entire process is based on the understanding that a sense of recognition and purpose and opportunities for further growth, is the best motivation a firm can offer to ambitious staff.

5.3.3 Advancement of "Diverse Minds"

Being able to support executives across the globe in both industry and public institutions in solving complex issues requires talent, perspective and an open mind. Thus, diversity among its employees is an essential element of Booz Allen Hamilton. Specific recruiting concepts meet this concern. Cultural diversity among employees is promoted actively: regular communications of coordinated measures concerning the issue of diversity as well as mandatory training to raise awareness are standard. Furthermore an annual "Diversity Award", has been established firm-wide, honoring particular commitment of employees in this field.

Great attention is given to the *Advancement of Women*: it is Booz Allen Hamilton's ambition to attain a well-balanced proportion of male and female consultants, for example by way of attracting young academics. In 2002, Booz Allen Hamilton thus established a scholarship program for highly gifted female students in cooperation with the German National Academic Foundation (Studienstiftung des deutschen Volkes). In this context, both institutions fund a year abroad in a European country for scholarship holders; additionally, goal-oriented career advice, internships and advice given by selected female mentors at Booz Allen Hamilton are offered to them. Booz Allen Hamilton has been honored several times for its commitment to diversity. "Working Mother" magazine for instance, has repeatedly placed the firm in the "Top 10" of "100 Best Companies for Working Mothers" in the United States.

5.3.4 Work-life Balance

Booz Allen Hamilton makes high demands on its employees. An open and flexible attitude towards the client's expectations at all times counts among these. Nevertheless, the consultancy endeavors to offer its employees flexible solutions, which in turn enable them to strike a successful balance between their working and their private lives.

The firm offers a variety of flexible work arrangements which support the work-life balance concept. One of these is a leave of absence or part-time work, where 60% can mean working three days a week, taking additional holidays during the school holidays or maybe at the end of a project. Nevertheless, working fewer hours during a regular working day can prove to be quite difficult in an environment in which the "nine-to-five" rule does not exist.

Furthermore, the firm also offers employees the opportunity to give something back to the community through firm-sponsored volunteer activities and pro bono assignments at non-government, non-profit organizations. The pro-bono projects often have an additional benefit of enabling employees to accomplish personal objectives through their professional activities.

5.4 Conclusion

Ninety years of service to the world's leading corporations have shown that work as a consultant offers an ideal environment for strategic thinkers, those with an ability to solve problems, show flexibility and have a desire for continued professional training. The range of activities is challenging. It requires of each individual that he or she is aware of these demands. The „Booz Allen Way" offers attractive and demanding work, an international corporate culture, a supportive environment – and inspires every individual.

6 Managing Human Resources at Metaplan

Wolfgang Schnelle †

Metaplan GmbH

6.1 Metaplan

Metaplan's human resources management is strongly related to the specific approach of its consulting procedure and its consulting concept of organizational change. It is a sociologically guided consultancy with a solid foundation in advanced organizational theories. This has to be explained to make the ways and means of recruiting and training our consultants understood.

6.1.1 The Metaplan Consulting Procedure: Moderating Processes of Reaching Shared Understanding

The Metaplan consulting procedure is a process of group communication. In discussions with groups of people from affected areas, the problems are brought to light which are to be the focus of the consultancy process. The suggestions for solving these problems are also elaborated in group discussions and workshops at which those involved participate.

The consultants intervene in the group discussions either indirectly or directly. 'Indirectly' means that they formulate the questions and propositions which form the subject of the discussions. They intervene directly by taking part in the discussion, introducing their own opinions and recommendations in a provocative manner. They always do this if the indirect method is not successful in breaking open closed thinking and fixed interests. These indirect and direct interventions are the points where consulting takes place: Metaplaners are simultaneously both moderators and consultants.

6.1.2 The Metaplan Consulting Concept of Organizational Change

Three mechanisms interlock in the Metaplan consulting concept. The first mechanism is to create a common conceptual framework to replace the ingrained points of view trapping the members of an organization. This is a prerequisite for communications amounting to more than mere compromise. The second mechanism is to form viable connections between the participants' divergent interests; this entails a power play. The third mechanism concerns creating trust. The partners should be able to make advance concessions in the hope of receiving returns on their investment in the project at a later date.

6.1.3 The Metaplan Consulting Approach Is a Sociologically Guided Consultancy with a Solid Foundation in Advanced Organizational Theories

These are the theories most influential on Metaplan consultancy:

- Decisions in organizations have to be made under conditions of **bounded rationality** and **ambiguity** (*Herbert A. Simon, James G. March*). This opens the door for communication processes in which the participants try to build up shared understanding and an arrangement of their interests.

- **Rule following**: self-generated or social rules are followed in organizations to absorb insecurities of decision-making, even if they are economically disadvantageous (*James G. March, John W. Meyer* and *Brian Rowan, Paul J. Dimaggio and Walter M. Powell*). Metaplaners are aware of that and ask themselves whether such rules should be respected or challenged in the process.

- Organizations are arenas of **micro-political disputes** (*Michel Crozier and Erhard Friedberg* [in French], *Guenther Ortmann* [in German]). These disputes help to overcome deadlocks in the processes of organizational change. They have to be accepted to a certain degree.

- Subunits and departments in organizations develop specific "thought styles". They might be trapped in **"closed thinking"** which makes it difficult to build up shared understanding between different "thought collectives". (*Ludwik Fleck*, who in 1935 published a sociological investigation of the production of scientific knowledge, coined these terms, which found their way into the Metaplan method of working).

- Organizations themselves cause costs: costs of information, of transactions, of control, and of exerting influence. **Economic theories of organization** allow Metaplaners look at those costs mostly neglected or underestimated by managers (the best known in this field are *Oliver E. Williams* [in English] and *Arnold Picot* [in German]).

6.1.4 Typical Projects and Strategic Clients

We are engaged by corporations, associations and public institutions. They come to Metaplan because Metaplaners support the process of reaching shared under-standing among the parties involved and refrain from imposing "solutions" on them.

This happens when there is a need for strategic and/or organizational planning or for new options for taking action. Such projects might last several months.

Almost all kinds of industries are among our clients: engineering works, the automotive industry, insurance companies, and banks.

Strategic clients include, in particular, big pharmaceutical companies making use of our ability to moderate meetings with medical researchers, hospital and of-fice-based physicians, in nearly all languages spoken on both sides of the Atlantic.

6.1.5 Facts and Figures

Metaplan is an international moderation and consulting institute that was founded in Germany in 1972. We have a conference center in Quickborn (Hamburg) espe-cially designed for workshop moderation.

We have had an office in Paris (France) since 1985. In 2001 we opened our of-fice in Princeton, NJ, in the United States.
In 2002 we had a total of
- 6 Partners
- 13 Consultants
- 19 Back-office staff
In that year our total turnover was €5.5m.

6.1.6 Recruitment

From time to time we place advertisements in the national press describing the graduates we are looking for:

We are an international moderation and consultancy company. Founded in 1972, we now have offices in Quickborn (near Hamburg), Paris, and Princeton, New Jersey. Our clients are well-known international businesses and institutions.

Our consulting procedure is based on moderation of processes of reaching shared understanding in organizations.

We lead discussions between players with different interests and perspectives towards the "blind spots" in the organization. We open up the thought processes of those involved, make their logic transparent, and get them to interact. In addition to the company's economic viewpoint, we also include sociological and cultural aspects in our reflections. We lead those involved to new ways of thinking, and from the organization we develop joint solutions and strategies for taking action. In this way new possible courses of action are revealed, which are supported and implemented by all those involved.

Consultants as intermediaries between different ways of thinking

The successful candidate will have the following qualifications:

You have a university degree with a broad subject base which illustrates your intellectual curiosity.

You have at least 5 years of professional experience with leadership responsibility; you have found that the social reality in organizations is multi-layered and that leadership often takes place laterally.

You can easily put yourself in the shoes of other players and understand their interests and ways of thinking.

You are sensitive to situations involving power relations and trust relations in organizations, and can communicate with people on higher or lower levels as equals.

You are ready for a change in your career and are open to the ways of thinking and the methods upon which our work is based.

You speak German and English fluently (and possibly another language), since you have spent prolonged periods abroad which have given you competence in the languages and culture of different countries. You are excited by the idea of working on projects in the USA and Europe.

Fig. 6.1. Job Advertisement

6.1.7 Training

All new consultants will be trained in the Metaplan Moderation Method. They will be enabled to conduct Metaplan Moderation Trainings for clients. From 1992 to 2002, 19 internal seminars were held on topics in organizational and social science by academic lecturers (see Table 6.1.). Participation is obligatory for everybody, even for Partners.

Tab. 6.1. Training

1	20-21March 1992	Lose Kopplungen (Loose couplings)	Prof. Guenther Ortmann, Wuppertal
2	1 June 1992	Mikropolitik in Organization (Micropolitics in organizations)	Prof. Guenther Ortmann, Wuppertal
3	31 Aug. 1992	Is it sensible to be rational? Beyond rationality: organizations as social constructions	Nils Brunsson, Professor of Management, Stockholm
4	30 Oct. 1992	1. 'The triumphant march of the computers' or 'About computers, fishing-nets and a bunch of big fish' 2. Reduction of complexity: why you should prescribe a cure of losing weight to your EDP? 3. Information systems and reformability of organization 4. CIMsalabim: promises of a magic formula and doubts	Prof. Guenther Ortmann, Wuppertal based on an article by Wolfgang Dernbach, Diebold Deutschland GmbH Arthur Francis, Professor of Corpor. Strategy, Glasgow Prof. Willi Küpper, Hamburg
5	5-6 Feb. 1993	Strategische Analyse von Organisationen (Strategic Analysis of Organizations)	Prof. E. Friedberg, Paris
6	6 May 1993	Unternehmensnetzwerke (Corporate Networks)	Prof. Joerg Sydow, Wuppertal
7	24 March 1995	Kooperationsspiele (Cooperation Games)	Prof. Guenther Ortmann, Wuppertal
8	15-16 June 1995	Die Vernunft der Moderne Teil I: individualistische und universalistische Rationalität (Reason in the Modern Age, Part I: individualistic and universalistic rationality)	Prof. Wolfgang Kersting, Kiel

9	15-16 Dec. 1995	1. Strategisches Management und wissens-intensive Unternehmungen (Strategic Management and knowledge-intensive undertakings) 2. Unternehmensnetzwerke *(Corporate Networks)*	Prof. Guenther Ortmann Wuppertal, Prof. Joerg Sydow, Berlin
10	23 Feb. 1996	Die Vernunft der Moderne Teil II: Diskursethik; Klugheit und Moralität auf dem Markt, in der Ökologie und im Wohlfahrtsstaat (Reason in the Modern Age, Part II: Ethics of discourse; Smartness and morality on the market, in ecology and in the welfare state)	Prof. Wolfgang Kersting, Kiel
11	10 May 1996	Ästhetik in der Architektur *(Esthetics in Architecture)*	Titus Bernhard, University of Applied Sciences, Augsburg
12	27-28 June 1996	Forms of Intelligence: Rationality and Rule-following; Institutions as Rules; The Construction of Organizations; Administrative Reforms	Nils Brunsson, Professor of Management, Stockholm
13	28-29 Aug. 1996	Ökonomische Theorien der Organisation Property-Rights-Theorie, Transaktionskostentheorie, Principal-Agent-Theorie (Economic Theories of Organization Property rights theory, Transaction cost theory, Principal agent theory)	Prof. Arnold Picot, Institute for Information, Organization and Management at the Munich School of Management
14	03 Oct. 1996	Zirkularität als Standpunkt Der formale Aufbau der Modernen Systemtheorie, ihre Argumentationstypik und Stoßrichtung (Circularity as a Standpoint The formal structure of Modern System Theory, its typology of argumentation, and thrust)	Prof. Theodor M. Bardmann, Niederrhein University of Applied Sciences, Moenchengladbach

15	10-11 Jan. 1997	Das Konzept der Organisation als auto-poietisches System auf der Basis von Ent-scheidungen (The concept of the organization as an autopoietic system based on decisions)	Prof. Niklas Luhmann, Bielefeld
16	1-2 May 1997	Selbstorganisation, Fremdorganisation, Organisationsberatung (Organization of self, organization of others, organizational consulting)	Prof. Alfred Kieser, Mannheim
17	5-6 July 1998	Soziologie der Handlungsmuster Sociology of patterns of taking action (in French)	Claudette Lafaye, Philippe Corcuff, Paris
18	31 Oct.- 1 Nov. 1999	Rollen der Beratung 1. Phänomene des Management Consulting 2. Organisationsberatung in der Automobilindustrie 3. Die Rolle der Beratung bei Metaplan (1. Phenomena in Consulting Roles management consulting 2. Organizational consulting in the automotive industry 3. The role of consulting at Metaplan)	Dr. Andreas Werr, Stockholm School of Economics Dr. Roland Springer, DaimlerChrysler, Stuttgart Dr. Thomas Schnelle, Metaplan
19	14-15 Jan. 2001	Unterschiedliche Denkwelten in Organisationen (Divergent 'thought worlds' in organizations)	Prof. Dirk Baecker, Witten/ Herdecke

Furthermore, several internal seminars have taken place where consulting projects were presented by Metaplan consultants. The focus in these seminars has been to show the application of Metaplan consulting methods and procedures.

6.1.8 Remuneration

When consultants begin they all receive a fair salary which increases according to their experience and performance. Depending on Metaplan's business performance, they may get several extra salaries. The Partners receive a percentage of annual profits.

6.1.9 Principles and Guidelines of Partnership

Financial Principles

Our partnership is an association based on economic solidarity. The Partners all work to produce a financial profit, which they share.

Distribution is made according to a scheme that is determined in advance. It does not depend on personal successes or failures in the period of calculation (which is the business year).

Every Partner may take the initiative to make alterations to the scheme for distribution. Any such proposal must be discussed by all the Partners at a joint meeting, which aims for a unanimous decision. The decision on whether alterations are to be made and if so, which, will then be taken by the Partner with decision-making powers within the company.

Mutual Obligations

Every Partner shall select his/her own activities and means in such a manner that the goals and interests of the others are respected and taken into account, and s/he shall not exploit his/her opportunities for his/her own benefit to the disadvantage of his/her Partners.

Whenever Partners work together, no-one shall attempt to raise his/her profile to the detriment of the others. In order to reinforce trust in behavior based on solidarity, all Partners shall allow the other Partners insight into their activities. They shall explain how they use their time, they shall make their documentation on their projects available, they shall inform the others of what they are planning, etc.

Consensus

The Partners take part in the processes of forming a consensus and express themselves if they have a differing opinion. A consensus is to be found concerning the following issues: on appointing new Partners, if a Partner is to be criticized because his/her behavior gives cause for calling into question whether s/he should remain in the partnership, if a Partner is to be requested to leave the partnership, or if s/he is to be excluded from it, on the question of to whom the position of Managing Partner should be offered, if the current Managing Partner relinquishes this responsibility or wishes to leave, on changes and further development of methods and forms affecting the work of the Partners at a fundamental level, on changes to the messages and advertising signals that ensure a consistent identity on the market, on price positioning, on matters on the 'moral borderline', for example concerning the acceptance of commissions that are incompatible with the moral views of a Partner.

At all times it remains within the remit of the Managing Partner to decide whether s/he will follow the majority view, or take and implement a decision that differs with it. In such cases s/he shall explain his/her actions to the other Partners prior to taking such action.

7 Human Resource Management at Roland Berger Strategy Consultants

Burkhard Schwenker

Roland Berger Strategy Consultants

7.1 Introduction

Roland Berger Strategy Consultants is one of the world's leading strategy consulting companies, and the only one of European origin in the top segment. Our roots are firmly centered in Europe, with its wealth of languages, cultures, legal systems and markets. Our corporate culture combines European respect for diversity and individual cultures with American pragmatism, performing with professionalism and entrepreneurship. We blend rigorous analysis, competence and creativity, operating globally without losing sight of local particularities.

Roland Berger Strategy Consultants is active in all relevant markets, serving our clients with nearly 1,630 employees located in 31 offices across Europe, Asia and the Americas. Mr. Roland Berger founded the company in Munich in 1967, and served as its Global Managing Partner until he became Chairman of the Supervisory Board in July 2003. It was not long before the young company started expanding abroad – initially in neighboring Western European markets, but soon in Latin America as well. The company has been globalizing rapidly since the end of the 1980s. Roland Berger Strategy Consultants now also operates in Japan, China and Central and Eastern Europe. In addition, we have established two offices in the US since 1998.

We have grown rapidly and organically right from the outset. Today, our company has sales of EUR 530 billion (2004), making us number two in the German consulting market, number 3 in Europe and number five worldwide.

Roland Berger Strategy Consultants' clients include some 30% of the Global 1,000 and more than 40% of Europe's leading companies. We advise around 90% of Germany's top 50 manufacturing and trading firms, as well as 60% of Germany's leading banks and insurance companies. We maintain close relationships with our clients and they appreciate our work, as demonstrated by the fact that 78% of them return to us for support with additional projects. The way we see ourselves is based on our value proposition, expressed in the words, "Creative strategies that work." The standards we work to are as follows:

- We believe there are many individual ways and methodologies to achieve success.
- We deliver not standard advice, but tailored solutions that make a real difference.
- We support our clients in implementing these solutions, and thus ensure that they can be applied.
- We believe in local delivery backed up with global knowledge and experience.

The secret of our success is our ability to cover all the relevant topics with interdisciplinary teams. To do this, we are organized in global Competence Centers (CCs). Functional CCs develop innovative functional concepts and business approaches, while industry CCs customize functional topics for industry application and design concepts for each industry and company. We tailor our work and the applied methodologies to each individual assignment to fully meet our clients' needs. For each consulting project, we put together a dedicated interdisciplinary and, where appropriate, international team of experts with functional and industry-specific knowledge. This puts us in a position to develop creative strategies and support their implementation.

Our broad-based service portfolio covers strategic issues such as:

- Wrowth strategies, portfolio optimization and value-based management;
- post merger integration and corporate restructuring;
- marketing and brand management strategies;
- strategic alliances and internationalization strategies.

7.2 Basic Principles of Our Human Resources Work

It is our staff who makes the difference. It is their performance, innovative ability and flexibility that set us apart from the competition and that have put Roland Berger Strategy Consultants where we are today. In short, we consider our people to be our capital. Roland Berger Strategy Consultants recruits, develops and retains the most outstanding, analytical and creative minds in a way that enhances their value to our clients, to themselves and to our firm. We have realized a truly international working environment, with consultants of 32 nationalities and from a wide range of educational and professional backgrounds. We are dedicated to a common working style around the world, based on respect for and openness toward all individuals, both our clients and our employees at all levels. Our non-hierarchical and entrepreneurial spirit encourages our employees to come up with outstanding innovative ideas and watch them become reality.

The backbone of our successful human resources work is a clear human resources strategy and its practical implementation by our human resources management. Above all, this must be guided by the specifics of human resources work at a consulting firm, which arise out of the specific nature of "consulting" as a product. For all a consultancy's methods and tools, and for all its extensively documented research and recommendations, it does not "produce" things for its clients, but rather changes things by communicating knowledge. And that change is brought about solely by the people involved.

This is where human resources work comes in, creating the foundations of quality in a consulting firm's value chain. Human resources development is vitally important to the strategy of any consultancy, because it provides the foundation for success: clients are unlikely to call in consultants if they believe they can find the same skills in-house. It is this advantage in terms of knowledge and experience that gives consulting firms their raison d'etre.

However, it is not just the fact that our staff is our only real production factor that makes human resources development the number one task and challenge in managing a consulting firm. It is also the need to manage human resources: adjusting skill sets to constantly changing market demands or planning how many consultants are needed at each functional level to handle business and create a balanced seniority pyramid. This often goes hand in hand with rapid corporate growth, while staff tend to move on more quickly and have higher career expectations than employees at industrial companies. All this combines to make this work both complex and exciting.

To be the "employer of choice" for top talent, you need not only an excellent reputation and a challenging working environment, but also world-class HR work. At Roland Berger Strategy Consultants, this refers to two aspects: On the one hand, we have a comprehensive system of mentorship that supports each employee during his/her entire career with our company. On the other, our HR strategy is implemented by our Human Resources Department, pooling all essential HR functions (see Figure 7.1.):

- Developing HR strategy and implementing innovative actions;
- university and business school contacts;
- human resources planning and recruiting;
- staffing;
- human resources development;
- training;
- team and company events.

HR DEPARTMENT

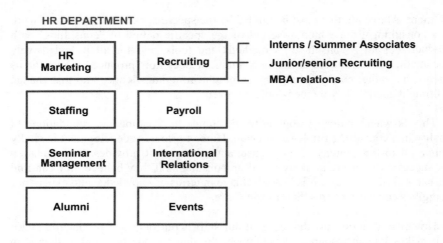

Fig. 7.1. Structure of HR Management

Our centralized setup ensures that our HR activities are consistent worldwide, and that our employees find uniform standards regardless of where they may be employed (even if they transfer within the company under our International Staff Exchange Program, for example). It also allows us to present a consistent profile in human resources marketing.

In the following sections, we will look at selected aspects of our human resources policy and human resources management in greater detail. We will follow the typical "career" of a member of our staff. In other words, I will start when they are first hired, look at their development opportunities and then cover a number of specific key aspects.

7.3 Selection and Appointment Process

To a top-quality candidate, the things an employer must offer are a good reputation, an exciting working environment and good development prospects. You could say this is the supply-side "limitation" on human resources work: only a positive image attracts the best talent.

To a consulting company, the aim is to take thousands of applicants and filter out the right ones, take highly qualified staff and swiftly equip them with the consultant's arsenal of tools, turn brilliant lone warriors into a successful team, and create the right career path for each individual.

To cover the permanent demand for consultants at source, in terms of both quantity and quality, companies must begin investing in corporate consulting's target groups well before an employee joins the company. This means that we need to get in touch with top talent early on. Since a high proportion of new hires are graduates of universities and business schools, we invest in target universities and chairs through workshops, case studies and grants. Another human resources marketing tool is our *TOPICS* event, which attracts considerable attention in the media: every summer, we invite some 60-80 internationally selected students to simulate a consulting project for a weekend. This is not about invented or made-up projects, but about real cases, in which well-known companies commission a project on a current issue. The students learn first-hand what everyday consulting work in direct contact with clients is like.

In addition to such conventional measures, we have also begun to establish chairs in key business management fields, particularly at the INSEAD business school in Fontainebleau (Business and Technology chair) and the Technical University of Munich (Internet-based Information Systems chair). By exchanging content and ideas, we can influence the education of future generations of consultants, and identify and address promising consultants sooner than other companies.

To get an early start in forging ties with future colleagues, internships are the most efficient way to get to know one another: students can gain practical experience – typically after their intermediate exams – and learn what it is like to apply the knowledge they have acquired to real project work. This usually gives them a very good idea of whether consulting in general and our company in particular meet their expectations in terms of career development, interests and inclinations, and whether we offer the working environment they seek. From the company's point of view, we can get a good idea of whether the interns have what it takes and whether they will fit into the team.

To really ensure a "return on investment" on internships, however, it is important that the company and the colleagues the intern has come to know remain in contact with the prospective candidate throughout the rest of their studies, until they complete their final examinations and decide which profession they want to enter. We do this through our *Students' Club*, which the top 10% of interns in each year are invited to join. We also offer successful interns the opportunity to have one of our consultants supervise their thesis or doctoral work. Therefore, depending on the year, as many as two-thirds of our new hires are already familiar with our company and how we work from their student days, thus shortening the expensive orientation phase.

In addition to the purely quantitative aspects of securing "new blood", the wealth of talent also represents a key element of our strategic marketing and recruiting activities. Succeeding with our clients depends not least on our ability to assemble a team of consultants with an optimum mix of functional know-how, industry experience and other qualifications (e.g. statistics, legal matters, etc.). Business management specialists are not the only people that meet the high quality requirements profile of a consulting company: they also need engineers, IT specialists, lawyers and specialists in natural sciences and the humanities. Different perspectives, ways of thinking and analysis are often the key to success in consultant teams. That is why 49% of our staff hold a degree in business administration or economics, 40% are engineers and IT specialists, and 11% graduates of other disciplines (medicine, law, humanities, psychology, etc.).

One question that concerns me in this context is why, in Germany at least, we don't seem to be able to interest more women in consulting than the meager 15-20% industry average. Roland Berger Strategy Consultants is trying to do something about this, through our FORWARD program (For Women: Attracting, Retaining, Developing), launched in the fall of 2002. This initiative has two aims:

First, we want more women to apply for positions with us. To achieve this, we specifically target female university graduates, for example through private information events at universities and by offering women interns specially tailored support.

Second, we want to boost employer loyalty among the women who have joined us. To this end, we have developed a special option for a coaching relationship between more experienced and less experienced female employees, and we have introduced new working time schemes for mothers with young children. Furthermore, we organize network meetings at which we work to further develop and refine FORWARD programs. For example, working groups are examining suggestions for areas in which mothers can work during their parental leave, or what a suitable career path might look like for female consultants.

This program has received a remarkably positive response, both internally and externally. We believe that we can use it to decisively boost our attractiveness as an employer. We are thus doing everything we can to develop and refine FORWARD. This also includes maintaining and expanding the interfaces between the working groups and company management.

In addition to the young novices, the old hands – that is, candidates with a longer track record of employment and extensive industry experience – are becoming increasingly important among our new recruits. As I mentioned earlier, clients expect us to send them experienced consultants; in many cases now, they expect more senior teams.

All prospective consultants, including those who have already completed an internship with us, have to pass through a clearly defined two-stage process (see Figure 7.2.).

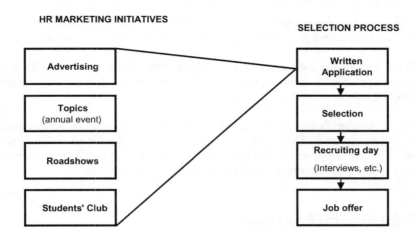

Fig. 7.2. The Hiring Process

In stage one, our Human Resources Department sifts through the applications we receive. Around 15% of them are then invited to stage two, one of our recruiting days.

We employ a considerable amount of specially trained resources to ensure that our recruiting process avoids one key error: hiring a candidate, only to have one of the parties realize that they made the wrong decision. There are two reasons why we focus on this: From the company perspective, staff have to stay with us for at least two years, because we invest substantial resources in training them, and we can recover this investment only in the form of output (for which clients pay). But we are also concerned for the *welfare* of the employee: it takes them at least two years of consulting work before they have accumulated the know-how they need to advance their position on the labor market.

The basic skills and abilities we look for in our future consultants are as follows:

- Basic evidence of above-average academic performance and expertise,
- plus analytical and creative abilities and
- the capacity to present and communicate complex issues in a clear and structured format.

But consulting is an interactive business, and only consultants who have outstanding interpersonal skills and are highly intelligent will succeed. First, these attributes determine the mood and quality of work within the team itself. Second, a consulting project stands or falls with our ability to integrate the client's staff in analyzing and resolving problems and get them to take responsibility for implementing our recommendations. We do not need arrogant know-it-alls – we want consultants who can listen and who are willing to learn from our clients.

Good consultants must be able to get things done, know how to handle resistance and be able to enforce unpleasant decisions. Without these abilities, they will not be able to meet clients' demands.

We try to identify these skills through interviews and case studies in the course of our recruiting days. These events are conducted centrally for all positions to be filled in a given country. This ensures that we do not have differing evaluation standards and new consultants with varying performance profiles.

7.4 Evaluation Principles

Like any other business, consulting companies strive to keep their best staff and grow their own managers in-house. However, unlike conventional companies, consulting firms must assume that not everyone *wants* to be regarded as a potential future manager, at least not when they join the company. Many people see consultancy not as their life's work, but more as a "fast track" that will qualify them, in three to five years' time, for a subsequent career with another "traditional" company or for working on their own. We do not consider this to be a negative attitude, nor do other consulting firms. In fact, it is a commonly accepted part of the way we do business. This makes it all the more important for human resources management to identify the real top candidates from among our staff and encourage them to make their career with our company.

This is where human resources development comes in, helping us continuously monitor each and every employee and keep them informed as to whether and to what extent their performance is consistent with their status and what clients expect. Employees who perform well can advance continuously and above all quickly – after all, that is one of the main reasons why working for a consultancy is so attractive. Both sides – staff and management – want to see progress on the career ladder, and as the next level approaches, both consider systematically whether they will succeed.

Obviously, this principle involves some winnowing. Many of our competitors use the expression "up or out". We, too, demand continuous high performance, and reward high performers with career advancement. However, we also believe that not everyone is equally suited to be, for example, a Project Manager. We believe that there are also specialists we need on client projects, and whom we thus encourage to some extent. But even employees who take this path and who are not affected by the principle of continuous promotion after a certain point in their career are subject to continuous evaluation. We very much believe in taking responsibility for developing staff, especially given the fact that a stagnating career makes people lose interest, both in the recruiting market and for individual em-ployees: it puts them in a "gilded cage" in which their age and income level make them unattractive to industrial companies.

An individual's career at our company is based on a clearly structured system in which we define individual hierarchy levels in terms of the performance we ex-pect. We lay down at the outset what consultants can achieve when they expand their competence, experience and scope of responsibility. For each of these stages, we define what we expect and what we reward, not only in professional and meth-odological terms (the so-called "hard skills"), but also in terms of "soft skills". We also define how long it should take to advance from one stage to the next, and make it clear to staff.

Our basic system has 4 elements (see Figure 7.3.):

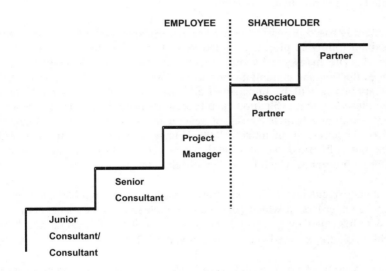

Fig. 7.3. Professional Levels

- New consultants join at the Junior Consultant or Consultant level, de-pending on previous experience. In their first one or two years, they are primarily involved in research and analysis work, expanding gradually until they work independently on smaller project modules.
- The first major development step is when, as a Senior Consultant, a member staff is allowed to independently manage project modules and is given management and control responsibilities within their team. This is also the entry level for staff with professional experience in other indus-tries.
- The next level up is Project Manager, with full responsibility for project content and management, and for follow-up acquisition.

- On joining the firm's management team, first as Associate Partner and later, if they are successful, as Partner, employees take on responsibility for acquisitions through long-term client relationships, managing an area of competence, and product and staff development.

This system of development stages is tightly linked to a performance assessment and evaluation tool. This very important and transparent tool is shaped by our corporate culture and is used right from day one at all hierarchy levels. Continuous career development calls for constant monitoring and regular review and evaluation of how consultants are meeting the various criteria of their requirements profile. Since the outcome of this evaluation decides whether and when a consultant will reach the next level, our system must be capable of generating valid statements about staff performance, that is, about the quality and efficiency of their professional work, their commitment and their ability to communicate with the client and within their own team.

This system is based primarily on the Project Manager individually evaluating each consultant following project completion, and providing them with constructive feedback. The managers making these evaluations must receive intensive training in evaluation and communication techniques, so that what are necessarily subjective appraisals will be understood and accepted. Twice a year, Mentors summarize these ongoing evaluations and present them to the respective regional Evaluation Committee, which consist of several members of the local management and is supported by members of the Human Resources department. This Committee makes the final decision on all promotions, bonuses and admission to special internal programs, which I will come back to later.

At the management level, this "top-down" evaluation is supplemented by its "bottom-up" counterpart, in which consultants regularly evaluate managers in accordance with management guidelines. To achieve a full 360-degree view, a "peer group" evaluation may be used at the management level.

Employees who have achieved outstanding results in our evaluation process are invited to join our Challenge Club. This club has three aims:

First, it aims to motivate its members. They have all been identified as constituting our management reserves, and they should actively be made aware of this. Members generally participate for two years, within which time they can expect to climb to the shareholder rank. However, it is also possible for a member to be dismissed for failing to perform adequately – in other words, our performance philosophy also applies here.

Second, the club aims to provide its members with special training above and beyond our internally established seminar program. We want to permanently boost their individual know-how. However, while technical expertise is important, preparing members for the management tasks that lie in store for them is also a very critical factor in their training.

Third, the members collaborate on internal task forces and help develop issues that are important for the entire company. In other words, they already take an active role in developing the firm whose future they will later be expected to control.

The Challenge Club meets once a year for its main event, which has been held in previous years in such cities as New York, Shanghai and Moscow. The agenda includes a mix of seminars, company visits and extensive opportunities for networking with our management, who consider the event a great occasion to meet and chat with our future managers. In addition to this main event, there are also various smaller meetings aimed at focusing on specific issues and facilitating more direct contact with other top candidates.

The program enjoys wide recognition as a career-boosting opportunity, and the participants are highly appreciative. One of the key results from the firm's perspective is that we have seen a significant decline in the number of exits – club members are more loyal because they receive an immediate sense of how much our firm appreciates their work.

7.5 Project Work

One of the key aspects of human resources work in consulting firms is staffing and capacity planning. One of the challenges to management here is that this involves three factors that may be in conflict with each other:

- Clients must be provided the most suitable team to meet their needs, in both professional and personal terms.

- It is in the consultancy's best business interest to have consultants consistently work with the same clients.

- Consultants want to work on interesting projects, with varying content and moving from place to place, to help them develop.

We are constantly striving to improve the professionalism of our capacity planning while taking these factors into account. Three years ago, we introduced a virtual end-to-end IT system that all project coordinators can use to manage their resource requirements. This tool integrates three elements:

1. An overview of each consultant's education and experience profile, which they update and manage themselves to increase demand for their services.
2. A capacity planning module that shows which of the selected consultants is available and when, and books them for a project at the simple press of a key.

3. A controlling tool that allows consultants to enter their working hours directly, and Project Managers and management to assess productivity, capacity utilization and other factors at any time.

Project Managers can plan their own capacity utilization, or they may delegate this task to our staffing unit, which is particularly efficient at putting together international teams. The system as a whole has achieved a high level of maturity and reliability, so that our human resources management has been massively strengthened in this key area.

7.6 Compensation

Compensation is another key lever in implementing a performance-based culture at consulting firms (see Figure 7.4).

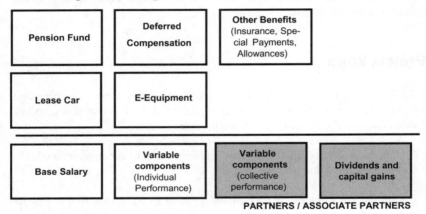

Fig. 7.4. Components of Compensation

We believe it is not mainly how much people are paid, but also the structure of their compensation – that is, how it breaks down into fixed and variable components and special payments – that gives companies a competitive edge. As far as our salary levels are concerned, we know from market studies that we are on a level that sets us significantly apart from much of the competition. Roland Berger consultants are generally at the upper end of the relevant earnings spectrum in the respective countries.

Our supplementary compensation components also make us an attractive employer. We recruit staff at all levels of seniority, and the maximum variable component achievable increases as they climb the ladder. The reason for this is easy to understand: first, it stresses the performance principle, and second, if staff is appointed to management level, their compensation model consists largely of variable components. The variable component, in turn, breaks down into a personal performance-based component and a collective performance-based component, which is usually based on results at the company or divisional level. Most lower seniority levels use a variable component based on individual performance, the variable bonus being linked directly to the individual's performance evaluation, further emphasizing how important and effective this tool is.

Further up the hierarchy, especially at the Partner level (as Partners are also shareholders in the company), compensation is based largely on the collective performance-based component, as this encourages Partners to collaborate. In addition, our Partners benefit from our company's growth through dividend payments and capital gains.

We also use compensation components that are not paid directly in cash, but depend on employees achieving a given seniority level, to promote loyalty to the company. We also have pension plans tailored to meet the requirements of a profession that does not, and should not, normally continue through to retirement age, given the stress involved. This makes us partly responsible for staff in the post-employment phase: we ensure that some of what they earn today is available to them tomorrow, however far off that may be, so they do not lose out when they retire.

One of the main secondary aspects of an attractive compensation package for hard-working employees is that they can largely take their pick of company cars and use high-performance equipment (laptops, mobile phones, PDAs, etc.).

7.7 Continuous Training

We invest heavily in developing our staff, focusing our efforts on two main goals. First, we aim to share our cumulative knowledge with new staff quickly and/or to promote knowledge sharing between staff. Second, it is our duty to support staff at all levels in acquiring the abilities we will expect of them at the next level.

Most continuous development does, of course, take place "on the job", in everyday project work under the guidance of suitably experienced colleagues, and is promoted by assigning employees to projects on a variety of subjects, especially at the start of their careers. Based on analyses of training requirements and years of experience, we have designed a supplementary internal training program that is closely connected with our career and evaluation system. Attendance at specific seminars is a requirement for promotion to the next level, while other seminars are recommended as a result of individual performance evaluations and are designed to promote professional and personal development (Figure 7.5.).

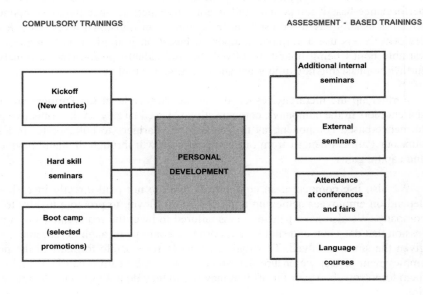

COMPULSORY TRAININGS   ASSESSMENT - BASED TRAININGS

Fig. 7.5. Qualification Opportunities

To give some details:

- New consultants start with basic training at a two-week introductory seminar soon after they are hired. This basic training focuses mainly on essential consulting tools for analyzing and interpreting business data and drawing conclusions for further action. We complement this largely content-driven element with aspects that are rarely taught at universities. These include skills that are essential for interacting successfully with clients and colleagues, such as communications skills, workshop techniques, or moderating and presentation skills.

- Once consultants have built up a certain amount of experience, their development requirements shift toward the technical aspects of project management: management and control, structuring problems into project modules and specific "to-dos", and planning the use of time and resources. At this stage, interpersonal skills become more important. A Project Manager must be able to precisely identify clients' needs, manage clients and their team, deal with delicate corporate policy matters and motivate both the client's and their own staff throughout the life of the project. Taking on management responsibilities at the project level may turn into a springboard for a management role with the company.

- The qualifications required at the management level are multifaceted. On the one hand, this is due to the specific skill set that makes a successful manager.

On the other, it is the result of the wide and varied range of tasks associated with acquiring and managing projects, and leading and managing your own company. We expect our managers to safeguard our sound financial basis through marketing and client management, and we expect them to be just as skilled at managing projects as they are at solving content problems.

As ideal "role models", they should also have the personal and professional characteristics required to encourage consultants to be loyal to our company, and to develop and promote them. But we also need to manage our own company, to develop and pursue strategies and initiate and control processes. Like any other company, ours demands structure and planning, control and administration.

On average, we expect our staff to spend around 10 full days a year on continuing development from their second year onward. To provide clear guidance for all employees, we have developed a "qualifications passport" that outlines mandatory and optional seminars for each functional level. Our internal seminar program offers around 200 individual events each year, led by internal experts and external specialists in the relevant field, including many university lecturers. In some cases, our in-house seminars on business management topics are designed and conducted in cooperation with business schools. The wide range of tasks involved means that continuing development at the management level needs to be much more individual and sophisticated, so we often use individual coaching here.

7.8 Additional Programs

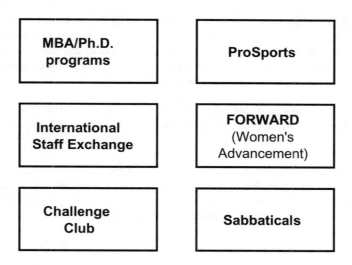

Fig. 7.6. Additional Skill and Motivation Enhancement Measures

7.8.1 MBA and Ph.D. Programs

In addition to our continuing development programs, we offer our consultants two special programs that allow them to work toward an MBA or a Ph.D. while working as a consultant. Candidates must have been with us for at least two years and must obtain their mentor's approval.

Employees selected for these programs are released from work – for one or two years for the MBA program, depending on which business school they select, and one year for the Ph.D. program (with an option to extend for 6 months). Participants either receive a postgraduate scholarship, or are reimbursed for their course fees and living expenses. These disbursements are made in the form of a loan that is deemed repaid in full when the employee completes two years of consulting work following the program.

We assist our program participants wherever possible by offering permanent contact through our **Academic Network** program. This organization combines our ongoing partnerships with a number of international chairs at universities and business schools. We share practical and academic know-how with college representatives (Academic Circle), conduct joint studies and publish books and Ph.D. dissertations on management theory and corporate management. Our Ph.D. candidates can use this channel as an opening into university research projects.

7.8.2 Working Abroad

For employees who wish to gain longer-term experience working abroad above and beyond the occasional project assignment, our International Staff Exchange Program (ISEP) offers them the opportunity to relocate to one of our international offices for a period of around two years. The initiative for such a move has to come from the individual consultant: they must apply to an office abroad and successfully complete its local selection process.

As a central support function, the ISEP team within our HR Department supports the entire transfer process, assisting with contracts and visas or organizing language courses, for example.

Over the past few years, an average of 80 employees have participated in the transfer program each year. Management regards it as explicitly desirable that would-be managers gain extensive international experience through the projects they are involved in or through spending time abroad.

7.8.3 Other Activities

The broad spectrum of personal development activities we offer is rounded out by the option to take a sabbatical for personal reasons. The requirement for this is the mentor's approval. If approved, staff can take up to six months off to spend time with their family, learn, travel, etc.

Senior Consultants and Project Managers who have been with our company for at least two years can also switch to working part-time, reducing their working hours by up to half. They can opt either to work 2.5 days (or more) each week, or reduce their annual working hours by up to 50%, to take time out after a project, for example. This option is also an explicit component of our women's development program FORWARD, which I mentioned earlier, and is also available for anyone who wants to devote some time to raising their children.

Last but not least, if a company aims to attract, promote and retain employees, it needs to nurture an environment in which a positive corporate culture can grow. Primarily, this means staff developing ties to the company and their colleagues above and beyond their contractual or working relationships. One explicit aspect of our human resources work includes a number of activities that promote such ties. For example, we offer our colleagues the chance to participate in sporting events at attractive locations (ProSports), or invite them to attend exciting team events, often including their partners.

7.8.4 Development Is for Support Staff, too

So far, I have concentrated mainly on our consultants, but we also offer attractive continuing development programs for our support staff. For instance, all professional support staff (that is, our in-house Editing, Language Service, Research and Knowledge Management staff) enjoy essentially the same benefits as consultants, i.e. performance-based bonuses, access to all seminars, sabbaticals, and participation in the MBA and Ph.D. programs and ISEP.

As with our consultants, we have built up a career model for our support departments, and employees whose personnel committee gives them an above-average evaluation can take on more responsibility over time. Here, too, increasing seniority comes with an increasing share of variable salary components.

7.9 And When Staff Leave ...

Compared with other businesses, consulting companies have a relatively high turnover rate. People often have their own agenda, such as prospects of taking on management responsibilities in industry. A consultancy's attitude to people leaving is therefore very different from the norm elsewhere.

And so it is with us, too. If someone lets us know that they see their future outside of the consulting business, or if our evaluation procedures indicate that they are not meeting our performance standards, we offer to help them look for a suitable position. We do this because, as a consulting company, we have a first-class network of contacts with our clients' management, and we usually have a very good idea of what attributes and abilities employees need to succeed with them. Not only that, but having worked with and trained our staff intensively for several years, we are in a very good position to assess them, which puts us in an ideal position to "match" job offers. The benefits here are obvious, to both staff and clients: clients know that the consultants they have come to know and appreciate from project work are "high flyers", and our employees can take up the position that is best suited to their personal and professional abilities.

We see this support as investing in our own future. After all, it is highly likely that employees who leave us will, in the foreseeable future, be in a position to decide on consulting contracts. And what would then be more obvious than to call their old employer and ask them to submit a proposal? In other words, each former employee is also a potential future client!

With this in mind, we also cultivate our **Alumni Network** as a platform for former employees to exchange news and views among themselves and to keep in touch with current employees. Former consultants not only retain their emotional ties to their old company, but also continue to benefit from the information and know-how we generate. The network has its own password-protected website, ensuring that our alumni are always up to date on our company's current products.

7.10 Conclusion

Surveys show that we are perceived as an extremely attractive employer. This pleases us, of course, but it also obligates us. We must constantly develop our human resources work in such a way that we can continue to offer our employees the outstanding opportunities that will keep them excited about our firm.

Our human resources work has not stood still in recent years, and it is not going to do so any time soon. Similar to a client project, we continuously monitor current benchmarks for outstanding, motivating human resources development activities. We take the elements we consider to be reasonable and relevant – both for the satisfaction and growth of individual employees and for the firm's objectives – and develop internal concepts for implementing those elements in harmony with our particular environment. We regard this form of innovative and active human resources work as our duty.

8 How Students Manage Human Resources

Kathrin Günther[1], Frederike Harms[1], Mareike Schilling[1], and Lorraine Schneider[2]

[1] University of Paderborn, Germany

[2] Capgemini Deutschland GmbH

8.1 The BDSU: Students Consult Companies

The German Confederation of Junior Enterprises (**B**undesverband **D**eutscher **S**tudentischer **U**nternehmensberatungen – BDSU) is an incorporation of Junior Enterprises. These are autonomous operating organizations from all over Germany which are working in the consultative sector.

The idea of Junior Enterprises was established in France during the 1960s. Its main purpose was to connect theory with practice. This gave and still gives highly motivated students the opportunity to use their theoretical knowledge by independently carrying out consulting projects and thus gaining professional experience. Since the concept was successfully established in Germany in the mid 1980s, an increasing number of newly founded Junior Enterprises was recorded. In 1992 the BDSU was formed as the German Confederation of Junior Enterprises to encourage the continuous cooperation and the knowledge transfer of the different academic initiatives. The BDSU already includes 29 German Junior Enterprises with approximately 1,600 students today.

The initial idea and long-term tasks of the BDSU have been summarized into the following **mission**:

The BDSU as the incorporation of the leading German Junior Enterprises creates surplus value by

- Guaranteeing continuous transposition of knowledge and experience as a platform,
- demanding, encouraging and securing quality,
- supporting the interaction between students and the economy as well as
- arranging and developing actively the idea of "students consult companies".

The **vision** includes business objectives and guidelines and thus presents the course of the BDSU´s strategic and operative planning:

- The BDSU thrives to become Germany's most recognized academic initiative.
- The membership in the BDSU stands for high graded, professional and innovative consulting performance.
- The established seal of quality of the BDSU serves for its members as a profitable reference.
- The BDSU guarantees a structured and organized transposition of knowledge and experience.
- The BDSU is a working network, which is marked by each individual student of the member initiatives.

In order to achieve the ambitious goals and guidelines, the BDSU needs high commitment, creativity and strategic thinking of the Junior Enterprises, their associates and Executive Boards. The Board of the BDSU consists of six students who honorarily take over responsibility of the confederation for one year. Every Board member undertakes and supervises independently one specific working scope during his tenure. There is also an advisory committee which supports the Executive Board in a controlling and advising way.

In addition the BDSU disposes of a widespread network, which consists of the following components:

1. JADE (Junior Association for Development in Europe)
At the moment, the JADE[2] represents confederations of seven European countries and four Consultative Members. Altogether the network is composed of more than 250 Junior Enterprises with over 20,000 students. A close cooperation with Brazilian Junior Enterprises makes the JADE the world's second largest academic network. With the objective of developing an international strategy, it provides the BDSU the opportunity to operate on a global basis.

2. Kölner Runde
The so called ´Kölner Runde` is an incorporation of the six most recognized academic initiatives of Germany.[3] The national Board members are meeting up regularly to work out possible collaborations on a national level and to organize collective events such as symposiums.

3. Cooperations with existing companies
The BDSU has a close partnership to a range of well-known companies, which assist the confederation as curators and sponsors. The following companies are currently part of the curatorship: AXA, Cap Gemini Ernst & Young, Microsoft, MLP, PalmOne, Volkswagen Consulting as well as ZF Friedrichshafen.

---

[2]For further information see also www.jadenet.org
[3]The "Kölner Runde" includes MARKET TEAM, MTP, AIESEC, bonding, ELSA and the BDSU.

These companies support the BDSU both in a financial and idealistic way in terms of workshops, trainings, events and external consulting projects.

Through regular events like for example the BDSU-Meetings with working groups and workshops or even nationwide projects, each associate gets the possibility to exchange knowledge and socialize with interesting people.

The idea of Junior Enterprises prospers from the readiness and capability of the BDSU Board as well as every single academic initiative. Customer satisfaction is the most important factor in the everyday live of a consultant, which demands a high degree of professionalism and awareness of quality. Therefore the BDSU Board defined a common quality control requirement, whose compliance is controlled annually. Consequently, the BDSU as a seal of quality is taken into account.

In comparison to common Management Consultancies, the academic initiatives see the fundamental key of success in the knowledge of their associates. Basically every student irrespective of the branch of study gets the possibility to work in a Junior Enterprise. Premises are team spirit, a high commitment and the fact of having pleasure in transforming theoretical knowledge into practical experience. The Junior Enterprise thus lives on its associates, who bring contemporary and interdisciplinary knowledge from the universities to the Enterprise. This knowledge ranges from business and computer science to psychology, law and natural sciences. Especially the mixture of knowledge and willingness among the associates represents an indispensable competitive advantage and enable the academic initiative to provide a broad field of consulting service. The offer contains custommade solutions essentially in the sectors Management Consulting like for example Quality Management, Optimization of Processes and Market Researches as well as IT-Consulting and Training. The customers of the Junior Enterprises are as diverse as the operating areas: They vary from sole proprietorship to well-known large-scale enterprises out of each branch.

Every Junior Enterprise is an independent and autonomous construct with partly very dissimilar forms of organizations although the BDSU as a confederation provides certain standards and requisitions. For this reason it is not astonishing that there exist different concepts and approaches in human resource management in a Junior Enterprise.

8.2 Students Deal with Personnel Matters

In the following the possibilities of a Junior Enterprise in the segment of their internal human resource management will be displayed:

Junior Enterprises are organized in non-profit associations, which means that they are basically open to any student who is interested and committed. Nevertheless, a human resource planning is indispensable for an effective analysis of the labor-pool. To realize short-term, medium-term and long-term goals Junior Enterprises have to revert to a top-quality staff pool. Its composition relates to the requirements of the market as well as to the maintenance and the advancement of the association. Evidently, human resource planning is a central requirement, in order to carry out a selective human resource management.

8.2.1 Staff Marketing

Both, the fields of activities of the Junior Enterprises and the development potentialities of every associate, are visualized at informational events at participating universities, which take place continuously. The publicity of Junior Enterprises and the interest in cooperation is also brought forward through attendances at lectures. Interested students furthermore receive the crucial information through flyers, annual reports and individual field reports, which are meant to inspire them to work for a Junior Enterprise. Posters and reports in daily- and student papers also are viewed as effective advertising material. The most successful procedure to acquire new staff still lies in the word-of-mouth recommendation. Nothing furthers an efficient acquisition of new staff like the demonstration of individual career options through a person in charge.

8.2.2 Selection of Personnel

Even though the Junior Enterprises are open to every student, the economic orientation and the awareness of quality, which is an outcome of the mentioned orientation, make a well directed selection of new staff indispensable. To gain membership in a Junior Enterprise, every student has to pass through a regulated procedure of admission, which consists of three stages:

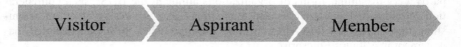

Fig. 8.1. Three Stages to Become a Member

After the first contact with the Junior Enterprise, the interested student is classified as a visitor and registered in the staff database. The visitor is also admitted to the mailing list, through which he constantly receives information about internal developments of the association and current projects. Once the visitor shows serious interest and commitment as well as a desire to be integrated into the association for a period of time, he is asked to file an application for membership. From that moment on the visitor turns officially into an aspirant. This stage is similar to a qualifying period and can last up to a year. Every aspirant has to fulfill a set program, which consists of various aspects: The aspirants have to prove their ability of working independently and their sense of responsibility. Further on, they should participate in obligatory trainings and carry out at least one internal project.

At the end of the qualifying period there is an interview between the Executive Board of the Junior Enterprise and the aspirant. Here, he can point out his personal preferences and goals. Both sides get the opportunity to voice possible criticism. Afterwards the aspirant gets the opportunity to present himself and his previous activities during a meeting in front of all members. The aspirant should receive feedback from the members within a two week period. Finally, the Board decides on the admission.

Associates get information about every project at the regular meetings and via e-mail. Thus each interested person has the chance to apply. The Board, then, will screen application on the basis of the following criteria:

- Experiences gained in previous project work,
- professional knowledge,
- performance at the customer,
- team spirit,
- prior commitment,
- status of the applicant (members are first choice).

In order to secure a continuous knowledge transfer, the Board pays particular attention to a well-balanced mixture between experienced consultants and interested and motivated aspirants when determining the project team members. That way, new associates without deep professional knowledge will still participate in projects. Nevertheless, the compliance of internal quality standards has highest priority. Every candidate who would like to become Project Manager needs to be a member of the Junior Enterprise and has to dispose of appropriate practical experience and soft skills.

At the kick-off-meeting, important issues like general documentation, workflow-based project controlling processes, as well as the contractual and legal conditions are discussed. Along with team members, the Quality Manager and Executive Board for Finances participate in this meeting. During the whole project, relevant field reports of previous projects are at the team members' disposal. Furthermore, the team is in close contact with experienced, seniors as well as the Board and the Quality Manager.

8.2.3 Staff Commitment

The Junior Enterprise offers a range of different events in order to strengthen its bonds with the contributor and to increase team spirit. Since every contributor may leave the Junior Enterprise at any time, events like these are of great importance.

These events are varied nature: First of all there is the 'Strategic Weekend', at which all associates come together to define the strategic direction of the particular financial year. These meetings ensure that associates are actively integrated into the conceptual development process. Solidarity between contributors of the Junior Enterprise is furthered through collective activities at the so called 'Social Weekend'. In addition to this there are weekly meetings to inform everybody about latest developments.

Furthermore, regular staff dialogues play an important role in committing the staff to the Junior Enterprise. The long-term commitment of associates is intensified through the continuous recapitulation of developing perspectives as well as constructive criticism.

8.2.4 Staff Development

The Junior Enterprise organizes a great number of training sessions in the course of every semester. The training program is prepared half a year in advance. Exceptional about it is to be emphasized that most of the tutors are active members of the Junior Enterprise. Every training session is evaluated by means of a web-based evaluation sheet to guarantee a Continuous Improvement Process (CIP).

Staff dialogues are another method of developing personnel and can fulfill various functions. Thanks to this classical management tool particular problems and suggestions for improvement as well as target agreements can be verbalized and reviewed.

A Junior Enterprise concentrates mainly on external and internal projects. For the advancement of cooperative and autonomous learning they are used systematically. Internal projects are a special feature of Junior Enterprises, which focus on the development of staff and also on internal organization. Documentation is handled as in external projects. It helps to familiarize associates with the general conditions of consulting projects and to prepare them for assignments in external projects.

An additional chance for individual development lies in the possibility of taking over a position in the Executive Board or the direction of a department. This work prepares students to assume responsibility and to make decisions in work life.

8.2.5 Leaving the Junior Enterprise

The past has shown that access to job life is easier for students with experiences in practice. It usually leads either to self-employment or an employment in a renowned company. Consequently, it is very important for Junior Enterprises to keep in contact with their former associates – the so called 'Alumni'. Maintenance of Alumni relations has a social as well as an economic component: In many cases, close contact has lead to consulting projects and internships. Herewith an interior solidarity is maintained beyond the association membership.

8.3 Students Develop Concepts

After a global overview of the internal human resource management a detailed insight into the various conceptual works of Junior Enterprises is delivered. Especially the selection of personnel, staff bonding, advanced training and different alumni appendages attract interest.

8.3.1 Selection of Personnel

As a result of the high expenditure of human labor, students who are less engaged leave the Junior Enterprise of their own accord. Self-selection is therefore an appropriate instrument of selecting personnel. Nevertheless Junior Enterprises are endeavored to reduce the costs of vocational adjustment and further education by using pre-selective measures.

The consultants of Junior Beratung Bayreuth (JBB) (www.jbb-ev.de) present themselves at relevant university lectures. Approximately a hundred visitors attend the bi-annual road show. In the framework of this meeting JBB tries to give a realistic description of their daily tasks to avoid deficient expectations on the part of the visitors.

On a regular basis, Recruiting Workshops simulate real projects. They provide potential junior staff with the opportunity to gain insights in a consultant's everyday life. Furthermore, such workshops speed up the integration of future members into the association and common work. Since participation takes time and organizational input, it demands high operational readiness right at the beginning: Self-selection happens in the process of dedication. As a result, the workshop has a good chance to win long-termed devoted and motivated members for the association.

The following dimensions serve as a basis for the decision process and further planning. Here, the attention is put less on professional than on multidisciplinary skills:

- Capacity for teamwork,
- time management,
- task arrangement,
- analytic and process orientated thinking,
- concentrated working under time pressure,
- structured proceeding,
- working and analyzing information efficiently,
- creativity at detecting solutions,
- presentation techniques and rhetorical skills.

Before the actual project simulation, a presentation technique training (PowerPoint® application included) as well as an informal lunch with as many JBB members as possible takes place. The case and a classification of all participants depending on determined characteristics (i.e. number of semesters) will be presented. All fresh aspirants are confronted with the following standard problem: A huge Swedish furniture manufacturer plans to expand to New Zealand. In the context of a market analysis the participants shall advice the client and estimate risks and chances. They receive information material as well as analysis tools for working out the results. These outcomes should afterwards be presented to the board of the manufacturer, which consists of three-four members of JBB.

In approximately four hours the individual teams have to generate a proposal all by themselves. Their only support is a limited access to the internal database. During this process time the President and the Head of Human Resources offer their help in resolving problems and questions once. Sixty minutes later, usually towards nine pm, the cooperating customer signals its acceptance of the project via a telephone call. He makes it known that he expects results within four days. One of the next team meetings is observed by a member of JBB who takes notes according to the before defined dimensions. His mere presence poses a stress-factor. Two days later the project manager is informed, again via telephone, that the final presentation has to be brought forward one day. In addition, during this presentation the teams have to face challenging tasks: The lecture is shortened from 20 to 10 minutes, the results have to be presented spontaneously in a foreign language and tricky problems are brought to the teams' attention. The process is rounded off through a group and personal feedback.

Striving for quality, the consultants of JBB try to concretize the dimensions in terms of behavioral anchored scales and to form a consistent feedback standard. Whoever has gone through this demanding selection process is usually characterized by enduring commitment and a high grade of working moral.

8.3.2 Staff Commitment Program

Finding, retaining and motivating qualified and committed students is one of the most crucial tasks of human resource management in a Junior Enterprise. Besides various positive aspects like practical experiences, trainings and contacts to other students as well as companies, a membership implies in particular the observance of responsibilities, an infinity to the spirit of the association and the contribution of personal ideas.

The Junior Enterprise Company Consulting Team (CCT) located in Berlin (www.cct-ev.de) is distinguished through an all-embracing staff bonding program. The association structure is as follows:

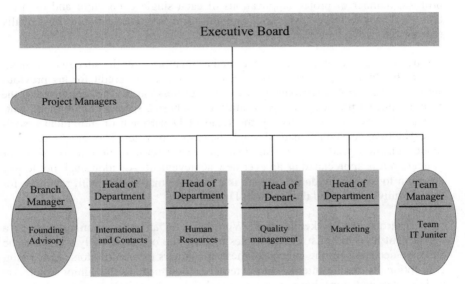

Fig. 8.2. Organizational Structure of the Association (Company Consulting Team)

In consequence of the association structure of CCT, visitors apply directly for a job posting at the respective department. In such a way, the major domains within the association as well as the specific task allocation are established. To facilitate co-operation and orientation, every new department visitor is assigned a 'buddy'. This buddy introduces new recruits into the association, encourages them to participate in meetings and provides kind support.

In discussions concerning agreements on objectives with the Head of Department, high and specific aims are fixed for the next three months. These allude to declared goals of the Balanced Scorecard as well as to individual requirements and the wishes of personal development of the contributor. Structured feedbacks are given in regular intervals to guarantee acknowledgement and to build up an open feedback culture.

CCT attaches special importance to a unique conversational standard. This is demonstrated both by a way of soft skills (e.g. techniques of moderation, presentation and work) and the consequent implementation in sessions and the assignment of coaches. Their task consists in auditing and if necessary correcting the way of communicating and moderating the team meetings.

When being a visitor and during the time of probation students have the possibility to collect external project experience. The project manager assures that the filling of projects takes place on the basis of professional qualifications and criteria of equity. This is warranted by taking into consideration the candidates' profiles, number of project applications of each single contributor and the rule, that – if achievable – visitors, aspirants and members should be equally represented in every project.

The associate is ceremonially appointed as member after the successful conclusion of his time of probation. As a means of giving him credit for his previous activities, the member receives presents and business cards. The 'employee of the month'-concept provides the opportunity to emphasize special commitment. Current candidates are nominated by the Head of Department or individual associates. The final decision is made through the casting of votes. The 'employee of the month'-election heads to underline that the successful operation is not taken for granted, but is appreciated as an ever new achievement. An additional tool to pay attention to each individual associate is a birthday mailing list with reminder for the Executive Board and the Heads of Department.

CCT arranges 'Workends' and 'Workdays' on an association as well as a department level to enlist the associates more to the operative daily work and the strategic decisions. In the context of these encounters the contributors are working conceptionally on the internal and external embodiment of the Junior Enterprise and develop new consulting approaches and fields. Associates moreover have the possibility to express their opinion anonymously through quarterly interviews and Board evaluations. Via this venue valuable change processes are implemented. The fact that the Executive Board gathers return information four times a year underlines the feedback culture mentioned above. It relates to the core-idea of the Junior Enterprise: The association is formed by everyone.

Weekly meetings not only assure the concurrence of all contributors but also review current issues and announce projects. The fact that external projects are exclusively presented during the meetings is a major incentive to attend the appointment.

To integrate new associates and to intensify the corporate feeling, pub outings following meetings and other 'Outside-Office-Events' are offered. These range from theatre, movie-theatre or concert visits to sportive events like bowling or climbing. Relaxed socialization is encouraged through

- Festivities (Christmas- and Summer-Parties, Alumni Days),
- the annual Social Weekend (Organized in common with the Austrian Junior Enterprise Uniforce),
- corporate trips to the BDSU or JADE meetings (A financial allowance is offered to the participants).

The two last-mentioned activities support a fortification of the European spirit and international exchange.

Since the financial resources of Junior Enterprises are rare, motivation is provided exclusively through intrinsic means.

8.3.3 Concept of Training

In the sector of human resource development the training concept of 'Campus Consult' from Paderborn (www.campus-consult.de) is introduced. From April 2003 to March 2004, 42 internal courses with various focal points were arranged. A total of 553 participants attended the training sessions, held by 23 different tutors.

A special department is responsible for the organization of further education. The head of the training department[4] together with the Board of human resources and the company management conduct a detailed demand analysis. Hereupon a training program is scheduled for the upcoming six months. This very plan is continuously updated and adapted. Further on, the head of the training department takes care of location and media acquisitions, surrounding the event. The particular tutor is in charge of the content of the training session. The head of department stays in close contact with the tutors to ensure that original requirements are met. New tutors actively participate in the composition and devolution of training session.

The upcoming training sessions are published on the homepage at a regular basis. Their posting provides access to all data concerning specifics of training, the tutor, date, time, preferable premises. Thus everybody has the opportunity to get informed about the actual courses. Enrollment into training is facilitated through a protected area of the homepage. It is the task of the head of department to check

---

[4]The association Campus Consult is divided into 3 positions within the Executive Board and 5 Heads of Departments. There also is a corporation (Ltd.) with 2 managers alongside.

the contingent as well as the suppositions of each registered person. He has the authority to accept or deny applicants. Thereupon an automatic e-mail is sent to the participant.

Because of the considerable increase of new associates, it has been deemed necessary to offer basic courses every half a year. By way of this a continuous social and professional integration of new contributors is guaranteed. Basic courses are classified and listed as follows:

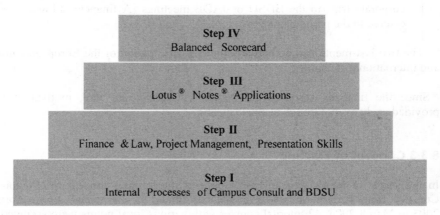

Fig. 8.3. Construction of Basic Courses (Campus Consult)

The training sessions of step I are meant to give visitors a first orientation. They are familiarized with the composition and devolution of the Junior Enterprise. This particular training is lectured by the Board of human resources. In step II young consultants learn important tools for a consultant's everyday life. The training sessions on this level take on a workshop character, which furthers the internalization process of newly gained qualifications. Step III helps trainees to use the office software. The internal data flow consists mainly of address administration, project management and e-mail communication, supported by Lotus® Notes® databases. Team Rooms are provided especially for project work. In step IV, finally, associates get to know the Balanced Scorecard, since the strategic assignation of the Junior Enterprise results from and the operative work is build up on it.

Every associate is given the opportunity to broaden his knowledge systematically after passing the basic courses. Specific courses on different subjects are offered every semester. They are divided into the following categories: IT, IT-application, management as well as soft skills. Based on the demand analysis the training session in these sectors are established. In order to prepare contributors for future projects, training sessions are generated from the current costumer demand. Training on Basel II may serve as an example. Often trainings arise from actual project work. Therefore, the annual report team is skilled in accordant application programs for layout and design. New courses often arise out of personal preferences and initiatives. A Junior Enterprise thrives thanks to the concurrence of students from different areas of expertise. Thus, generated knowledge can be passed on to associates foreign to the subject. Consequently everyone has the prospect of broadening his own horizon. The outcome is an interesting mixture of courses like leadership workshops, computer network training and internet security or even an introduction to service marketing.

Some topics are transmitted in a series of courses which build upon each other and take into account various fields of preparation. In the course of training sessions for Lotus® Notes® databases, i.e., basics are taught first, followed by an introduction to the autonomous development of databases.. Given that the tutor has worked himself a variety of projects, his knowledge and experience will be passed on. As soon as participants have gathered practical experiences they themselves are enabled to assist the next generation as tutor. Because of this cycle high class training sessions will also be offered in the future.

Quality control is maintained through course evaluation, for which a secured area of the homepage set up is reserved. Participation is anonymous and will be interpreted automatically.

Specific work groups allow associates to deepen their knowledge in different domains. These groups meet on a regular basis. They function as multiplying systems, in so far as single team members will be asked to prepare future group meetings. The resulting concepts will afterwards be discussed by the whole group. The goal of these study circles is to achieve deep knowledge in a particular branch as well as – if possible – collective preparation towards external certificates. The Microsoft Office Specialist Team, for example, is working to receive the correspondent certificate. There are also Competence Teams who are engaged in issues like Cost-Performance Calculation, Human Resource Management, Knowledge management and the so called Linuxcafé.

8.3.4 Concept for Alumni

The time a conductor works actively for the association varies normally from three to five years. Afterwards he has the option to support the Junior Enterprise in order to assure the consecutive knowledge exchange. In the following, possible ways of Alumni engagement are described:

With the allocation of projects, internships and job offers, the Alumnus shows confidence in his former association. Moreover the Alumni might provide training opportunities in interesting subjects. The Junior Enterprise 'Junior Business Team e.V.' from Stuttgart (www.jbt-ev.de) can be seen as pioneer in this respect. The team invites its Alumni twice a year to 'Working Weekends'. As part of these events the Alumni organize workshops in which knowledge can be transferred to associates. In addition, every conductor gets a chance to talk about the Junior Enterprise and potential job perspectives in a relaxed atmosphere.

Especially such informal conversations enable the Alumni to take part in the active work of the association. An Alumnus of the Junior Enterprise 'Junior Comtec' from Darmstadt (www.junior-comtec.de), for example, offers a sailing tour for associates every year. Furthermore the Alumni take part in 'Strategic Weekends' to work actively on the association's strategic direction. Besides that, a newsletter informs the Alumni continuously about actual developments. They also have access to a special Alumni-Intranet, where they can find out about current activities, internal matters as well as other Alumni. The Junior Enterprise Campus Consult encourages the support of their Alumni through cooperation in their Advisory Board. In the specific case of the Company Consulting Team an Alumnus provides the association with plenty of advertising resources at different German train stations.

Since much is to be gained from Alumni feedback, it is evidently important to invest as much time and power as possible into the perpetuation of contacts. Interchange creates synergy effects and proofs useful for both sides.

8.4 Conclusion

Given that Junior Enterprises are exclusively organized and sustained by students, they cannot revert to a constant team. For this very reason, a higher fluctuation is quite normal and the considerable burden for students who are engaged in intensive studies need to be recognized as a source of possible problems. This challenge requires a systematic and creative approach to the creation respectively conversion of concepts. The existence of Junior Enterprises since the 1960s shows that the chosen way leads to success.

9 Employer Branding through Preference Matching

Stephan Erlenkaemper[1], Tom Hinzdorf[2], Katrin Priemuth[3], and Christian von Thaden[4]

[1]Catholic University of Eichstaett-Ingolstadt, Germany
[2]BBDO Consulting Munich
[3]Sophus Consulting Ingolstadt
[4]BBDO Consulting Düsseldorf

Summary

Efficient employer branding requires innovative methods of personnel market research to control and target the employer attractiveness of consultancies. Preference matching can be used to determine the specifications potential applicants have for attractive employers and to define the selection and decision-making process of applicants as realistically as possible. The information gained from this matching process is then turned into precise recommendations for the successful employer branding of consultancies and other companies.

9.1 Objectives and Prerequisites for Successful Employer Branding

Employer branding is the marketing-oriented positioning of the employer as a brand, the exact determination of the relevant target group and the correspondingly tuned mix of measures to be taken. Where this target group is potential applicants, employer branding for the company has the task of making the company as attractive as possible to applicants. One result of this process is an increase in attractiveness as an employer.

For this purpose, employer branding has to close an information gap. By developing an image as an employer, top consultancies in particular tend to attract certain applicants without influencing whether these are the applicants the company actually wants to address. The fundamental question concerning employer branding for this industry is therefore: How should staff managers present their consultancy as an employer brand to animate - as far as possible - only those applicants who suit the company and its culture to submit their applications? Efficient employer branding must answer this question, as it is ultimately not just a matter of increasing the attractiveness of consultancies but to make sure that the right applicants apply to the right consultancies. Only thus can a win-win situation be established.

9.2 Controlling Information through Preference Matching

For the personnel marketing departments of consulting companies, the question at this point is what exactly brochures, flyers, trade fairs, internet, job interviews and advertisements should communicate in order to be as attractive as possible in the race for the best graduates. Such information is generally gained via personnel market research and the use of questionnaires. In these questionnaires graduates are asked directly about their preferences for certain company features such as image, salary, responsibility or location of the company. In addition, graduates are asked about the attractiveness of the company. Beside the fact that experience from market research has shown that direct questioning does not necessarily fulfill the criterion of validity, this method is also not realistic as it does not portray the decision-making process of potential applicants in their selection of attractive consultancies. This usually takes the form of a classic trade-off situation. This means that in their selection of an employer applicants must weigh up the advantages and disadvantages of the various consulting firms. For example, someone who wants to earn a high salary will usually also accepts a higher workload and be flexible about the field they are assigned to work in.

To gain as realistic a picture as possible of the decision-making behavior of graduates and thereby gain valid recommendations for employer branding, a method from consumer market research has been transferred to human resources: choice modeling (Thaden 2001) (see Figure 9.1.). In this method, the graduate being questioned has to rate fictive but realistic company profiles of consultancies according to their attractiveness. They are therefore forced to choose between the different companies presented.

The attractiveness of the rated companies is the sum of the quality of the following features:

- Team,
- company image,
- starting position in the company,
- management style,
- activity,
- working conditions,
- focus of the company / degree of internationalization,
- location,
- salary and social security contributions.

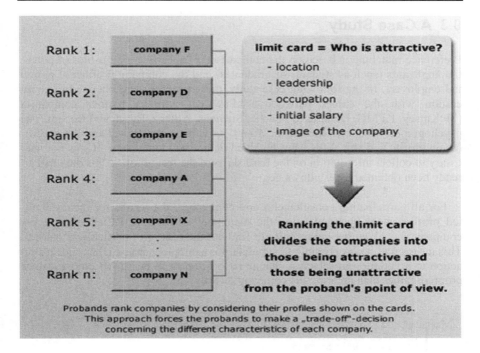

Rank 1: company F

limit card = Who is attractive?
- location
- leadership
Rank 2: company D
- occupation
- initial salary
Rank 3: company E
- image of the company

Rank 4: company A

Rank 5: company X

Ranking the limit card
divides the companies into
those being attractive and
Rank n: company N
those being unattractive
from the proband's point of view.

Probands rank companies by considering their profiles shown on the cards.
This approach forces the probands to make a „trade-off"-decision
concerning the different characteristics of each company.

Fig. 9.1. Preference Matching Based on Consumer Behavior Theory

As Figure 9.1. shows, the people questioned, the subjects, are forced by this method – as in reality – to assess the company as a whole according to their personal preferences. This makes it unnecessary to evaluate the attractiveness of individual company features but rather the attractiveness of a consultancy or the competitor company as a whole. If all profiles are rated, i.e. the preferences placed in order of importance, this still does not mean that the companies and consultancies assessed by the subjects are attractive enough for them to actually submit an application. This information is gained from an additional statement, in which the applicants have to say which of the profiled companies they would consider applying to. These could be all or none of the consultancies and companies presented.

By this method, one can assess what the ideal consulting firm should look like from the point of view of the subjects, which leads on to the question of which company fits the specification profile of the applicants. To find an answer, the subjects' specification profiles are matched with the previously compiled company profiles of potential employers using the tool TORP. The results allows companies to check how they are perceived on the applicant market and also enables them to search for a particular type of applicant and design their brand accordingly.

9.3 A Case Study

Preference matching is based on the comparison of specification profiles of potential applicants (such as students or graduates) and the company profiles of potential employers. In the following case study, these profiles were obtained in cooperation with the career network e-fellows.net and its partner companies (McKinsey, KPMG, Deloitte & Touche, Siemens, Allianz, Bosch and Roche). The psychographic characteristics of the 1,880 individuals questioned and the specification profile and soft skills were obtained on an individual basis. It was not necessary to collect information on the hard skills of the test group as this data had already been obtained by e-fellows.net.

For all participating consultancies and companies, the results for their submitted profiles were obtained using the matching software TORP. Further, every company was given the opportunity to find out the effects of particular scenarios. This means that it was possible to simulate, for example, a potential applicant's reaction to a variation in salary, a change in location or to being put onto a trainee program rather than entering the company directly.

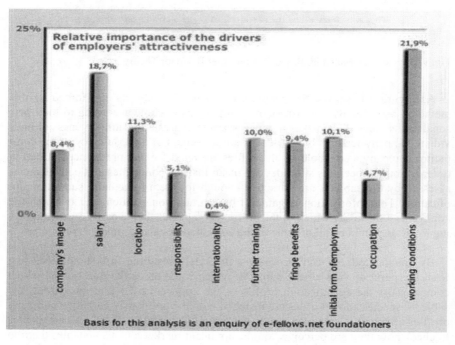

Fig. 9.2. Drivers of Employer Attractiveness as Rated by Students of Industrial Engineering

For a certain profile of one of the participating consultancies, for example, the result given by preference matching with TORP was an attractiveness of 82% among industrial engineering graduates who were scholarship holders of e-fellows.net. This means that 82% of the questioned graduates in this subject found the profile of the consultancy so attractive that they would apply. A TORP simulation revealed that the attractiveness of this consultancy would increase to 87% for this target group if the gross annual salary were increased to 5,000 €. To derive branding measures from these results, the drivers of employer attractiveness are then analyzed. These are determined individually for each company profile. In this process, the influence of each company profile feature on the decision to apply is determined. The relative influential weighting reveals how strong the influence of the attractiveness driver is on employer attractiveness. Figure 9.2. shows that in this study, salary influences the perceived employer attractiveness by 20.3%. This, however, is not to be seen as a valuation of this feature but as a quantification of its influence. Using the matching software TORP, such information can be gained for each company profile. Further, each company receives a psychographic description of the potential applicants questioned. In combination with the soft and hard skills of the potential applicants the question of whether I, as a company, address the target group I wish to address with my branding measures is answered.

In summary, for the purpose of controlling employer branding for companies and consultancies by means of TORP preference matching, the following questions can be answered:

- What percentage of the subjects questioned currently finds my company attractive and would also apply to work here?
- How high is the maximum recruiting potential for my company?
- For what reason are potential applicants interested in my company?
- Which factors should I work on to make more applicants interested in my company?
- How should I set up my employer brand using branding measures to address the right applicants?
- Which positive contributions do which employer branding methods entail?
- Which target group should I address and which communication should be communicated?

9.4 Conclusion

Efficient employer branding requires innovative methods of personnel market research to control and target the employer attractiveness of consultancies. Preference matching can be used to determine the specifications potential applicants have for attractive employers and to define the selection and decision-making process of applicants as realistically as possible. The information gained from this matching process is then turned into precise and therefore efficient recommendations for the successful employer branding of companies.

References

Thaden von Ch (2001) Conjoint-Analyse mit vielen Merkmalen. Peter Lang

10 Leadership Development at Accenture

Martina Beck and Ildiko Kreisz

Accenture - Austria, Switzerland and Germany (ASG)

10.1 About Accenture

Accenture is a global management consulting, technology services and outsourcing company. Committed to delivering innovation, Accenture collaborates with its clients to help them become high-performance businesses and governments. With deep industry and business process expertise, broad global resources and a proven track record, Accenture can mobilize the right people, skills, and technologies to help clients improve their performance. With more than 83,000 people in 47 countries, the company generated net revenues of US$11.8 billion for the fiscal year ended August 31, 2003.

10.1.1 Accenture History

Continuous innovation and rapid transformation have been themes throughout Accenture's history. Established in 1989 primarily as a technology consultant and systems integrator, Accenture soon began offering a new breed of business integration solutions to clients —solutions that aligned organizations' technologies, processes and people with their strategies.

Throughout its history, Accenture has expanded its offerings and capitalized on evolving management trends and technologies to benefit its clients. The company - under the name Accenture since January 2001 - pioneered systems integration and business integration; led the deployment of enterprise resource planning, customer relationship management and electronic services; and has established itself as a leader in today's global marketplace.

Joe W. Forehand, a partner with 30 years of experience, was named managing partner and CEO in November 1999 and chairman of Accenture's board of directors in February 2001. Under Forehand's leadership, Accenture became a public company in July 2001 when it listed on the New York Stock Exchange.

Today Accenture is one of the world's leading management consulting and technology services companies, working with 4,000 clients on nearly 18,000 engagements over the past five years. Of the Fortune Global 100, Accenture serves 92.

10.1.2 Accenture's Business

Every day, Accenture's professionals work with many of the worlds biggest, best and most innovative organizations, helping them identify and capitalize on business and technology opportunities. Accenture's different areas of business are:

Consulting

Companies are looking for more than "advice", they need total solutions. That's why Accenture has developed a comprehensive approach to consulting that moves clients forward at every level of their business, from high-level strategic planning to improved customer service, to day-to-day operations.

Technology

Technology underpins every decision organizations make, from the markets they enter, to the systems they deploy, to the skills they require of their people. Every day Accenture delivers new technology-based business solutions to its clients, leveraging the capabilities of the Accenture Technology Labs, the global solution centers and the deep technical skills of its people.

Outsourcing

In a world that demands greater shareholder value and new approaches to everything from day-to-day operations to long-term strategy, companies need to focus on activities that differentiate their business. Whether through a conventional outsourcing model - delivering long-term value through the management and operations of entire information technology departments, or through netsourcing - the new economy's Internet-based subscription model for outsourcing - Accenture focuses on bringing both business and technology skills to deliver life cycle solutions and bottom-line results to hundreds of organizations around the world.

10.2 Accenture's Structure

To achieve the number 1 goal—helping clients innovate to move the performance of their business to new heights – Accenture's structure is being geared to the structure of the markets it is serving. Accenture's business is structured around five Global Operating Groups:

- Financial Services,
- Products,
- Resources,
- Communications & High Tech,
- Post and Public Services.

The global operating groups together comprise 18 industry groups serving clients in every major industry. The industry focus gives Accenture an understanding of industry evolution, business issues and applicable technologies, enabling it to deliver innovative solutions tailored to each client or, as appropriate, more-standardized capabilities offered to multiple clients.

10.2.1 Accenture Locally

Accenture is an international company, which is reflected in the size of its network and in the capability to approach clients' challenges at global level. The international scope is strengthened by daily use of the new Internet and Intranet technologies and global knowledge management. Organizationally, Accenture is divided in Geographic Units, often comprised of several countries. Austria, Switzerland and Germany (ASG) form one such geographic unit.

10.2.2 Human Capital at Accenture

Accenture employees come from a wide range of cultural, educational and geographic backgrounds. The different points of view they bring lead to superior business solutions for Accenture and its clients. Their individual experiences promote creativity and innovation and contribute to Accenture's success. Accenture's employees belong to one of four different workforces, depending on the business area they work in.

Consulting Workforce	Solutions Workforce
Consultants design and deliver solutions that help improve Accenture clients' businesses, from strategic planning, to applying technologies to business needs, to day-to-day operations. Accenture's Consulting workforce is involved in business consulting, process design work and the application of technologies to business.	Accenture Technology Solutions employees build, deploy and maintain technology solutions for Accenture clients, focusing on application development, systems administration, and technology implementation. Solutions workforce employees are technology specialists who do application development, systems administration work, and develop and maintain software. Solutions workforce employees mainly work on projects at client sites or delivery centers.
Services Workforce	**Enterprise Workforce**
People working in this workforce manage and improve critical business operations for Accenture clients in areas such as IT, Procurement, HR, Finance and Accounting, Customer Contact Services, Insurance Services and Learning Solutions. The majority of the people who work in the outsourcing business are involved in client operations. They are responsible for providing long-term outsourcing services to one or multiple clients. They implement, manage, and ultimately transform the day-to-day activities associated with the above mentioned business functions.	These people manage and operate Accenture's own business functions and support client teams while working in areas such as Finance, Human Resources, Information Technology, Legal, and Marketing. They perform a variety of jobs, which are mainly situated in locations where they are most relevant to the work being performed. These locations are in any of the 48 countries in which Accenture operates, and may be at a client site, in a shared services center (e.g. a call center or a billing center), or in an Accenture office.

Fig. 10.1. Accenture Workforces

10.3 Human Resources at Accenture

Human Resources (HR) at Accenture is part of its Enterprise Workforce, delivering HR services to employees of all workforces. Operating in an international environment with complex company structures, Accenture HR is recognized as being at the heart of Accenture's business. HR provides critical expertise to integrate employee needs and business objectives, ensuring that Accenture has the people and organizational culture needed to deliver its business strategy.

10.3.1 Accenture HR Vision

HR is sought out as a strategic business partner, in all parts of the organization, with input on most business matters. HR professionals provide a valued perspective on key business issues and business operations, ensure that HR strategy and business strategy are aligned, and facilitate and expedite change.

HR is a 'people' expert, abreast of the latest market and strategic HR trends, provider of leading edge thinking into Accenture's business on 'people' issues and with a long-term vision for the HR aspects of its business. HR plays a lead role in organization development, including workforce strategy, and in monitoring and advising on culture and morale.

HR is a capability development expert, continuously increasing the skill level and knowledge capital of Accenture's people and with the ability to both rapidly fulfill current skill needs and anticipate, and meet, future needs for skills and professional development.

HR drives Accenture's employer positioning, which denotes the distinct place Accenture wants to occupy, as an employer, in the minds of Accenture employees and future talents, and which is understood and valued both externally and internally.

The Accenture HR organization is well integrated, both internally and with the rest of the business. Clear structures and processes are in place for governance and stakeholder management, operating effectively throughout the organization.

Accenture has an efficient, cost-effective and outcome-focused HR Service Delivery Model that makes optimum use of outsourcing, in-sourcing and shared services. HR structure, processes and systems provide cost effective services. Simple and efficient HR systems and infrastructure enable the streamlining of HR's transactional role, and top quartile (market) performance in terms of operational efficiency.

Accenture has a strong HR career model, which emphasizes both deep HR skills and strong business acumen.

10.3.2 Accenture ASG HR Organization

In Austria, Switzerland and Germany (ASG), the Human Resources department consists of approx. 100 employees working in the Frankfurt, Zurich and Vienna offices.

Most functions are centrally performed in the Frankfurt office, however to accommodate differences, mainly legal in nature, in the three countries, local HR professionals in Vienna and Zurich handle country-specific matters.

The ASG HR department, delivering HR services from the employees' first day until the handling of the termination, consists of two major HR divisions. One division is performing all comprehensive tasks that apply to all employees. This group consists of the following subteams: Training and Personnel Development, Strategy and Compensation, HR Operations (including HR Systems and Temps Management) and Partner Matters. The other division takes care of HR delivery. The structure of this division accommodates the workforce organization: Solutions Workforce HR, Services Workforce HR, Consulting Workforce HR and Enterprise Workforce HR. The Consulting Workforce HR team is further subgrouped by Operating Group (Financial Services, Products, Resources, Post & Public Services, Communications & High Tech).

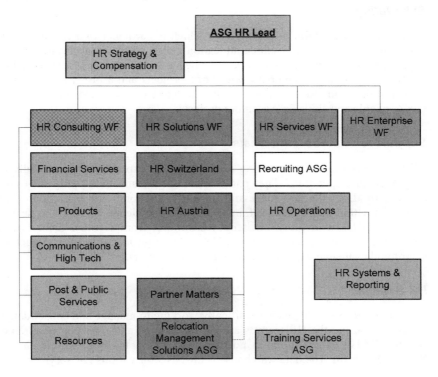

Fig. 10.2. High Level Orgchart Accenture ASG HR

As a growing and continuously developing organization, Accenture is constantly looking for a diverse range of professionals to have precise capabilities and to deliver solutions. Unlike most companies, Recruiting is not part of HR Operations. Recruiting exists as a separate department within the HR organization with recruiting specialists to deliver first-rate recruiting results.

The recruiting department consists of two subteams, Channel Management and Recruiting operations. Channel Management is responsible for ensuring that there is a pool of enough qualified, available candidates for all workforces and levels. In order to achieve this task, they utilize a variety of different personnel marketing instruments and channels. The recruiting operations team takes care of potential candidates throughout the entire selection process: from the first application to the signing of a contract. Corresponding to the workforce segmentation, the recruiting operations team is organized in a way to recruit by workforce.

10.3.3 Accenture HR Particularities

The nature of Accenture's business, especially for the consulting area, dictates how HR is structured and what functions it performs.

Scheduling

Scheduling is a function of HR delivery which is particular to a consulting business company. Effective resource allocation is crucial to the business, especially in consulting and outsourcing work. Excellence in scheduling is a success factor for HR in a consulting company with large projects and a broad range of skills. Highly skilled individuals, supported by the latest technologies, ensure the right mix of people and skills on Accenture projects.

Support for Outsourcing Deals

All HR teams support outsourcing deals with their expertise in successfully running Accenture operations. They partner with client teams in the early stages of an outsourcing deal to ensure successful transition and long term operation of business units within the Accenture framework. HR knowledge is critical to deal success, especially with given challenges stemming from German labor law. Involvement in numerous deals allows HR to leverage its experience in each deal and provide valuable expertise regarding people matters.

HR Systems

A team of HR professionals is specifically working to manage and consolidate HR systems, ensuring the HR team is always operational and reporting requirements are met. All HR data is stored in a data warehouse that has been built by the ASG HR Systems team. The data warehouse is the basis for various HR services.

The HR teams have access to a locally developed internet-based front-end tool to draw reports from the data warehouse in a quick and efficient way. In order to deliver state-of-the art reporting to the senior executives and decision-makers at Accenture, the HR data warehouse serves also as a basis for a unique business intelligence reporting.

Training Services ASG

The responsibility of Training Services ASG is to provide professional development through the delivery of training and new hire integration.

The department develops strategies to identify capability development needs to meet the market requirements in ASG and ensures that the needs regarding technical, industry and interpersonal development are addressed through comprehensive learning opportunities, taking the different backgrounds and career levels into consideration. To achieve this objective Accenture's global training strategies have to be aligned with the local requirements. Strategies and offerings are constantly revised to ensure that skill development meets market requirements in a consistent way.

Furthermore, Training Services ASG ensures the smooth integration of all employees starting with Accenture by offering Orientation seminars, welcome packages, New Joiner WebPages and networking opportunities.

The expertise of Training Services ASG is often used in proposals, and Training Services ASG designs and implements the training strategies of Accenture's outsourcing deals.

10.4   Leadership Development Program at Accenture

Accenture is committed to developing strong leaders at all levels of the company. The objective of the Accenture Leadership Development Program is a continuous investment in the improvement of leadership capabilities to support strategic business objectives.

The Accenture leadership development program has been designed by Global and Local Human Resources experts in cooperation with a Partner Steering Committee. The program was implemented in ASG in September 2002.

The program is driven by the Accenture Leadership Statement, which defines the imperatives for a successful leader and leadership roles relevant to Accenture. This Leadership Statement has been translated into a leadership competence matrix defining relevant behaviors and skills per level and leadership role. The development vehicles have been consequently designed on the basis of the defined competences and integrated into the existing and new HR processes.

10.4.1 Accenture Leadership Statement

The Leadership Statement represents a formal definition of leadership and the corresponding behaviors Accenture aspires to achieve as an organization. It describes the three leadership contributions that have been defined for Accenture - Value Creator, People Developer and Business Operator (which relate directly to the company's strategic imperatives). The statement is used as a basis for evaluating performance and serves as a common framework for career management decisions.

The Leadership Statement also includes definitions of Accenture's six core values: Client Value Creation, Best People, Respect for the Individual, Integrity, One Global Network, and Stewardship.

At Accenture, a leader is defined as an individual who...

- delivers results in each of three Leadership Contributions – Value Creator, People Developer and Business Operator;
- is a role model who people choose to follow and work with;
- conducts business while living the Accenture core values and upholding the Accenture Code of Business Ethics;
- sets direction with vision and is passionate about the business;
- is proactive and moves beyond his/her comfort zone in pursuit of Accenture's vision;
- projects confidence, optimism and energy to people in what they can achieve;
- develops strong and effective working relationships based on mutual respect and trust;
- strives to make others succeed;
- shows an active interest in others and cares about them;
- is a team player who removes barriers to working with others;
- shows character under pressure;
- takes charge and makes tough decisions;
- is an effective communicator;
- demonstrates a 'can do' attitude;
- is authentic in his/her leadership style;
- teams with other leaders;
- drives change.

Business results are essential but not sufficient to be a successful Accenture leader. There needs to be a balance across the three areas of leadership (Value Creator, People Developer and Business Operator).

The definition of leadership is intended to encourage leaders to develop their own authentic leadership style. They are expected to develop their own leadership beliefs into their own 'teachable point of view' that they articulate for their teams.

10.4.2 Accenture Leadership Competency Matrix

To become a leader in terms of the Accenture Leadership statement, people at different career levels require different competencies. These competencies have been clearly outlined in the Competency Matrix, which is, together with the Accenture Leadership Statement, the basis for the Leadership Development Program. The competency matrix determines the way employees are assessed and developed. Training measures to build the required skills at each level are derived from this comprehensive tool.

10.4.3 Leadership Development Program Elements

The ASG Leadership Development Program is comprised of several modules covering all relevant leadership aspects.

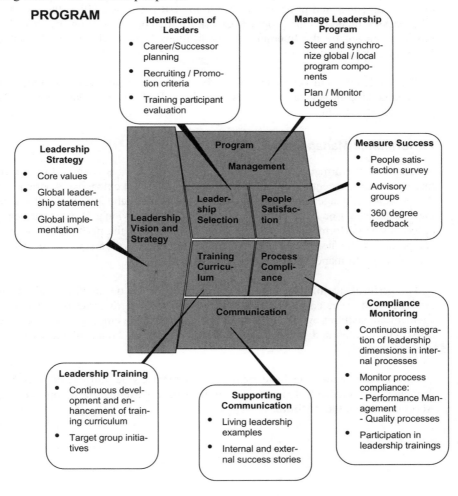

Fig. 10.3. Accenture Leadership Development Program, by Accenture

As already pointed out, Leadership Vision and Strategy are basis and backbone of the program. The other components are essential, intertwining parts of the program. For the different elements, tools and materials are provided on a global level. A high degree of standardization ensures comparability and consistency.

10.4.4 Integration of Leadership Development into HR Processes

The Leadership Development Program is a self-contained concept that provides unique opportunities for Accenture employees in terms of their professional and personal development as leaders.

However, the mere existence of a concept and its related tools is not enough. The idea needs to be brought to life. The Accenture HR organization has put the Leadership Development Program into action by integrating the leadership development guidelines and principles firmly in the HR processes. HR is the owner of all processes related to the program, except for the communication part, which is mostly managed by the Internal Communications Department of the Accenture Marketing Organization.

The guidelines and principles of the Leadership Development Program have been embedded in several HR areas, mainly in Performance Management, Recruiting, and Training.

Performance Management

A consistent performance management approach has always been part of Accenture's strength. Accenture HR can look back on long and extensive experience in Performance Management. Individuals receive regular and timely feedback on their assignments or fixed roles. Furthermore, each individual is assessed yearly based on the performance feedback received throughout the performance year in comparison to his/her peer group. An annual interview with a senior executive is part of the performance management process as well.

The performance management processes and tools all tie together, and are coordinated and executed by HR. All communications regarding performance management are sent out by HR, informing and educating the employees on the processes. HR creates and manages the necessary material, counsels and assists in decision-making.

Figure 10.3. shows the Leadership Development Cycle with its relevant Performance Management elements. The dimension regarding time is one year, at Accenture called the Performance year.

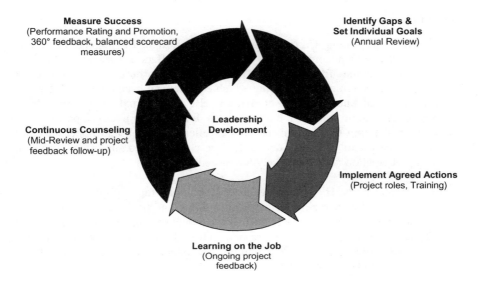

Measure Success
(Performance Rating and Promotion, 360° feedback, balanced scorecard measures)

Identify Gaps & Set Individual Goals
(Annual Review)

Continuous Counseling
(Mid-Review and project feedback follow-up)

Leadership Development

Implement Agreed Actions
(Project roles, Training)

Learning on the Job
(Ongoing project feedback)

Fig. 10.4. Performance Management Leadership Development Cycle, by Accenture

Since the introduction of the leadership development program, performance and appraisal factors are based on the competency matrix and the new guidelines and principles have self-evidently been incorporated in all performance management related work. HR makes sure that the leadership dimensions are taken into consideration for performance rating and promotion decisions. The leadership development progress of each employee is discussed during his Annual Interview.

The performance of each individual with regards to the leadership criteria must be documented in feedback forms and annual review documentation. The general quality of performance documentation is regularly surveyed by HR, with special attention to the notation of the leadership criteria.

Recruiting

In the recruiting process, the leadership capabilities of a potential candidate are taken in to consideration when taking the decision whether to hire the candidate or not.

All people involved in the recruiting process (personnel from the recruiting department and executives from the workforce the candidate is recruited for) have a common understanding about leadership at Accenture. The Accenture Leadership Statement with its definitions of the three leadership dimensions builds the basis to evaluate candidates regarding their skills and potential as Value Creators, Business Operators and People Developers. The candidate's leadership capabilities are evaluated during the entire recruiting process, from the screening of the application until the last personal interview.

Training

The Leadership Training Curriculum is rigorously designed to support the development of leadership competencies and herewith offers a variety of different learning opportunities for each career level. Those opportunities consist of local and global training courses depending which complement each other in a comprehensive way. The knowledge of internal e.g. HR and external sources have been combined to design state-of-the-art vehicles for leadership development. The Leadership Training Curriculum receives excellent feedback and is permanently adapted to new and changing demands. For compliance monitoring purposes, training participation rates are closely monitored.

On a regular basis, HR gathers feedback on the program, by questioning advisory groups and by analyzing feedback on training and the Leadership Development tools (e.g. the 360° feedback tool). The conduction and analysis of employee satisfaction surveys lies also in the responsibility of HR. Survey results are analyzed by HR professionals and key findings are incorporated in the improvement of the Leadership Development Program.

Local HR teams continuously work with the Global teams to align the global and local components of the Leadership Development Program and to fill identified gaps. HR implements or accompanies flanking measures to the program that is tailored to the different workforces. In HR reports to the senior management, leadership development is incorporated in Training Reports and other reports and presentations.

The fast and smooth integration of the leadership development program in HR work ensures the permanent success of the program. As a strategic business partner, HR gives advice on the program and its components to employees on all levels. HR keeps the employees informed about the introduction of new tools and processes in the context of the Leadership Development Program.

10.5 Conclusion

The Accenture HR organization has played a significant and driving role in the creation, roll-out and execution of the leadership development program. Even though each employee is responsible to develop his own leadership capabilities with support of his/her leadership team, HR ensures functioning and continuous improvement of the program. The rate and easiness with which the Accenture HR teams have incorporated the Leadership Development Program is a proof for the professionalism and the flexibility of the Accenture HR organization.

The Leadership Development Program is a comprehensive concept. Its elements are consistent and coherent for employees on all levels. The HR-driven processes which integrate the principles of the Leadership Development Program make Accenture HR best practice regarding leadership development.

11 Knowledge Management: A Way to Make a Difference in Our Field of Industry

Jane Aubriet-Beausire and Sophie Gaïo

Lee Hecht Harrison

11.1 Introduction

In the highly competitive market within which career management companies operate, the leaders distinguish themselves by offering high quality services, that are flexible to the needs of their clients, but that are also consistent across borders.

In the following article we will present the case of Lee Hecht Harrison, one of the leading firms in global career management services. Following a description of the company, we will discuss how the HR practices build corporate capability by focusing on the Lee Hecht Harrison methodology, by emphasizing quality and by supporting the growth of a culture based on being a learning organization. Finally, we will discuss two specific aspects of HR practice that make the company stand out, the first being the emphasis on orientation and certification of new hires and the second, long-term training and development of talent.

11.2 The Company

Lee Hecht Harrison (LHH) is a high quality, innovative, global outplacement and career services firm. Established in New York in 1974 and now headquartered in Woodcliff Lake, New Jersey, LHH has grown from a regional to a national, to a global organization.

Today, LHH has offices in more than 150 cities throughout the world. It employs more than 600 full-time and 700+ part-time employees and maintains close business relationships with Global Partners in many other locations, allowing it to serve organizations and their employees virtually anywhere in the world.

LHH is a subsidiary of Adecco S.A, a \$15 billion international human resources company headquartered in Lausanne, Switzerland. Adecco is the worldwide leader in employment staffing services, with the highest revenue, cash flow and market capitalization of any firm in the industry, now operating over 5,000 offices in more than 55 countries. Its stock is publicly traded on the Zurich, Paris and NASDAQ Stock Exchanges.

The association with Adecco has provided for significant global synergies and substantial capital investments, particularly in job search technology, in addition to making available more and better market research employment opportunities for clients. Importantly, the goals of the two businesses have always been complementary in their desire to help people to adapt to changing work environments, to sustain their employment value and to connect to jobs.

11.2.1 Structure of the Organization

In 2003, LHH's full-time staff totals over 600 employees, of whom approximately 67% are professionals and roughly 33% are support staff. The overall professional staff profile of consultants is about 50% male/50% female. Over half of the General Managers (those who run offices) are women, as are about 60% of LHH's senior management team, including the Chief Operating Officer.

LHH strives to be as flat an organization as possible, believing that customer responsiveness, service delivery and revenue and profitability growth are best achieved when « owned » at the local level. At the same time, they recognize the importance of firm-wide program and service development, quality assurance, and the capacity for providing national and international project management to corporate customers.

Major downsizing projects are coordinated by LHH's Project Services Division. Project Services was established in 1985 as the industry's first practice area dedicated to the delivery of career services for large numbers of people. Because the capabilities required to plan, deliver and manage a major downsizing/closure are quite different from those required to counsel an individual in career transition, the company has recognized these special skills and has created separate functions. Today, LHH's Project Services Division has developed the most sophisticated project management capability available anywhere in the career services industry.

Other corporate functions include Development and Delivery; Marketing, Sales, Information and Financial Services; and a small corporate headquarters staff.

All of LHH's offices are wholly owned and provide a full range of outplacement, career development, executive coaching, retention and workforce consulting services. There is no franchising or licensing of any of the programs or services which enables the company to fully define and monitor quality standards, as well as shift priorities/resources as required.

11.2.2 Company Mission

LHH's mission is to be the global leader in career consulting by building enduring business partnerships with customers and by providing innovative solutions that focus on the needs of each individual client. To attain this mission, the company philosophy has four major components:

1. To offer programs and services that is customer-focused, results-oriented, measurable, and flexible.
2. To maintain high internal standards for program quality, customer service, and resource and expense management that result in high levels of client satisfaction.
3. To lead the industry in integrating advanced technology and delivery, and to add value through a responsive, hands-on human touch.
4. To hire superior people, and provide them with the opportunity to succeed in an environment that values and rewards creativity, innovation and personal commitment.

11.2.3 Company Philosophy

The company believes that senior management has a special responsibility to ensure a positive environment that encourages only the very best, most professional behavior from all employees. They strive to be worthy of the support of their customers, clients and of one another by attending to their mission and values.

11.2.4 Company Values

The company values that underlie all activities are to:

- Commit to providing high quality customer service to clients, customers and staff, constantly improving performance and work force flexibility;
- reward achievement and initiative and hold one another accountable for results at all levels;
- respect one another as partners who bring talent, intelligence and compassion to business tasks, knowing that teamwork and constructive disagreement can result in exceptional accomplishment.

11.3 LHH Global Management Services

There are three main global career management services offered by LHH:

11.3.1 Outplacement

Outplacement is the structured process of helping unemployed individuals evaluate their career opportunities, implement a job search and manage the transition to new employment, whilst receiving personal support and job search productivity tools.

11.3.2 Leadership Development & Coaching

Leadership development is a systematic consulting process that helps individuals and teams achieve business results through improved leadership strategies and behaviors. Leadership development programs are designed to produce outcomes that drive current business operations and develop high potential leaders for the future. Coaching is a learning process that leads to behavioral change to improve individual performance and business results. It involves observation of specific patterns of behavior, giving feedback and developing an action plan to help individuals become more effective in their work environments.

11.3.3 Career Development

A process by which individuals evaluate their career and life plans, determine their existing and potential skills, interests and talents , learn how to adapt to the constantly changing job market and world of work , consider which options « fit » them , and establish and implement plans for achieving their goals.

Leadership development, coaching and career development services are provided to individuals employed within customer organizations, whilst outplacement is provided to employees who have recently been terminated, either collectively, or individually.

11.3.4 LHH's Customers

LHH has experience of working with companies of all sizes, both public and private, both internationally and nationally, from a very wide range of industries including: Aerospace and Defense; Banking and Financial Services; Computer, Software and Peripherals; Consumer Products, Sales and Electronics; Energy, Utilities, Petrochemicals and Natural Resources; Food, Beverage and Tobacco; Hospitality and Travel; Hospitals and Healthcare Services; Industrial Manufacturing, Products and Services; Insurance; Media and Entertainment, New Media and Dot-coms; Not-For-Profit, Government and Associations; Pharmaceutical; Professional Business Services; Retail and Wholesale; and Telecommunications.

11.3.5 LHH's People

LHH consultants come from diverse careers in business, executive search and self-employment. The minimum selection criteria for LHH professional staff and Certified Associates are the following:

- Bachelor's degree (60% hold a Master's degree or PhD);
- experience in a corporate/professional services environment and/or have owned a business;
- one-on-one counseling experience and group training and facilitation skills;
- career transition expertise/experience for individuals who deliver outplacement services; career development and/or organizational development experience for individuals who deliver career management/retention services;
- personal commitment to the career transition/career management field;
- strong client relations skills and professionalism;
- highly developed sense of ethical behavior, integrity and client confidentiality.

A number of LHH offices employ staff who is dedicated to the delivery of services to senior executives. These individuals, former senior executives themselves, understand the unique and often visible issues faced during high level transitions. They are equipped both personally and professionally to provide the type of strategic assessment, consultation and introductions expected by senior executives.

11.3.6 Profiles of Common Positions

LHH has clearly defined roles that are commonly used across the company and worldwide.

General Manager

The General Manager's primary responsibility is to build a financially successful business that delivers high quality career management services.

Director of Professional Services

The primary responsibility of the Director of Professional Services is to ensure that the highest quality of career management services is delivered through the Local Office.

Business Developer

The Business Developer's primary function is to profitably increase sales within the local office trading area, concentrating on new or expanded account relationships.

Consultant

The Consultant's primary responsibilities are to deliver career management services to program participants.

Business Manager

The primary responsibility of the Business Manager is to ensure that the highest quality administrative support services are delivered to each local office client.

Certified Associate

Certified Associates are trainers who deliver outplacement and career management services, typically in a group setting.

Job Market Consultant

The primary responsibility of the Job Market Consultant is to provide overall leadership and coordination for the job development effort at the local level.

Administrative Assistant

The primary responsibility of the Administrative Assistant is to provide essential computer and office functions for clients and office personnel.

Some consultants may specialize in a specific area or industry because of prior experience in that industry or because of expertise with clients from that industry. Many of the consultants come from careers in finance, human resources, information services, manufacturing, marketing, sales, strategic planning, technology and other disciplines.

The General Manager and/or Director of Professional Services of the local office makes the decision on specific consultant assignment after his/her initial meeting with the client. They seek to align clients with skilled consultants with personality type and similarity of background as the key criteria. A good match is always the objective, and it is important to note that the resources of all consultants in the office are available to all clients.

11.3.7 LHH Certified Associates

LHH employs more than 700 Certified Associates throughout the world who are selected, trained and formally certified to deliver programs. These individuals typically have long-standing relationships with LHH. Many are former employees who have opted for part-time work. Others enjoy varied assignments, and are willing to travel to, and to work in, on-site locations for clients.

LHH Certified Associates must complete a rigorous, multi-step certification process which includes indepth training in LHH methodology. They are also trained and certified on new programs and are recertified when content/material revisions are made. Each trainer's performance is monitored on an ongoing basis via evaluation forms completed by participants after each program. Periodic client surveys are also taken to gather feedback on Associates.

Evaluations of LHH seminar delivery are completed by all participants and then monitored for service quality and improvement suggestions. The evaluation scores are carefully tracked, and action is triggered whenever a consultant receives two 3s (out of 5) in two consecutive seminars. At that point, the individual's performance is reviewed, s/he is counseled and performance continues to be monitored. If feedback continues to fall short of LHH standards, changes in staff are made.

11.4 LHH Human Resource Practices

As can be seen from the presentation of the company in the previous section, Lee Hecht Harrison distinguishes itself as a leading career management company by building enduring business partnerships with customers and by providing innovative solutions that focus on the needs of each individual client.

The sheer nature of the LHH offer means that its value is based upon the intellectual capital, the emotional intelligence and the market knowledge of its consultants. As in most career management companies, people join the company with a tremendous variety of professional and personal backgrounds, bringing with them a richness of competencies, qualities and experiences. These must then be captured, modeled and developed so that the company can deliver a variety of high level services that are not only consistent in terms of quality and content across different businesses, but also nationally and internationally. Without this consistency, LHH would not be able to continue to build and reinforce its reputation as a global leader in the industry.

One of the challenges with this process, however, is that it must neither suppress the individual talents of the consultants, nor diminish the freedom of the businesses to tailor make aspects of the offers to meet the needs of individual clients. LHH therefore seeks to empower its employees to continuously develop themselves and their talents, to develop new offers where changing client needs can be met and where the quest for the best possible quality continues: not as a by-product of the process, but in everything that is done.

The goal of HR is to create a pyramid of knowledge where foundations are provided to ensure that all consultants understand the LHH methodology, the company's emphasis on quality and the overall goals and culture driving what the company considers to be a strong 'learning organization'. At the top of the pyramid, the goal of the company is to empower individuals to use their individual talents to adapt their skills and talents to meet the needs of a wide variety of clients, but with the support and ongoing commitment of the organization. By building the corporate capabilities in this way then the company can deliver high quality services that are globally consistent but able to be tailor made to the changing needs of clients.

Fig. 11.1. How Lee Hecht Harrison Human Resource Builds Corporate Capability

How Is This Achieved?

It is important to acknowledge that the LHH methodology, the corporate focus on quality and the learning organization culture are all interrelated, each one contributing to the success of the other. For the purposes of this paper, it seems interesting to briefly discuss each aspect as a way of introducing a more in-depth discussion of the HR best practices that make LHH stand out.

11.5 The LHH Methodology

The LHH Methodology describes the skills, actions and methods used by consultants to deliver each of LHH's products and services. All programs are described in detail with support documents and training to ensure that all consultants deliver the program consistently across businesses. Training in all programs leads to consultants being 'Certified' and this process begins as soon as candidates join the company. The process will be described in greater detail in the next section.

11.5.1 The Focus on Quality

Quality was the driving force in the founding of Lee Hecht Harrison and for the past 29 years, the focus has remained as the company has moved to a leadership position in the career management industry.

- *Organizational Design* – Quality is emphasized structurally, functionally and operationally. The company's organizational structure is designed to keep a focus on excellence in everything that is done and designated individuals exist at national, regional and local levels to ensure that quality standards are incorporated into performance. In addition to this, a Corporate Director of Quality is responsible for ultimate quality control, client satisfaction and organization-wide implementation of quality measures, with support from management. The culture of quality is reinforced in new employee orientations, ongoing training, certification programs and professional development conferences. Numerous awards at local and national levels have proved LHH's commitment to quality. Ultimately, the best measure of quality is the level of satisfaction and the return of clients.

- *Quality Indicators* – A variety of methods are used to measure client (the individual employee receiving LHH services) and customer (the sponsoring company paying for our services) levels' of satisfaction. It is done on a continuous basis with evaluations mid-service and end-of-service. Results are used to determine what (if any) actions need to be taken. In addition, an annual survey of corporate customers is undertaken to review quality at a broader and more comprehensive level.

- *Using Quality Measurements to Improve Performance* – There is little value in evaluating quality if the information gathered is not used to drive process improvements and consultant development. Consultants are evaluated by their general managers and by the Director of Professional Services whose sole responsibility is to oversee the quality of service delivery in each office. In addition to this, quality indicators that demonstrate client and customer satisfaction are used to determine performance and if a consultant is below expectations, the client can be reassigned a new consultant and a portion of the fee charged can be reimbursed. Finally, an annual business review ensures that LHH activities are reviewed from a business perspective leading to potential refinement of services, adjustments in procedures or other action. The goal is for LHH to gain business based on capability but to keep it based on performance.

- *Performance Guarantees* – LHH guarantees satisfaction with their services. If customers or clients are not satisfied then they will either not be charged, or a credit will be made for future services.

11.5.2 LHH as a Learning Organization

"The rate at which organizations learn may become the only sustainable source of competitive advantage"
                                                                    Dr. Peter Senge

Learning organizations can be defined as organizations that are 'designed to build collaborative relationships in order to draw strength from the diverse knowledge, experience, capabilities and ways of doing things that people and communities have and use (Addleson 1998). The idea is that organizations are evolving away from being purely performance based and towards a central theme of continual adaptation to an ever-changing environment. Where knowledge management focuses on the use of specific tools, often technological in nature, to capture organize, distil and distribute information (Corporate Leadership Council 2001), organizational learning seeks to enhance employees' motivations and embed particular core competencies within their skill sets, rather than simply making information available. It is the quality, not the quantity that counts.

The shift towards organizational learning requires cultural change to create a culture that embraces and encourages learning. In 'The 12 Building Blocks of the Learning Organization', Joan Kramer Bennet and Michael J O'Brien describe factors that have been identified as key to becoming a learning organization. The following table demonstrates the 12 building blocks with examples of the activities and initiatives undertaken by LHH, in its commitment to becoming a leading learning organization:

In this section we have gained a greater understanding of how LHH HR builds its corporate capability. For the purposes of this paper we would like to focus on two aspects that we believe are specific examples of HR best practice in this industry.

The First Is:

- The orientation and certification of new consultants and associates within Lee Hecht Harrison.

The Second Is:

- Continuous learning and the development of talent long-term.

Table 11.1. Lee Hecht Harrison and the 12 Building Blocks to Becoming a Learning Organization

	Building Blocks to Becoming a Learning Organization	Lee Hecht Harrison
1.	Draft a vision of the company's goals, so it can anticipate the types of learning that need to occur to reach this end state.	The LHH *Business Practices Handbook*, provides outlines of the company values and guiding principles to all new employees.
2.	Create an executive "covenant" with employees – company leaders should actively and visibly support learning activities and hold their people accountable for continuous learning.	Company wide certification, continuous learning activities and internal and external networking events including membership of the Association of Career Management Professionals.
3.	Act in accordance with principals of continuous learning – particularly in managerial practices.	Emphasis on quality with detailed assessment and support provided through all levels of the organization.
4.	Support a climate in which the individual and collective values and attitudes emphasize openness, trust and a willingness to share information.	New Employee Orientation meetings and LHH Business Practices all emphasize individual contribution, integrity and development.
5.	Provide fluid job descriptions and flexible organizational structures that can quickly adapt to changing organizational and learning needs.	Clear job descriptions allow for flexibility within roles to meet needs of clients. Flat organizational structure.
6.	Use technology to promote smooth information flow and easy access to all forms of knowledge relevant to the company's learning goals.	Support provided by LHH Information Services, Business Information Centre and LHH Learning Centre.
7.	Encourage individuals and teams to share knowledge – so that learning becomes an integral part of teamwork and cooperation.	GAP networking events and monthly teletutorials.
8.	Ensure that company work practices support continuous learning – through information sharing, benchmarking or problem-solving techniques.	Professional development sessions, internal and external networking events in addition to strong focus on quality with continuous feedback from customers and clients.
9.	Align performance and learning goals with customer needs to guarantee that learning is contributing directly to the company's bottom line.	Annual business review and client/customer satisfaction surveys.
10.	Design training programs that emphasize experiential learning and creative problem solving.	LHH certification and train-the-trainer events.
11.	Seek to develop both individuals and teams – organizations can only learn when groups of people learn collectively, not just as individuals.	Includes certification training, orientation meetings and professional development sessions as well as external group programs.
12.	Create rewards and recognition programs that promote and advocate continuous learning.	Program certification and awards.

11.6 Employee Orientation and Certification

11.6.1 Trends in Orientation Programs

According to the literature, to be successful, new hire orientation programs should include the following five components (Tyler 2001): (1) Pre-arrival reading materials, (2) a systematic and thorough introduction of company, department and job functions and responsibilities, (3) formal training to facilitate an understanding of company processes and practices; (4) coaching and mentoring and (5) measuring and evaluating of orientation, before, during and after programs.

The HR function of LHH has developed its orientation of new hires, both permanent and associates, around the LHH Certification process which teaches the LHH methodology used in the delivery of different LHH products and services. Although certification is the key component of the process, all other components of the above employee orientation are addressed including pre-arrival reading materials, local office orientations, a three day orientation at corporate for professional staff, one-on-one coaching and feedback from participants.

The benefits of ensuring an integrated approach with a strong emphasis on certification include the following for individuals, the company and its customers and clients:

Individuals

- It sets the tone in terms of their experience of the organization and impacts their motivation and retention long-term.
- They become a living part of the corporate culture and participate in building the learning organization from day one.
- They are encouraged to share their own talents and professional experience but within the LHH methodology.
- They understand the emphasis on quality and are given the confidence and tools to deliver the quality and approach expected from customers and clients.
- By learning the methodology in a clear and detailed way, with excellent support from both material and supervisors, they adapt quickly, adopt the methodology and time to productivity is kept at a minimum.
- They meet other members of the company and begin to form networks that are critical to a successful integration and long-term retention.

LHH

- Individuals understand their roles and responsibilities understand the broad picture and are keen to participate in making the company successful as quickly as possible.

- Quality and consistency remains extremely high across the business and contributes to the long-term retention and satisfaction of people, as they take ownership of their responsibilities.
- Sharing of information begins and a corporate culture based on learning is demonstrated.

Customers and Clients

- All consultants at LHH are able to deliver over and above what is expected in the most professional, yet personal manner, across the entire business. This capability is what makes LHH stand out as a leader.

11.6.2 The Certification Process

Certification meetings are held for a wide range of LHH products and services, including Career Transition Seminar, Developing Personal Resilience, Talent Builder, Career Focus, Moving Forward with Change, Road to Entrepreneurship, Job Search Work Team, and the Productivity Seminar.

The programs and services have been designed by specialists within the Development and Delivery Group at LHH's Head Quarters in New Jersey. They are created with the support of external specialists such as the Management Research Group (MRG) and emphasize feedback and ideas gathered from members of LHH, and especially from customers and clients of the company. Senior management play an important role in the creation of these programs and services also.

To support the launch of the programs and services, detailed preparations are made to certify members of LHH who will deliver them to customers and clients. All members involved will be certified with only slight modifications to the process being made, in the case of an update of a program or service.

Detailed training manuals, support presentations and evaluation forms that are consistent across the globe will be created to ensure that trainers across regions are delivering the same certification.

Certification varies according to the program but normally includes:

- Formal training in a group setting delivered by a leading member of the region's training group. This can range from a single day to a total of seven days split into modules;
- detailed support materials that individuals will own;
- additional support materials available on the company's electronic learning center;
- evaluation in the form of an observation (presentation of a topic in front of peers and the regional leader).

When successfully completed, individuals are awarded certificates by their hierarchy in formal presentations to ensure that reward and recognition is acknowledged. If individuals are considered to be below expectations, then remedial steps are taken to ensure that they achieve certification as soon as possible.

All new members of LHH participate in this process in the first couple of weeks of their arrival within the company and depending upon the stage of life cycle of the program/service, they may participate in certification with members of LHH who have been within the organization for some time, allowing for greater networking opportunities.

11.7   Training and Professional Development

As has been shown in the previous paragraphs, training is a priority from day one at LHH. The desire to continue to grow LHH as a learning organization has meant that continuous learning at both a formal and informal level must be a priority.

LHH exposes individuals to a wide variety of experiences, including local, regional, national, and international professional development events, external training programs, task force assignments, program delivery certification, and public conferences.

The formal training opportunities available include:

- Professional Development sessions that are held twice a year in each region for the sales and consulting staff. These are developed and delivered by LHH's Development and Delivery team to ensure consistency across the regions.

- New Employee Orientation meetings that are held three times a year for new professional staff as a way of introducing them to the LHH philosophy and resources, to create a personal network and to meet the senior management of LHH.

- A regular schedule of monthly teletutorails, training and professional development that are offered as a way for individuals to develop their understanding and skills in using the technology available within LHH.

- National contracts with external providers such as CompUSA, so that staff members can attend training classes on a variety of software packages.

- LHH's Information Services team and the Business Information Center who are available to help staff members with individual needs.

- An integrated e-learning platform from which individuals can gain materials and training on a variety of topics.

- Certification and Train-the-Trainer meetings as described in the previous section.

- Contracts with companies such as MRG to certify LHH staff in *Leadership Effectiveness Analysis and Personal Directions*, two instruments used in our Leadership Development/Coaching services.

- LHH pays for an employee's membership in the Association of Career Professionals (ACP International) and for certification in ICC International – an independent, international certification body for Career Management Professionals. LHH currently has more individuals certified than any other career management firm.

These initiatives have been designed to build on the competencies/skills of talented staff, to build the learning organization and to enable the Company to continue providing quality services whilst continuing to grow the business. It also contributes to a low turnover with most consultants staying for over five years and an annual turnover figure of below 10%, below industry average.

11.8 Conclusion

The purpose of this chapter has been to describe what makes Lee Hecht Harrison one of the leaders in its field. By building its corporate capability on its methodology, its focus on quality and its culture as a learning organization, it continues not only to deliver programs and services in line with customer needs, but it also maintains a committed, creative and dynamic team.

References

Addleson M (1999) What is a Learning Organisation?. The Learning Organisation Literature Review, Corporate Leadership Council, August 1999

Corporate Leadership Council, Building Orientation Programs and Tyler K (1988) Take the New Employee Orientation off the Back Burner. HR Magazine, May 1988. Quoted in: CLC New Hire Orientation Programs, March 2001, p. 1

Tyler K (1988) Take the New Employee Orientation off the Back Burner. HR Magazine, May 1988. Quoted in: CLC New Hire Orientation Programs, March 2001, p. 1

Part III:

HRM as Employee Champion

12 Gender Diversity Management in Consulting Companies

Uta B. Lieberum

Helmut-Schmidt-University/University of the Federal Armed Forces Hamburg, Germany

12.1 Introduction

According to research on diversity in organizational contexts, the mix of female and male employees in organizations and especially in management ranks is seen as an inherent source of innovation and hence as a value driver for companies. It is seen as a key factor in achieving a competitive advantage and in realizing strategic goals in a better way (Andresen, Hristozova and Lieberum 2005; Thomas and Ely 1996). However, when analyzing the proportion of women in management positions in companies it becomes obvious that they represent only a very low percentage, and that companies are still far from realizing and profiting from a gender mix in many countries. This result does not only apply to those companies which have a very low proportion of women but also to those that have an almost equal distribution of men and women in their overall workforce. In the case of consulting companies we can assume that there is a moderate number of female employees in general.

On the basis of various investigations it may be assumed that around 20-30% of the total numbers of those working in consulting companies are female and that this proportion is increasing (Rudolph, Theobald and Quack 2001; Hördt 2002; Okech and Rudolf 2003). One effective solution to solve the problem of female under-representation and to achieve a better gender mix within management is to eliminate all discriminatory features within company policy and to actively promote women's careers.

These activities will be investigated in this paper, with the focus being on whether within consulting companies such policies are communicated internally or externally, together with the nature of the methods of implementation. First of all the terms Gender Diversity and Diversity Management will be analyzed with regard to their terminology and meaning. Following this, the significance of corresponding measures will be categorized so that they can be used as reference points in a survey which we carried out on the 25 largest German consulting companies.

12.2 Gender Diversity

The motives encouraging firms to consider supporting more women in management ranks should include the achievement of the following (Andresen, Hristozova and Lieberum 2005):

- *Affirmative action* with respect to women. The focus of this strategy is to create an even playing field regarding their access to national as well as international management positions; this is to be achieved by a favorable treatment of women which might imply a temporary discrimination of men. Affirmative action is aimed at satisfying legal requirements and to remedy abuses (e.g. Kovach, Kravitz and Hughes 2004; Wright et al. 1995).
- *Equal opportunities* for domestic management positions. Equal opportunity activities seek to eliminate discrimination in the workplace by removing / overcoming structural and procedural barriers preventing women from taking advantage of opportunities regarding jobs, development, promotions, compensation and so on (e.g. Pérotin, Robinson and Loundes 2003; Whitehead 2001). This aim is consistent with the corporate values of many companies. The extremely competitive economic environment forces companies to select the very best people available, irrespective of their gender.
- *Gender diversity* related to the combination of female and male employees in such a way as is apt to create more value for the firm than would be the case with homogeneous groups. Well-managed diversity, including gender diversity, is seen as an inherent source of innovation which is a key factor in achieving a competitive advantage and in realizing strategic goals in a better way.

Whereas affirmative action and equal opportunity initiatives will lead to a balanced proportion of women and men on an organizational level (quantitative approach), gender diversity aims at a mixture of women and men on a team, departmental or hierarchical level in such a way as to maximize the potential advantages of diversity in the sense of, for example, innovativeness or effectiveness (qualitative approach). Hence, diversity does not necessarily lead to an equal proportion of women and men in a team or at other levels. In other words, the diversity approach shifts the focus from eliminating difference (due to structural and procedural barriers) to valuing similarities as well as differences between men and women that can be traced back to socialization. Managing diversity is more strategically than legally driven.

The investigation of the initiatives taken in order to achieve affirmative action, equal opportunities and/or gender diversity was the starting point of the empirical study, and this will be described in the next part. Although the focus is on gender diversity, affirmative action and equal opportunity activities were also analyzed; this is because the initiatives taken by companies regarding these goals are similar or even identical, as the implementation of equal opportunities in the long run is a prerequisite to achieve gender diversity.

According to several authors and companies there are numerous positive benefits for organizations that implement diversity initiatives in order to achieve gender diversity within their workforce and especially within their management ranks. These economic benefits include the possibility for firms to recruit and capitalize on the contributions of talented human beings; lower operating costs due to lower absenteeism, turnover, and job dissatisfaction in the work force; enhanced reputations with potential customers who also benefited from the value of diversity; more creativity and better problem-solving capabilities; and strong community and institutional support due to the level of culture within their diverse work forces. Furthermore, companies that voice their support for and run management practices that serve to achieve gender diversity experience a significant and positive improvement in their stock price. The above mentioned economic benefits can be classified into external and internal effects. The first-mentioned external effects concern the market and customers, shareholders, labor market and community. The internal benefits have an effect at three levels: individual level, level of interpersonal relations and organizational level (Andresen, Hristozova and Lieberum 2005).

Overall diversity is viewed as an instrument which can be used to increase the level of success within core business areas and to gain strategic competitive advantages (e.g. Balser 1999; Köhler-Braun 1999; Lau and Murnighan 1998; Stuber 2002 and Wright et al. 1995).

However, if diversity is not effectively managed, is it possible that higher levels of diversity could perhaps also bring about potential disadvantages, such as, for example, breakdowns in communication, increased levels of ambiguity, complexity and confusion as a result of different perspectives, higher staff turnover levels and levels of absenteeism among minority groups, as well as less integration and community support in consequence of internal group influences, irreconcilable views etc., as well as lower job satisfaction and motivation of diverse individuals (e.g. Milliken and Martins 1996; Zenger and Lawrence 1989).

While some researchers conclude that diversity, when managed in a professional manner, increases organizational performance and thus, ultimately, organizational success, (others point to an inverse connection between obvious differences and teamwork or performance results In the literature studies have shown positive, negative and zero effects, and it is thus very difficult to draw any certain conclusions regarding the connection of, for example, diversity with gender and performance (e.g. Gilbert and Ivancevich 2000; Richard 2000; Stumpf and Thomas 1999; Pless 2000; Tsui, Egan and O'Reilly 1992).

12.3 Gender Diversity Management

The potentially constructive or destructive influence of diversity on organizational performance does not result automatically from diversity but is instead a function of the management of such diversity; this is - ultimately - a mirror image of the organizational culture (e.g. Gilbert, Stead and Ivancevich 1999). The costs and gains companies encounter will vary, depending on how they manage diversity (Dass and Parker 1999). They define Diversity Management "as a complete organizational cultural change designed to foster appreciation of demographic, ethnic, and individual differences". That includes the modification of existing procedures and practices, beginning with human resource management function. The aim is to empower members of groups to contribute to the organizational targets and to develop their full potential, unhampered by group identities such as culture or ethnicity, age, gender, etc.

Thomas (2001) differentiates between three stages of maturity with regard to diversity. Organizations with a high degree of maturity view diversity as important and profitable. They understand the difference between integration and diversity. Companies with a low level of maturity see no connection between diversity and its influence on the organization. Any intervention occurs only in crisis situations and the main motivation for this is political correctness. Organizations with a medium level of maturity are aware of the nature of diversity and its dynamics, but they do not transform this knowledge into practice frequently enough. Such companies tend to emphasize the value of harmony.

In the literature there are numerous models which attempt to categorize the approaches to diversity management (e.g. Dass Parker 1999; Thomas 2001; Thomas and Ely 1996; Wagner and Sepehri 1999; Köhler-Braun 1999). In their 1996 model, Thomas and Ely distinguish between 3 different perspectives when dealing with diversity. A fourth perspective (the resistance approach) was added by Dass and Parker (1999): In the *Resistance Perspective* diversity management is regarded as an issue which is neither relevant nor threatening. These organizations aim to retain their existing homogeneity and monoculture. This strategy is reactive, and is characterized by denial, avoidance or manipulation (Dass and Parker 1999).

The *Discrimination-and-Fairness-Paradigm* is intended to achieve equal opportunities and fair treatment for all employees. The aim is to achieve a demographically representative workforce. This approach relies primarily on court rulings, but it does involve more than just a basic interest in statistics.

In contrast, The *Access-and-Legitimacy-Paradigm* is based on the acceptance and celebration of differences. The aim here is to achieve a situation in which the characteristics of the employees correspond so closely to those of the important clients that access is thus gained to various markets and customers, thereby generating a competitive advantage on the market.

The *Emerging or Learning Paradigm* encompasses aspects of the second and third approaches. As with the second approach, it promotes equal opportunities for all employees; it also resembles the third approach in that it recognizes both the differences amongst employees and the value of such differences. In addition this approach connects diversity with approaches to work. The aims which can be achieved by diversity include efficiency, innovation, customer satisfaction, personnel development and social responsibility. The learning and effectiveness approach aims at integration, whereby differences are recognized, together with their respective value (Dass and Parker 1999; Thomas and Ely 1996).

The first two approaches correspond to a lower degree of maturity, the third approach to a medium stage and the fourth approach to a high stage of maturity.

The different approaches include the implementation of different diversity measures. Various measures are involved in reaching a high degree of maturity. Central for the estimation of the maturity levels are the intensity, implementation and efficiency of possible gender diversity measures. These measures will be presented in the following section.

12.4 Gender Diversity Measures

The proportion of women in higher management levels at consultancies represent between 0 and 10%, on average nearly 3% (Hördt 2002). These figures for the consulting sector reveal that there are more barriers in progression to management positions for women than men. As a result of these additional barriers, that exist both inside and outside the work environment, women need more support on the part of the company in developing their careers. Aspects such as the attainment of equal opportunities for women and men and gender diversity, are central to our study.

Here both internal and external communication with regard to gender diversity are imbued with great significance, so that all participants can be kept informed and become involved. Only if the aim is formulated clearly as company policy can changes take place in the attitude of the employees and management. The potential of internal and external communication are manifold and serve to increase the acceptance and promote the implementation of the measures introduced.

There are many methods of communication and these can be integrated into already existing information and communication media.

The internal information and communication policy should cover all of the supporting policies the company offers to promote the combination of family commitments and career. It should, however, also provide information on active "father support" to promote the acceptance of fathers wishing to spend more time looking after their children, as well as external sources of information and events for parents and employees with career responsibilities. Positive examples should be given of how such support has already been implemented within the company, as well as ensuring that employees receive updates on the company while they are on their parental leave; details should also be given regarding any innovative suggestions made by employees, and of any such ideas that have now been adopted and implemented.

This information can be provided in individual discussions, on pinned-up notices and circular letters, and by means of the intranet. In addition, internal informative events such as company or departmental meetings could be planned to focus on a certain topic, or demand-oriented meetings and consultation hours with relevant personnel could be organized. Seminars could also integrate aspects of the company's "family-friendly" policies. The mission statement should be actively communicated, and someone in the company should be assigned the role as the person to contact on such issues. Company brochures and employees' newspapers focusing on specific topics could also be distributed. A policy ensuring active information and communication channels should lead to employees becoming proactive in finding out about their own needs.

External communication should be oriented towards a family-friendly company image, integrating the company's own concept of family-friendliness as well as individual measures and any awards which may have been won for family-friendly policies. This can then be supported by publishing internal and external job advertisements which are non-gender-specific, and which, for example, refer to the possibility of part-time work and explicitly state that applications from women are welcome, "even" for technical and management positions. Advertisements which promote the company's image can be placed in newspapers and specialist magazines, and articles in the press (specialist magazines, conferences, brochures) as well as membership of forums, working groups and networks focusing on the issue can be utilized. In addition this topic could be developed as one of the company's main consulting focus points and thus attract exactly those clients who have an equally positive attitude to this issue.

On the one hand the company's supporting measures will be used more, which means that the advantages already mentioned will begin to take effect. On the other hand the image of the company as an attractive and progressive employer will be improved. This does, however, mean that the formulation of the specific aim of gender diversity must put in an appearance somewhere, for example in the company's mission statement or as a general long-term goal of the company. This policy of communication and information can be supported by various measures.

Examples of these practices that serve to achieve gender diversity include (Andresen, Hristozova and Lieberum 2005):

- The employment situation of women in the company: increasing the number of women in higher management positions; no differentiation between women and men in part-time or full-time work and on parental leave; realization of equal pay for women and men.
- Staff recruitment and selection: gender neutral job advertisements; same selection criteria and methods for women and men; reintegration of women and men after their parental leave.
- Personnel development and further education: personnel and career development of part-time workers; support of women regarding expatriation as this helps to reach top management positions; equal career paths for women and men; (more or different) career counseling, mentoring and coaching programs, cross mentoring programs; support of mixed leadership.
- Flexible working hours: part-time work in higher management positions; enabling change from part-time to full-time work and vice versa.
- Information and communication policy: internal policy on equal opportunities; internal statements of co-operation between women and men in the workplace; institutionalization of equal opportunities and partnership-based behavior in the workplace.
- Service for families: support of child care; support for families and contact during parental leave; guidelines for coming back after parental leave.
- Flexible job organization: working at home; telework, mobile telework, teamwork.

Companies have to be aware of the fact that the failure of organizations to provide such support may deprive women of avenues for organizational success. In addition, companies need to make use of the abilities and experience of women. This last-mentioned control mechanism is required if we are to find out which of the support mechanisms proves to be the most effective and efficient for companies, and to determine and steer an optimum level of diversity.

The idea of categorizing gender diversity approaches and the practice of gender diversity measures leads to the following possible categorization where internal and external communication is deemed to be a necessary prerequisite for a high stage of maturity. The lowest level of intensity describes companies who do not implement any measures or communication activities. Whilst at level four the goal or the possibility of taking advantage of such measures is communicated, these measures do not factually exist in the company. At level three, also, communication is both internal and/or external, but only general measures are implemented, which have not only the goal of gender diversity. These measures are generally limited to flexible working hours or the possibility of part time work, which can be desired for other reasons. The second level includes internal as well as external communication, but at the same time also ensures that several measures are implemented which are aimed at fulfilling the requirements of gender diversity. The highest level is ultimately reserved for those companies who have aligned their entire personnel policy in accordance with the need for achieving gender diversity, and who communicate these successes both internally and externally.

This leads to the following intensity levels, which have been summarized in the table below:

Table 12.1. Levels of Intensity

Levels of intensity
Level 1: Very high intensity Companies which communicate gender diversity internally and externally as a company goal and which additionally implement consequently measures in all personnel functions with respect to gender diversity.
Level 2: High intensity Companies which communicate gender diversity internally and externally as a company goal and which additionally implement explicitly measures with respect to gender diversity, such as supporting the recruitment of women employees or networking for women.
Level 3: Middle intensity Companies which communicate gender diversity internally and/or externally as a company goal and additionally implement general measures not only with respect to gender diversity, such as e.g. flexible working hours and the possibility of part time work.
Level 4: Low intensity Companies which communicate gender diversity internally as a company goal but do not carry out any measures to promote women in managerial positions.
Level 5: Very low intensity Companies which do not communicate gender diversity as a company goal and do not carry out any measures at all to promote women in managerial positions.

Compared with the categories applied in the previous section, the lowest level five could be classified as the resistance perspective or a lower stage of maturity; levels four to three would correspond to the fairness approach or a medium stage of maturity, and levels three to two could encompass the access approach or a medium to a high level of maturity. Levels two to one could then be classified as the learning approach, in other words a high stage of maturity, whereby a decisive factor would be the willingness of level two companies to continue their development as a company. Exactly what this classification would look like for consulting companies will be discussed in the next section.

12.5 Practical Evidence in Consulting Companies

2004 we run a survey within the 25 largest management consultancies in Germany. The aim of the empirical study presented in the following sections is to investigate which initiatives are being taken by companies within selected fields of activity to achieve gender diversity in management ranks in general. The following questions should be answered through this investigation:

1. Do consulting companies in Germany pursue the goal of obtaining equal op
    portunities and/or do they aim at profiting from gender diversity in their or-
    ganization?
2. Do consulting companies communicate the goals of equal opportunities
    and/or gender diversity (a) externally and/or (b) internally?
3. Do consulting companies proactively take initiatives in general that serve to
    achieve the objectives of equal opportunities and gender diversity?

The survey started with the analysis of the homepages of these consulting companies with respect to public statements and documents about gender diversity. In
addition, we investigated whether the 25 consulting companies implemented activities to support gender diversity in general and/or promoted this topic by communicating it internally to their employees and/or implemented measures to support women. For this investigation we used structured telephone interviews as well
as an analysis of the contents of internal documents and brochures of these companies. The survey attained a response rate of 36% for the consulting companies
(n=9).

12.6 Results

In most of the consulting companies the proportion of female employees was on
average around 20 – 30%. However, the percentage of female managers at partner
level is not higher than 5%. These results prove the assumption that companies do
not take advantage of the potential of their entire internal staff to fill management
positions.

Table 12.2. summarizes the results in relation to external and internal communication of the goal of gender diversity, and the implementation of measures to
reach the goal of gender diversity. In comparison, the results of the same investigation of banks and insurance companies are shown, where the majority of employees are female, but also where on average not more than 7 % of the top management level are female.

Table 12.2. Empirical Results

	Consulting Companies		Banks		Insurance Companies	
Statements on their homepage	3 (n=25)	12%	5 (n=50)	7.7%	1 (n=28)	3.6%
Internal communi-cation	7 (n=9)	77.8%	15 (n=18)	83.3%	3 (n=10)	30%
Internal measures to foster gender diver-sity in general	7 (n=9)	77.8%	12 (n=18)	66.6%	3 (n=10)	30%

12.6.1 Importance of the Goal of Gender Diversity

Some companies, especially the larger ones, have partially recognized the need for and the need to pursue appropriate measures. The comparison with banks as a sector with a high proportion of female employees, especially with reference to the larger German banks, shows that consulting companies are on a par with them as far as their activities towards achieving equal opportunities are concerned. The insurance companies, on the other hand, generally reveal fewer activities within the area of gender diversity. It should be noted here that, especially with reference to the interviews, only a small number of companies could be included. Nevertheless, there are signs of strategies being introduced within the sectors considered. The following section will show the extent and type of the measures which are being implemented and pursued.

12.6.2 External Communication of Gender Diversity

The investigation regarding statements of gender diversity on homepages shows that 12% of the investigated consulting companies have placed statements which refer to this topic on their homepage, e.g. how to combine family and work or the "Total Quality Award" (in comparison 7.7% of the banks and 3.6% of the insurance companies). This kind of external communication is completed by a few of the companies with public events and/or articles placed on the internet or in newspapers and magazines (see Table 12.2.).

12.6.3 Internal Communication of Gender Diversity

By analyzing the responses of nine consulting companies with respect to the question as to whether internal statements which declare the support of gender diversity exist and what kind of measures have been established in the companies, the results showed that internal statements regarding gender diversity had been made by 78% of the consulting companies surveyed (in comparison 83% of the banks and 30% of the insurance companies) (see Table 12.2.). Of those companies that do not give evidence of their commitment on their homepage, some limited their communication to internal interest groups. Most of the companies use internal brochures to show for example the possibilities of flexible working hours or organize internal road shows to discuss the possibilities and to find individual solutions.

12.6.4 Gender Diversity Initiatives

78% of the consulting companies implement specific measures to achieve the objective of gender diversity (in comparison 67% of the banks and 30% of the insurance companies). Here it can be assumed that precisely those consulting companies responded to the qualitative section that has actually themselves already implemented measures. One of the reasons given by companies declining to take part in our survey was that either they had no interest in this topic or that in principle their company would not take part in surveys. Furthermore, several companies who took part in our study were large consulting companies who have made themselves well-known in the media. This means that the results we obtained could be quite different in the case of smaller consulting companies, of which there are very many in Germany. This would have to be the subject of further research.

In order to gain the advantages of gender diversity the organizations in the sample work on several aspects of human resources management. The most important initiative is the implementation of flexible working hours in connection with part-time work, which has also been implemented to some extent in higher management positions. A few companies have implemented measures to improve the recruitment of female applicants, and also measures concerning personnel development, such as mentoring and coaching programs, as well as supporting women's networks within the companies.

In the banks and insurance companies measures had been implemented concerning more flexible job organization schemes, providing the opportunity to work at home, or telework, as well as special services for families, such as child care support, active contact during parental leave and guidelines for coming back after parental leave, and, albeit rarely, supporting women employees in their applications for expatriate positions. Based on the above presented framework and these results the companies can be subdivided into five different intensity levels related to the goal of gender diversity.

These intensity levels, described in a previous section (especially levels 1, 2 and 3) depend on the kind and the number of measures which have been realized in the company, and on the effectiveness of the measures implemented. According to the results there are only a few companies which implement activities designed to promote equal opportunities, and that these companies very seldom reach the highest intensity level. This means that they will not reach their potential level of success (in terms of gender mix and organizational success).

Table 12.3. Categorization of the Companies Surveyed

Intensity	Very high 1	High 2	Middle 3	Low 4	Very low 5
Consulting companies (n= 9)	0%	33.3%	44.4%	0%	22.2%
Banks (n=18)	5.6%	16.7%	44.4%	16.7%	16.7%
Insurance companies (n=10)	0%	0%	30%	0	70%

It is striking that the consulting companies who do actively support women employees usually implement several measures to do so. Here there are differences to the banks and insurance companies studied. Banks on average achieve a somewhat lower level of intensity; however, there are more banks in this investigation and therefore also smaller companies have been included. The difference in comparison with the insurance companies is more obvious: only 30% of insurance companies can be classified in the medium group and they therefore pursue gender diversity to a lesser extent on average.

In the interviews with the consulting companies it was also established that in principle there should be no distinctions made between men and women in personnel policy, but that only the qualifications should count. This finding is also supported by interviews carried out in 2002, where representatives of the largest consulting companies were also interviewed on the subject of women within the consulting sector (Hördt 2002). In spite of this, measures were implemented, as the proportion of women managers at top management level was and still is extremely small. In addition it was stated that resistance was particularly strong from women, once special programs had been introduced, with the reasons for this being given as the fact that these measures would instead have the opposite effect and hinder women's progress.

This evaluation reveals the special culture which seems to predominate in consulting companies: the focus is on the high qualifications of the employees and on their level of involvement with regard to the company's clients and the projects that have been taken on. It is at precisely such high level positions that a part-time position is untenable, thus making the combination of family and profession more difficult, and thus leading to there being fewer women in higher positions, even though in principle the opportunities for men and women are equal. The roles allocated by society or by the family are decisive here, whereby in most cases the traditional form of the division of labor in the family prevails. Nevertheless there would still be other ways in which consulting companies could provide more support, thus enabling concurrent family and professional commitments to be a feasible prospect, even in senior positions. The project work to be done could be distributed among more people or simply distributed differently, so that both men and women would be able to develop their careers successfully within a consulting company, irrespective of the fact that they have a family as well. Hördt's study (2002) on the topic of women in the consulting sector provides similar findings. Her investigation shows that the only significant criteria for working in this sector are performance and efficiency, which are supposed to be non-gender specific. The small proportion of women is explained as being due to the smaller proportion of women on the labor market. However, other criteria were also identified which were explained by internal factors, such as, for example, gender specific assignment procedures and a lower level of access to informal networks. Problems with acceptance of women among clients were also mentioned (Hördt 2002).

This points very clearly to the fact that although there are no official barriers for women, internal unofficial barriers do prevail, which could be related to the allocation of roles within the family and to the everyday attitudes toward and interaction with women in the workplace; these are therefore factors which are not compatible with the working conditions in the consulting sector.

One possibility would be to consider the concept that there are no differences regarding gender within the companies questioned and therefore that no measures need to be implemented. Instead the goal to promote more women to senior positions should be actively integrated into personnel policy, with all departments oriented towards this goal. This would call for changes to the company culture in such ways that behavior and attitudes, management style and career opportunities would be explicitly analyzed for discriminatory aspects and amended in the sense of a change process. In addition, the goal of gender diversity should be communicated clearly and pursued using those methods described in the introductory sections of this paper.

12.7 Résumé

There are many possible approaches for supporting gender diversity in companies.

However, several companies do use external and/or internal information platforms to communicate the goal of gender diversity to the public and/or to their employees. They also make arrangements for specific activities to implement measures to reach the goal of gender diversity. There are differences between the companies themselves and between the fields of activity, and these will have to be examined more precisely.

Referring to this empirical study, we are able to state that consulting companies use external and/or internal information platforms to communicate the goal of gender diversity to the public and/or to their employees. They also implement specific activities that serve to achieve the goal of gender diversity. Although suggestions on how to ameliorate the situation are frequently given in the literature, the number of initiatives introduced by organizations in practice to support the taking up of management positions by their female employees are somewhat sparse and insufficient.

The number of women in senior positions is still low, and shows the minor effect such measures can have, should there be no appropriate changes made to the company culture and if the management level is not included in the measures introduced. The qualitative investigation could be based on a 360° analysis of a tangible diversity practice, including as many perspectives as possible from within the organization (for example employees, management, HR department, works council).

In a detailed analysis the companies which have a middle, high or very high intensity level have to be split into different sections depending on the amount, content and effectiveness of the implemented measures.

Further research should also involve other industries in order to investigate potential differences between companies with a high, middle or low proportion of female workers. Also, measures contributing to gender diversity should be analyzed with respect to their efficiency and effectiveness. Additionally, consulting companies of various sizes should be included in the study in order to gain meaningful results for the consulting sector as a whole. It would also be important to establish Best Practices and then to quantify the costs and usefulness effects. There is also still a need to determine an optimum level of gender diversity in management ranks with respect to its impact on organizational success.

References

Andresen M, Hristozova E and Lieberum UB (2005) Gender Diversity and Organizational Success: The Contribution of Female Foreign Assignments. Morley M, Hearty N, Collings DG (eds) New Directions in Expatriate Research. Palgrave Macmillian (forthcoming)

Balser S (1999) Abschied von der Monokultur: Diversity als Spiegel der Welt. Personalführung (5), pp. 14-16

Dass P, Parker B (1999) Strategies for Managing Human Resource Diversity: From Resistance to Learning. Academy of Management Executive 13(2), pp. 68 – 80

Gilbert JA, Ivancevich JM (2000) Valuing Diversity: A Tale of Two Organizations. Academy of Management Executive 14 (1), pp. 93 – 106

Gilbert JA, Stead BA and Ivancevich JM (1999) Diversity Management: A New Organizational Paradigm. Journal of Business Ethics 21 (1), pp. 61 – 77

Hördt O (2002) Frauen in der Unternehmensberatung: Empirische Analyse zur geschlechtsspezifischen Segregation. Deutscher Universitätsverlag, Wiesbaden

Köhler-Braun K (1999) Vielfalt führt zum Erfolg. Personalwirtschaft (10), pp. 74-79

Köhler-Braun K (1999) Durch Diversity zu neuen Anforderungen an das Management. Zeitschrift Führung und Organisation (4), pp. 188-194

Kovach KA, Kravitz DA and Hughes AA (2004) Affirmative Action: How can we be so lost when we don't even know where we are going?. Labor Law Journal 55 (1), pp. 53 – 61

Lau D, Murnighan JK (1998) Demographic Diversity and Faultlines: The Compositional Dynamics of Organizational Groups. Academy of Management Review 23 (2), pp. 325 – 340

Milliken FJ, Martins LL (1996) Searching for Common Threads: Understanding the Multiple Effects of Diversity in Organizational Groups. Academy of Management Review 21 (2), pp. 402 – 433

Pérotin V, Robinson A and Loundes J (2003) Equal Opportunities Practices and Enterprise Performance: A comparative investigation on Australian and British data. International Labour Review 142 (4), pp. 471 – 505

Okech J, Rudolf H (2003) Nonstop im Einsatz: Vom Klonen des Menschen: Verbot oder Tabu?. WZB-Mitteilungen 102, pp. 12 – 15

Pless N (2000) Diversitätsmanagement: Geschäftserfolg in den USA. Personalwirtschaft (5), pp. 51-57

Rudolph H, Theobald H and Quack S (2001) Internationalisierung: Ausgangspunkt einer Neuformierung der Geschlechterverhältnisse in der Unternehmensberatung. Discussion Paper FS I 01-102, Wissenschaftszentrum Berlin für Sozialforschung, pp. 1 – 21

Stuber M (2002) Diversity als Strategie. Personalwirtschaft (1), pp. 28-33

Stumpf S, Thomas A (1999) Zusammenarbeit und Kommunikation: Management von Heterogenität und Homogenität in Gruppen. Personalführung 32 (5), pp. 36-45

Thomas RR (2001) Management of Diversity: Neue Personalstrategien für Unternehmen, Wiesbaden

Thomas DA, Ely RJ (1996) Making Differences Matter: A New Paradigm for Managing Diversity. Harvard Business Review 74 (9/10), pp. 79 – 90

Tsui AS, Egan TD and O'Reilly AC (1992) Being Different: Relational Demography and Organizational Attachment. Administrative Science Quarterly 37 (4), pp. 549 – 579

Wagner D, Sepehri P (1999) Managing Diversity: Alter Wein in neuen Schläuchen. Personalführung 31 (5), pp. 18 – 21

Whitehead S (2001) Woman as Manager: A Seductive Ontology. Gender, Work & Organization 8 (1), pp. 84 – 107

Wright P, Ferris SP, Hiller JS and Kroll M (1995) Competitiveness trough Management of Diversity: Effects on Stock Price Valuation. Academy of Management Journal 38 (1), pp. 272 – 287

Zenger TR, Lawrence BS (1989) Organizational Demography: The Differential Effects of Age and Tenure Distribution on Technical Communication. Academy of Management Journal 32 (2), pp. 353 – 376

13 Managing Employability in the German Consultancy Industry

Maida Petersitzke and Elena Hristozova

Helmut-Schmidt-University/University of the Federal Armed Forces Hamburg, Germany

13.1 Introduction

After decades of rapid growth, the consultancy industry is currently experiencing a slowdown, which commenced in 2001 (Kipping 2002). For the first time, employees in this industry are faced with personnel reduction (Graubner and Richter 2003), hiring freezing (Bornmüller 2005) or other alternatives to downsizing (Fritzel and Vaterrodt 2002) at such scale. According to employee data from 2001 to 2003 for Germany, five of the largest IT consulting companies have reduced their personnel by 1,315 heads (Lünendonk 2002, 2003 and 2004). Now that consultancies are planning to hire again, they are faced with one of the consequences of these personnel reductions: the decrease in job security has in turn caused a decrease in employer attractiveness (BDU 2005). This example serves as an illustration of the negative consequences personnel reductions within the consultancy industry has had for both employee and employer. Consequently, both parties have an interest in finding an alternative to job security. The alternative currently on offer is called employability. Very generally, employability refers to the ability of a person to obtain and maintain a job now and in the future. Ideally, employability is based on a principle of responsibility shared between the organization and the individual and if the idea of employability is embraced fully by employer and employee it has potential for creating Win-Win situations for both parties. We argue that under certain conditions, offering support to staff that enables them to develop their individual employability does present a viable alternative to job security. We also argue that fostering employability of staff in a proactive manner will have a positive effect on employer attractiveness in the consultancy industry.

To the best of our knowledge there is no contribution addressing the issue of employability within the consultancy industry. Therefore our aim is to close this gap and deliver first insights based on a pilot study that we carried out in the German consultancy industry. For the purpose of the present article we offer some further reasons for the relevance of employability for the German consultancy industry and then highlight activities both employers and employees can engage in to develop individual employability.

In the following sections of this article, we first focus on the industry-specific demand for employability within the German consultancy industry. Then we present some background information on the concept of employability and employability development referring to a conceptual framework for analyzing individual activities and organizational offers enhancing employability. Finally, we will present the results of the pilot study. More specifically, the pilot study has three research objectives: (A) to identify areas of strength and weakness regarding employability activities for both employers and employees in the consultancy industry; (B) to investigate differences between consultants and back office employees in the context of employability and (C) based on these results propose several starting points for consultancies that want to strengthen their efforts with regard to employability development.

We have put the focus of our contribution on the large IT and management consultancies in Germany for three particular reasons. *Firstly*, Germany is the second largest consulting market in Europe (BDU 2005). *Secondly*, large German consultancies are currently experiencing the consequences of the above-mentioned slowdown to a greater extent than small and medium-sized firms (BDU 2005). *Thirdly*, IT and management consulting represent 88.5% of the consulting market in Germany (BDU 2005).

13.2 Employability Demand in the German Consultancy Industry

In this section we focus our attention on the industry-specific *demand for employability* caused by the relevant business context of the German consultancy industry. Certain driving forces in the business environment may influence the demand for employability. Such drivers can be developments in the industry and characteristics of the market where firms operate. In this context, Riddell and Sweetman (1997) distinguish between four major developments: *technological, organizational, economical* and *demographical* (see Figure 13.1.).

These phenomena and market characteristics influence the *demand for employability* in the German consultancy industry to differing degrees. In order to specify the influence of the above-mentioned driving forces on the demand for employability within the German consultancy industry we have used data mainly from the annual reports of the Federal Association of German Management Consultants Bundesverband Deutscher Unternehmensberater (BDU 2005; BDU 2004) and annual market studies (Streicher and Lünendonk 2004a; 2004b) which are focused on the 25 largest players in the management and IT consultancy market.

Fig. 13.1. Driving Forces Shaping the Demand for Employability

13.2.1 Technological (Know-how) Development and Product Market

In an economic environment characterized by globalization technological development is becoming more and more important with respect to organizational success. Due to such development job-specific skills can become obsolete fairly rapidly (Blechinger and Pfeifer 2000; Neuman and Weiss 1995). Thus employability is crucial for bridging skills gaps and continuing labor market participation (de Grip et al. 2001). More specifically, technological development in the consultancy industry leads to the continuous emergence of new managerial vogues. Consequently, existing knowledge and skills regarding management concepts and techniques have a short half-life (Kubr 2002). Furthermore, consultancy firms are continuously confronted with market pressure to keep a balance between the capacity to offer new services and the ability to stay specialized in one area in order to guarantee in-depth know-how (BDU 2005; BDU 2004). To sum it up, the intensive know-how development and market pressures can be expected to have a steady impact on the employability demand within the consultancy industry.

13.2.2 Organizational Developments

Organizational developments demand a high degree of flexibility, which can be accomplished by being employable (Dielmann 1999; Riddell and Sweetman 2000). Organizational developments can be reorganizations and/or changes in the position of the organization that take place in a larger configuration like parent company or franchise (De Grip et al. 2001). The more employees are involved in such developments the stronger is the need for organizational and individual flexibility. For 2004, the BDU reports a high number of reorganization activities within the big consultancies concerning internal structures and reorientation towards new services and clients (BDU 2005). Internal reorganization and new market orientation are typical strategies in turbulent times. Thus employability is particularly important during times of crisis: on the one hand external employability can be used as an alternative to job security and on the other hand internal employability contributes to better organizational flexibility. Due to current organizational developments in big German consultancies the need for flexibility and respectively for employability is relatively high.

13.2.3 Economic Developments (in Competition)

Recent competition in Western economies is focused on knowledge and innovation capacity. In an international context firms are forced to adapt to changes more rapidly (de Grip et. al 2001) and this leads to an increased demand for a flexible and innovative workforce (e.g. Brown 2003; Bollérot 2001; Dielmann 1999). The degree to which an industry is influenced by its international context depends on how open it is. Openness of an industrial sector can be estimated by looking at export shares of the industry's production (de Grip et al 2001).

According to market studies carried out annually by Lünendonk, in 2003 the top 25 IT consultancies made 14% (1.1 billion EUR) of their total turnover with foreign clients (Streicher and Lünendonk 2004). The same study reports less than 10% (304 Mio EUR) export shares for the top 25 management consultancies. Although export shares do not differ to a great extent, Kipping (1996) as well as Streicher and Lünendonk (2004) consider management consulting a "local business". On the other hand, the consultancy industry in Germany considers increasing internationalization as an important driver for turnover in 2005 (BDU 2005). This development could lead to a higher export-orientation also for management consulting. In summary, openness of the IT consultancy sector can be considered moderate, whereas openness of management consultancies is lower and therefore less relevant to the demand for employability. However, increasing internationalization is seen as a driver for turnover. This may positively influence export-orientation of German management consultancies in the near future.

13.2.4 Demographic Developments and Labor Market

In Europe the aging workforce and a decreasing labor market inflow of younger employees lead to two challenges where employability could contribute to a solution. *Firstly*, European employers, especially those in Germany, need to retain their personnel longer (Commission of the European Communities 2005). A look at the German consulting market reveals the following picture: While the number of consultants and junior consultants has decreased, the number of senior consultants, project managers and partners has increased (BDU 2005). This development in the German consultancy sector underlines a general tendency in the European labor market. *Secondly,* knowledge-driven industries more than others experience a skills shortage due to the above-mentioned demographic development and are forced to participate in a "war for talent" (Chambers et al. 1998; Leitl et al. 2001). In 2005, the battle for outstanding talent within the large consultancies in Germany is likely to continue. Furthermore, people development and alternatives to job security will be of central relevance for recruitment strategies (BDU 2005). Employability also plays a central role with regard to career transfers. Due to a "grow-or-go" policy (Kubr 2002) and a high number of separations in the recent past (Graubner and Richter 2003) career transfers outside the organization are common in consultancies. In summary, current demographic developments in the German labor market have a strong impact on the need for employability in the consulting sector.

As we have seen various kinds of developments influence the demand for employability in the German consulting business. In the short run this demand reflects the need for finding an alternative to job security. In the long run, it reflects the need to build a flexible and innovative workforce possessing state-of-the-art know-how regardless of age. Thus, we see the concept of employability as highly relevant to the German consultancy industry.

13.3 Employability and Employability Development

Employability is very generally defined as the ability of an individual to enter working life, keep a job or to find new employment (Blancke, Roth and Schmid 1999). However, other definitions include a range of different perspectives and conceptual approaches, which are summarized in the following.

Employability may be understood as an organizational or as an individual concept. When it is viewed as an *organizational concept* it refers to the degree of flexibility of a specific organization's staff with regard to placement, i.e. highly employable individuals can easily be reassigned to jobs within the organization. The need for this kind of functional flexibility in the consultancy industry has been highlighted above. But more frequently, employability has been discussed as an *individual concept* where employability refers to an individual's ability either to obtain or to maintain a job, i.e. enter the workforce or stay in it. Additionally, as an individual concept employability may refer to an employee's capacity to find a different position with his or her current employer when necessary or desired (*internal employability*) or it may refer to finding new employment with a different employer (*external employability*). For the purpose of the present contribution we focus our investigation on the individual concept of both internal and external employability.

An important question with regard to employability is how individual employability can be fostered and facilitated. While the aim of employability is to find and maintain a job, employability development is seen as a tool (Bollérot 2001) or strategy serving this aim. In this context, we understand employability development as an action-oriented concept taking into account efforts of both employee and employer aimed at obtaining and maintaining a certain degree of individual employability.

Thus we differentiate here between (A) employability activities: employees' activities that contribute to individual employability and (B) employability offers: organizational measures aimed at enhancing individual employability. In the following we present a framework that encompasses both possible employability activities and employability offers.

13.4 Employability Development Framework

This model, on which the remainder of this article is based, has been adapted from a very similar model proposed by Andresen and Petersitzke (2004) which is in turn based on a framework proposed by Lombriser and Uepping (2001). The framework we use here has several advantages: Firstly, the model integrates employee and organizational efforts contributing to employability. Individual activities can largely be matched to corresponding organizational offers, which are also framed as activities. Secondly, this framework illustrates the principle of shared responsibility, which most authors in this field agree on: It is the organization's responsibility to provide opportunities and an environment that allows employees to craft their employability. It is the individual employee's responsibility to then make use of the opportunities available. Thirdly, this framework is specific enough to derive fairly concrete management recommendations. However, this framework also has some disadvantages. Most importantly, it disregards that employability efforts have to be embedded in an organizational culture, which encourages employees to care for their employability in a proactive way.

The employability development framework we use here divides activities for individuals and organizations into four categories of tasks: Identity Growth, Self-Organization, Qualification and Self-Marketing. Table 13.1. provides an overview of the different categories and sub-categories. In the following two sections we will describe individual and organizational activities in more detail.

Table 13.1. Employee and Employer Activities (Andresen and Petersitzke 2004)

	Employee	Employer
Identity Growth	Assess status quo	Provide assessment instruments
	Identify direction for development	Provide Guidance
Self-Organization	Gather information on careers, market, opportunities and requirements	Provide information on careers, openings, market and requirements
	Develop strategy	Offer assistance with strategy, training plan and access to career advice
	Make time for learning	
Qualification	Engage in learning: Strategic level	Offer training and development: Strategic level
	Engage in Learning: Operational level	Offer development: Operational level
Self-Marketing	Maintain visibility	Provide platforms
	Develop networks	Offer training on networking
	Share learning	

13.4.1 Employability Activities

To enhance their employability, individuals engage in four sets of tasks or activities, which can in turn be divided into subtasks with associated activities. Table 13.2. - 13.5. detail the specific individual activities required. The first set of tasks, labeled Identity Growth, includes all activities related to the individual taking stock of his or her current professional situation and identifying a direction in which to take his or her professional development based both on individual strengths and preferences as well as on market demands.

Table 13.2. Employee Tasks, Identity Growth

Assess Status quo	Identify and Evaluate Direction for Development on the Basis of Own:
Asking for feedback on performance	Professional Goals
Get guidance from trusted third parties	Skills and Knowledge
	Strengths and Weaknesses

The second set of tasks details activities related to Self-Organization which involves processes of information gathering, for example on present skill requirements for positions of interest, skills in demand on the labor market now and in the future, career paths, and getting organized about when, how and what to learn.

Table 13.3. Employee Tasks, Self-Organization

Gather Information on	Develop Qualification Strategy	Make Time for Learning
Career paths and labor market	Set learning objectives	On the job
Opportunities for qualification inside and outside the organization	Identify milestones	Off the job
Skill requirements for positions of interest		

The third set of tasks, labeled Qualification, describes the actual learning process where different learning strategies complement each other to ensure employability in the short and in the long term, whereas reactive and preventive learning strategies are closely tied to current and impending business needs, proactive learning is geared at new knowledge that may influence the direction of the business through its availability.

Table 13.4. Employee Tasks, Qualification

Engage in Learning: Strategic Level	Engage in Learning: Operational Level
Reactive Learning: Update knowledge and skills to maintain current levels of performance	Job Enlargement
Preventive Learning: Extend existing knowledge and skills adapting to changes already planned	Job Enrichment
Proactive Learning: Acquire knowledge and skills that may become relevant to the business	Job Rotation
Independent of business needs: Acquire completely new areas of expertise	Project Work
	Training off-the-job

The fourth set of tasks refers to Self-Marketing aspects of individual employability. In order to become an attractive candidate for a new position being well qualified does not suffice. Ensuring that others within or outside one's organization know one's profile of skills, knowledge and interests will increase the likelihood of becoming eligible for positions one would not have known about otherwise.

Table 13.5. Employee Tasks, Self-Marketing

Maintain Visibility	Develop Networks	Share Knowledge
Demonstrate new knowledge and skills to management and peers	Inside the organization	With others in your organization
Inform HR about recent qualifications	Outside the organization	With others in your professional network
Seize opportunities to make yourself known in the organization		

In order to foster their employability, individuals should initially work through these four categories engaging in the relevant activities. Once this process has been initiated and an individual qualification and marketing strategy has been developed and put in practice, the strategy adopted should be evaluated and updated regularly.

13.4.2 Employability Offers

Table 13.6. – 13.9. provide an overview of employer activities geared at supporting individual employability. The first set of tasks labeled Identity Growth involves all organizational offers that support employees with identifying the direction in which they want to develop. These activities are integrated in a range of organizational processes and vary from HR tools to facilitate self-assessment to providing HR services such as counseling.

Table 13.6. Employer Tasks, Identity Growth

Provide Assessment Instruments	Provide Guidance and Counseling
360° Feedback	Mentorship Programs
Online Tests	Feedback on Self -Assessment
Development Center	Individual Guidance by Internal or External Career Advisor

The second set of tasks labeled Self-Organization mainly consists in offering different kinds of updated information to employees and guidance on how to use this information.

Table 13.7. Employer Tasks, Self-Organization

Provide Information	Offer Assistance
Career paths	Develop individual training plans
Labor Market Trends	Access and support for external career advice
Skill requirements for positions in the organization	
Updates of requirements after innovations	
Learning/Training Opportunities within and outside the organization	
Job Openings within and outside the organization	

The third set of tasks, Qualification, entails traditional personnel development activities such as providing training to cover needs derived from current and future job requirements as well as offering job rotation, job enrichment, job enlargement and project work serving development purposes. Furthermore, organizations can offer a range of additional qualification opportunities that combine the organization's interests with labor market requirements.

Table 13.8. Employer Tasks, Qualification

Offer Training and Development: Strategic Level	Offer Development: Operational Level
Adapted to current business needs	Job Rotation
Adapted to future business needs	Job Enrichment
Adapted to potential business needs	Job Enlargement
Adapted to professional development needs	Project Work
	Training off-the-job

Finally, the fourth set of tasks for employers involves supporting Self-Marketing. In the literature, there are few recommendations as to how to do that practically in the context of employability. However, it is central to provide opportunities for networking within and outside the organization. This can be achieved by offering intranet communities for certain groups of employees, by encouraging those wanting to increase their visibility to participate in cross-departmental projects or by organizing internal career fairs where business units as well as individual employees present themselves.

Table 13.9. Employer Tasks, Self-Marketing

Provide Networking Platforms	Offer Training focused on Networking
Online	In-house
Face-to-Face	External provider

We have now presented the reader with a framework to analyze employability development from an individual and organizational point of view. For the remainder of this article we will focus on an *empirical pilot study* we have carried out in 2005 in five of the top 25 IT and management consultancies located in Germany. Five responsible HR professionals and 29 employees of these firms participated in this pilot study. Further we have run two more interviews with representatives from large consultancies also located in Germany. The outcome of these two interviews has been used to support interpretation of the main results of this study.

13.5 The Study

The first aim of this study was to identify areas of strength and weakness regarding employability activities and employability offers in the consultancy industry. In order to make our analysis and recommendations as specific as possible, our second aim was to check for differences in (A) degree of employability and (B) activities for those members of staff employed as consultants and those not employed as consultants, i.e. researchers and members of support teams in back office functions. The third aim of this study was to derive and present some industry-specific first recommendations on where and how organizations can strengthen their efforts in order to enhance employability.

To achieve our first aim, we asked employees to which degree they engaged in each of 34 employability activities calculating mean levels of activity. We also interviewed a contact from the HR department of the participating consultancy firms asking whether and to whom they offered each of 32 employability activities. Items in our questionnaire and interview guideline were derived from the employability development framework presented above.

To achieve our second aim we divided our group of participants into those working as consultants and those working in back office functions. We asked each group to rate their current employability on an eight-item scale, which checks the perceived likelihood of changing into different kinds of positions inside and outside the organization within the next twelve months (van der Heijden 2001). We then checked for significant differences in perceived employability between the groups using t-tests. We also investigated whether there are any significant differences between groups in levels of engagement in employability activities, also using t-tests.

To achieve our third aim, proposing some industry-specific and fairly concrete recommendations for developing organizational employability activities we combined three perspectives (see Figure 13.2.) in our research methodology: From the reported activity level of employees we identified those individual activities and sets where activity level was particularly low.

Fig. 13.2. Deriving Opportunities for Developing Organizational Offers

Furthermore, we asked employees which of these 34 activities they thought they would like to engage in more actively to ensure their employability identifying those activities that were indicated most frequently. We then identified those activities where activity was low *and* a need was indicated. If these activities corresponded to an organizational offer that was not provided across the board by most participating organizations to both employee groups, we singled those activities out as candidates which may usefully contribute to further developing employability offers in consultancy firms in Germany.

13.5.1 Investigating Activity Levels of Employees and Employers

Comparing the four sets of activities for employees we found that employees report significantly *less activity for tasks related to self-organization* than for activities related to identity growth, qualification or self-marketing. Looking at individual activities we found that regarding self-organization, there is little reported activity for *developing a learning strategy, identifying milestones for reaching one's learning goals* and managing time in a way that allows participants to *learn during working hours and outside working hours*. Regarding identity growth, there is little activity for *obtaining feedback from a mentor*. With regard to qualification and self marketing, showing interest in taking part in a *job rotation* and *keeping the HR department informed about one's skills and knowledge* are the activities where involvement is lowest. On the other hand, employees report *high levels of activity for achieving awareness of own skills as well as strengths and weaknesses*. Interestingly, awareness of skills, strengths and weaknesses is a lot higher than awareness of career goals. Furthermore, employees are highly active regarding learning that is necessary to maintain current levels of performance. They are very active in taking on new tasks that involve more responsibility for the purpose of development and actively share their knowledge with others in their organization. To sum up the above, on average participating employees show a *marked lack of activity regarding strategic and planning tasks (goals, learning strategy, milestones, time management) that would form the basis of a systematic endeavor to promote their employability*.

The five participating organizations, on the other hand, engage in between 9 (for back office staff) and 24 (for consultants) out of 32 employability offers. As the number of participating organizations is small, we are reluctant to overinterpret results. However, there is a general tendency for participating organizations to engage in those activities that are usually offered by HR for reasons not explicitly related to employability *such as communicating internal job openings and skill requirements for recently created positions as well as supporting development activities that are initiated by employees themselves*. Only 2 organizational offers are provided to both back office staff and consultants by all participating organizations: *support with creating a training plan and qualification to maintain current levels of performance*. For consultants, another 3 offers are provided by all participating consultancies: *communication of skill requirements for positions within the organization and information about internal training opportunities as well as qualification that covers not only current skill requirements but also future requirements that have already been decided on*. On the other hand, *mentoring* is offered to consultants in two participating organizations and *360° feedback* is offered to consultants in 2 participating organizations and to back office staff in one organization only. *Written tests for self-assessment* are offered to consultants in 1 organization. Furthermore, only 1 consulting firm provides its staff with *information on labor market developments* and no organization has invited labor market experts to talk about recent developments. None of the participating organizations support their staff financially when they want to get career guidance by an external provider. To sum up the above, participating organizations are *least active with regard to progressive instruments for self-assessment, offering career guidance (by way of mentoring or external providers) and offering information on labor market trends*.

13.5.2 Investigating Differences between Back Office Staff and Consultants

We investigated differences between back office staff and consultants with regard to three criteria: (A) degree of employability, (B) level of activity for the four sets of activities and (C) organizational employability offers available. Our back office group included researchers as well as staff in support functions provided they held at least a qualification at degree level. When we asked both groups to rate their own employability, we found that back office staff reports a significantly lower probability that they will change to a different position over the next year. Our measure includes various possibilities ranging from changing to a similar position in their current organization to changing to a position with more responsibility or at a higher management level in a different organization. This measure has been identified as a reliable measure of employability by van der Heijden (2002). Of course, self-reports of employability only represent one perspective out of several, but we think that the people concerned would generally be in a very good (if not the best) position to estimate the likelihood of changing jobs, especially because the difference in employability held true when we only considered those employees that reported that they are planning to change their jobs over the next 12 months. In summary, *back office employees in our study report lower probability of changing jobs. Based on these results we see back office employees as more vulnerable in terms of employability.*

However, this was the only global difference between the two groups that we identified. Groups did not differ in their general level of activity with regard to employability development nor were there any significant differences for the four sets of activities. However, there were a few significant differences with regard to individual activities: for example, not surprisingly, consultants were more involved in project work. This result probably reflects the way consultancy work is usually organized (Kubr 2002) rather than these individuals proactively seeking out opportunities for project work. All in all, our results do not indicate significant global differences in employee activities between the two groups.

With regard to employer activities, all organizations make at least as many offers to consultants as to back office employees. One organization, for example, offers 15 activities to both employee groups whereas another offers 23 to consultants but only twelve to back office staff. However, a greater number of participating organizations is needed to establish whether consultancy firms generally provide significantly more employability offers to consultants.

This leads us to the conclusion that *whereas consultants and back office employees do not differ significantly in their level of activity or focus of activity, back office employees in our study are more vulnerable in terms of employability,* i.e. they estimate their chances of changing jobs - even if they want to - worse than consultants do. What does that mean for HR management in consultancy firms? The tendency that we see in our data is that back office employees are offered less than consultants in terms of employability development. However, if their self report reflects their standing on the labor market well, this group of employees needs more support from their organization to generate higher levels of individual activity thereby compensating for lower self-reported employability. Furthermore, our data indicates that back office employees do not need offers different from those made to consultants but they need more of the same.

13.5.3 How Can Employability Offers Be Developed Further in Consultancy Firms?

Our third research aim was to identify specific needs for developing employability offers and derive some first recommendations. As mentioned above we are primarily defining needs as those activities where employee activity is low (A), where employees express a wish to be more engaged (B) and where a corresponding offer is not provided by all organizations for all employees (C).

Concerning (A), we have already identified the main areas of low activity for employees: *getting feedback from a mentor, developing a qualification strategy, identifying milestones, taking part in job rotations, making time for learning during and outside working hours* and *informing the HR department about qualifications obtained recently.* Therefore we now turn to (B), those activities where employees indicated a wish for more engagement. For the identity growth set of activities, employees indicated a need for *more feedback from mentors, more clarity about professional goals* and *evaluating regularly whether they are still on track to reach their professional goals.* For the self-organization set employees indicated that they wanted to gather more *information about different possible career paths* and indicated *a need to know more about trends, markets and industries.* They also indicated a *need for developing a qualification strategy* and planning their time in a way that allows for *learning in their leisure time* as well. Concerning organizational support that is not offered in every organization and for all employees (C), we have identified the following activities: *mentoring, external career counseling, information about the labor market, inviting labor market experts, trainings on networking, instruments for individual assessment, job requirements for positions outside the organization and training and development not focused on current or future job requirements.*

Figure 13.3. summarizes the above-mentioned results. Further, the figure pinpoints overlap between the three perspectives: self-reported level of employee activity, indicated need for more activity and level of organizational activity.

So what conclusions can we draw from the two perspectives – self reported level of activity and need for change? Generally, the two perspectives indicate that both identity growth and self-organization are areas which additional effort to facilitate employability should focus on. More specifically, there are three activities where low levels of activity and expressed wish for more activity coincide: getting *feedback from mentors, developing a qualification strategy and planning so that there is time for learning.* Additionally, there is the expressed wish for developing clearer professional goals and gathering information about market trends and career paths.

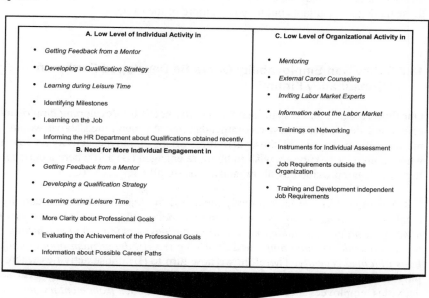

Fig. 13.3. Summary of Results regarding Individual Activities, Indicated Need for More Activity and Organizational Offers

There are various ways of combining organizational activities to cover for these needs. In our catalogue of organizational offers, these issues would be addressed by mentoring (e.g. Ragins 1997), coaching (e.g. Kubr 2002) and internal or external career counseling (e.g. Chung and Gforerer 2003). Additionally, some needs can be addressed by very specific activities such as providing information about labor markets online and inviting labor market experts to give talks to employees. However, these offers do not seem to be part of the standard repertoire provided by most organizations to all employees. *Mentoring is offered by 2 organizations* and only for consultants, new employees or highest potentials. *Internal career coaching* is offered by 2 organizations for all employees. Only 1 organization offers *information about the labor market* and none of the participating organizations *invite labor market experts* or support *external career coaching or counseling*. Therefore we think that these activities would be a good starting point to strengthen organizational efforts to facilitate employability (see Figure 13.3.). Inviting labor market experts and thereby delivering information that is industry-specific can be easily integrated into networking meetings inside the consulting firm. All except for one consultancy report to run several networking activities at different levels and for different functions.

Additionally, we see two general options that have the potential to address most of the issues described above: The first option is to introduce a mentoring system open to individuals from all professional groups in the organization. Traditionally mentoring is based on two behavioral aspects (Ragins 1997). The first aspect focuses on *career development behaviors* like coaching (Kubr 2002), i.e. "... sponsoring advancement, providing challenging assignments and protecting mentees from adverse forces" (Ragins 1997: 484). The second aspect of mentoring involves *psychological roles* provided by the mentor, which include "... friendship, counseling and role modeling" (Ragins 1997: 484). Our understanding of *employability mentoring* focuses explicitly on career development. The mentor's tasks with regard to enhancing employability include helping to identify career goals and strategies, supporting regular re-evaluation of strategies based on goals, advising on new skills that will become relevant in the future, helping to identify opportunities to acquire those skills on the job and identifying opportunities to change position within or – if necessary – outside the organization. In consultancy firms the challenge is to free up senior staff's time in order to make sure mentor and mentee have enough contact time.

A second option is to offer financial support if employees want to obtain career guidance from an external advisor. What could be the added value of an external career advisor? Coaching skills, knowledge of trends and changes in the labor market as well as the impact of changes on careers are central to the expertise of external career counselors or career coaches. Various tools for self-assessment suited to the needs of the individual can also be made available by career counselors. Also, in contrast to internal career counseling, external counselors can provide complete confidentiality (Chung 2003). Furthermore, career counselors can provide professional support with developing an individual qualification strategy and with making time for learning. In contrast to outplacement programs, career guidance has a proactive character and focuses on identifying career opportunities primarily with the current employer.

We now return to the difference between back office staff and consultants. We established above that back office staff generally *do not need support that is different* from that needed by consultants. They just need *more of the same*. In the context of consultancy firms, we understand "more of the same" as ensuring that special attention is given to those in the organization who are more vulnerable.

"More of the same" aims at giving special support to those who need to be more active because they are less employable.

To illustrate this, we would like to give two examples regarding the content of organizational employability offers: as consultants are significantly more involved in *project work* than non-consultants, organizations should take every opportunity to offer project work also to back office staff. The "more of the same" principle can also be implemented in access to mentoring: we propose that back office staff should generally be given priority over consultants in access to mentoring. BDU reports (BDU 2004) have shown that downsizing starts in the back office, but employability mentoring as described above may facilitate re-placement within or outside the organization only when it has been started early enough. Finally, "more of the same" also refers to ensuring that organizational employability offers are communicated proactively to back office staff.

13.6 How Can Employability Work in Consultancies?

At this point it is necessary to take one step back and shortly consider the concept of employability from a more abstract point of view. Is employability really a sufficient substitute for job security? Are employees going to accept this second-best solution to their security needs? Critics have proposed that employability is a cunning strategy to prioritize profit over people. We think that an employability development program will be faced with resistance from employees due to a loss of security, from the organization due to the apparent paradox of spending money on qualifying people to leave the organization and from managers when they are asked to prioritize learning over day-to-day tasks. Nevertheless, we think that an employability development program can work under two central conditions:

The *shift from job security to employability* has to be made explicit by the organization by way of *negotiating a new psychological contract* involving a new deal that is considered fair and balanced by the affected employees (Marr and Fliaster 2003). This implies the following: for many, job security still lies at the heart of the employment relationship and employability will be considered the poor brother of job security. Consequently, they may be incurring a significant loss when job security is no longer offered. It is therefore crucial that consultancy firms negotiate new deals by making the link between decreased job security and additional employability support offers explicit. This enables consultancies to minimize perceived losses of employees by offering tangible alternatives (Rousseau 1995; Hiltrop 1996). One of the aims of making an alternative offer is conserving the perception of fairness and respect for affected employees. The shift to employability and the new offers this entails should be communicated not only internally, but also externally. Such communication can be expected to absorb some of the consequences of decreased employer attractiveness observed in German consultancies (Bornmüller 2005; BDU 2005; Graubner and Richter 2003).

Organizations have to choose a whole-hearted approach to implementing employability practices. As we have seen above, facilitating employability development involves much more than the traditional personnel development activities. Renaming IT skill trainings or leadership development programs into employability practices will not suffice and is likely to have significant negative effects on trust and commitment through disenchantment of staff (Grant 1999). Organizational employability programs involve a wide range of practices, some of which may be new to the organization, such as facilitating access to skill requirements for positions outside the organization. Also, to make employability efforts effective, organizations need a culture that is coherent with and encourages employees to ask for training that incorporates employability goals and managers to act as coaches. However, this is what it takes in order to introduce employability as a credible follow-up model for job security. But why should organizations be interested in qualifying employees in a way that enables them to leave the organization? The idea behind employability is not that organizations provide all sorts of general qualifications to their employees in a selfless fashion. Rather, employability-oriented qualifications offered by the organization should be those that have relevance both to corporate strategy and to employees' professional development so that a Win-Win scenario can be created for both parties (Lombriser and Uepping 2001). Furthermore, the fear that highly employable individuals will leave the organization at the first opportunity may be unwarranted: Craig et al. (2003) showed how a "full throttle" approach to employability became a strong driver for employee commitment in the organizations surveyed.

13.7 Summary of Results and Conclusions

We found that back office staff and consultants differ in their self-reports of employability: consultants see themselves as more employable than back office employees. We found that from the perspective of employees there is room for improvement especially with regard to activities related to identity growth and self-organization. In other words, individual development activities are doubtless taking place but individuals do not seem to follow an employability development master plan where they have established clear goals and strategies for themselves. We also found that participating organizations mostly do not offer those HR instruments that are geared at offering support with developing such a master plan for all employees. We therefore propose for consultancy firms to engage in some activities that are introduced specifically for the purpose of facilitating employability. We also propose to provide support mainly on the basis of a vulnerability principle. Internal mentoring programs focusing on employability and/or supporting access to external career advisors present two options for further developing organizational employability offers in consulting firms.

References

Andresen M, Petersitzke M (2004) Employability: A New Challenge for Corporate Universities. Beitrag zur 4. Jährlichen Konferenz der European Academy of Management, St. Andrews

Blancke S, Roth C and Schmid J (1999) Employability als Herausforderung für Politik, Wirtschaft und Individuum. Eberhard-Karls-Universität Tübingen, Institut für Politikwissenschaft

Blechinger D, Pfeiffer F (1996) Technological Change and Skill Obsolescence: the case of German apprenticeship training. Discussion paper: Centre for European Economic Research, Mannheim

Bollérot P (2001) Two Actors in Employability: The Employer and the Worker. Employability: From Theory to Practice, International Social Securities Series 2001, pp.51-90

Bornmüller G (2005) Immer in Bewegung. Hhigh Potential May/June 2005, p.26-28

Brown P, Kesketh A and Williams S (2003) Employability in a Knowledge-driven Economy. Journal of Education and Work 16 (2), pp.107-126

Bundesverband Deutscher Unternehmensberater (2005) Facts and Figures zum Beratermarkt 2004. Bonn

Bundesverband Deutscher Unternehmensberater (2004) Facts and Figures zum Beratermarkt 2004. Bonn

Chambers EG, Foulton M, Handfield-Jones H, Hankin SM, Michaels I, Edward G (1998) The War for Talent. McKinsey Quarterly 3, pp.44-58

Chung BY, Gfroerer MCA (2003) Career Coaching: Practice, Training, Professional, and Ethical Issues. The Career Development Quarterly (52), pp. 141-152

Commission of the European Communities (2005): Green Paper "Confronting demographic change: a new solidarity between the generations", Brussels, 16.3.2005

Craig E, Kimberly J and Bouchikhi H (2003) Can Loyalty be Leased? Harvard Business Review 80 (9), p. 24

Dam van K (2004) Antecedens and Consequences of Employability Orientation. European Journal of Work and Organizational Psychology 13 (1), pp.29-51

Dielmann K (1999) Förderung von Employability in den Niederlanden. Personalführung (7), pp.52-55

Fritzel I, Vaterrodt JC (2002) Flexible Auszeit für Berater. Management & Training (2), pp.14-15

Grant D (1999) HRM, Rhetoric and the Psychological Contract: A Case of 'Easier Said than Done'. The International Journal of Human Resource Management 10 (2), pp.327-350

Graubner M, Richter A (2003) Managing Tomorrow's Consulting Firm. Consulting to Management 14 (3), pp.43-50

Grip de A, Loo van J and Sanders J (2001) The Industry Employability Index: Taking account of supply and demand characteristics. Research Centre for Education and the Labour Market (ROA), Faculty of Economics and Business Administration, Maastricht University

Heijden van der B (2001) Prerequisites to Guarantee Life-long Employability. Personnel Review 31 (1), pp.44-61

Hiltrop JM (1995) The Changing Psychological Contract: The Human Resource Challenge of the 1990s. European Management Journal 13 (3), pp.286–294

Joyce F, Elferdink MA (1992) A Collaborative Model for Community Workforce Excellence. Economic Development Review, Fall 1992, pp.9-13

Kipping M (2002) Jenseits von Krise und Wachstum. ZFO 71 (5), pp.269-276

Kipping M, Sauviat C (1996) Global Management Consultancies: Their Evolution and Structure. Discussion Papers in International Investment and Business Studies, Series B, IX (221)

Kubr M (2002) Management Consulting: A Guide to the profession. International Labour Office, Geneva, 4th Edition

Leitl M, Rust H and Schmalholz CG (2001) Ohne frische Talente sehen wir ziemlich alt aus. Managermagazin (10), pp.263-271

Lombriser R, Uepping H (2001) Employability statt Jobsicherheit. Luchterhand, Neuwied

Marr R, Fliaster A (2003) Bröckelt das Loyalitätsgefüge in deutschen Unternehmen?: Herausforderungen für die künftige Gestaltung des "psychologischen Vertrages" mit Führungskräften. In: Ringlstetter M, Henzler H and Mirow M (Eds) Perspektiven der strategischen Unternehmensführung: Theorien, Konzepte und Anwendungen, Gabler, Wiesbaden, pp.277-305

Neumann S, Weiss A (1995) On the Effects of Schooling Vintage on Experience-earnings Profiles: Theory and Evidence. European Economic Review 39 (5), pp.943-958

Ragins BR (1997) Diversified Mentoring Relationships in Organizations: A Power Perspective. Academy of Management Review 22 (2), pp.482-521

Riddell W, Sweetman A (2000) Human Capital Formation in a Rapid Change: Adapting public policy to a labour market in transition. IRPP (2000), pp85-141

Rousseau DM (1995) Psychological Contracts in Organizations: Understanding Written and Unwritten Agreements. Sage, Thousand Oaks

Streicher H, Lünendonk T (2004a) Lünendonk-Studie 2004: Führende IT-Beratungs- und Systemintegrations-Unternehmen in Deutschland. Lünendonk

Streicher H, Lünendonk T (2004b) Lünendonk-Studie 2004: Führende Managementberatungs-Unternehmen in Deutschland. Lünendonk GmbH

List of Figures

List of Tables

Notes on Contributors

Jane Aubriet-Beausire began her career in the New Zealand tourism and hotel industry before gaining an Honours Degree in Marketing and joining Fuji Xerox New Zealand. Following a move to Europe and a Masters in International Business (HEC Paris & Stockholm School of Economics), she became interested in HR marketing and joined SmithKline Beecham as a University Relations Manager for Europe based in London. She then joined Novartis International in Basle, as Head of Leadership Resourcing within the Global Talent Management team. Her responsibilities included recruitment of high potential talent from top MBA schools world-wide, the design and implementation of tailor-made management development programs and career coaching and development of global early promise talent. Today, she is a Senior Consultant for Lee Hecht Harrison within their Senior Executive and Executive Team in Paris and she qualified as a Master Trainer Coach for LHH Programs and Services in Europe. In addition, she is an external career coach for INSEAD MBAs and Executive MBAs, a lecturer in Proactive Career Management at HEC Business School and a member of the International Association of Career Management Professionals. Her areas of specific interest are cross-border career management and the development of high potential talent.

Martina Beck is the HR Team Lead for the Post & Public Services Operating Group in Austria, Switzerland and Germany at Accenture in Frankfurt. She graduated from the University of Bamberg with a degree in Business Administration with an emphasis on International Business and Human Resources. Her studies included a year abroad at the Ecole Supérieure de Commerce de Montpellier. She began her career at Accenture, managing Project Scheduling for the Financial Services Operating Group. This led to an assignment on-site at a Financial Services client project, providing HR support for more than 200 employees - many of them expatriates needing assistance on their first foreign assignment. To broaden her HR knowledge, she worked as a recruiter responsible for hiring employees with prior professional experience. She then took responsibility for HR Initiatives and Policies working on programs such as Child Care, Flexible Work Arrangements and Benefits Communications.

Rainer Bernnat is Vice President and Partner at Booz Allen Hamilton in the Information Technology Group and is based in Frankfurt. His assignments include IT strategy and architecture projects for global and regional financial institutions (retail, wholesale, insurance) as well as IT projects with a total budget of more than €1 billion and design of business processes for implementing an enterprise-wide IT-architecture department for a leading European IT provider. In addition to his experience in the financial services sector, Rainer is an advisor to the German Government (Federal Ministries and Agencies) in the area of e-Government, IT security and Information Society. Examples of his recent assignments include strategy planning and implementation for the German e-Government Initiative "BundOnline 2005", development of IT standards and architectures for e-Government applications for the Federal Ministry of the Interior and drafting the internet strategy for the German Chancellor Gerhard Schröder. Rainer is a member of the Executive Board of the largest German public-private-partnership "Initiative D21" and a member of the Advisory Board of the e-Government center for the German Fraunhofer Gesellschaft. He holds a diploma and a PhD in Business Administration and completed his degree at the J. W. Goethe University in Frankfurt and at the Universidad de Navarra, Pamplona in Spain.

Michael Dickmann lectures in the areas of international and strategic human resource management. He is the Director of the Cranfield MSc in International Human Resource Management and the Director of CReME, the Centre of Research into the Management of Expatriation. Before rejoining Cranfield, he worked as the Head of Human Resources in a multinational corporation based in Munich, Germany. His Ph.D. and much of his research focuses on cross-border human resource strategies, and the structures and processes of multinational organizations, including the ways they manage change and international mergers & acquisitions. Michael has a first class Honors Degree in Economics from London University and an MSc in Industrial Relations and Personnel Management from LSE. He has cooperated with the CIPD on a number of key projects. Michael has several years of work experience for major consultancies and in industry. He has conducted a variety of consulting and research assignments on people management with cutting-edge multinational organizations mostly from the banking, telecommunications, chemical, electrical engineering and electronics industries. Spanning his activities from Gemini Consulting to Cranfield he had clients from the private and public sectors. He has worked in his native Germany, Australia, the USA, Colombia, Spain and Britain, and speaks English and Spanish fluently.

Michel E. Domsch is a Professor of Management and Head of the Institute for Human Resource and International Management at HSU, Helmut-Schmidt-University in Hamburg. Since 2004 he is also Director of MDC Management Development Centre at the HSU. He was a research fellow at the Harvard Business School and received his Ph.D. and his postdoctoral degree "Habilitation" in Business Administration from the Ruhr-University in Bochum, Germany. Michel has worked 10 years in Germany and Great Britain for British Petroleum and more than 20 years as a management consultant. Michel's consulting assignments include projects on employee satisfaction, gender diversity and family friendly policies, work-life balance and leadership development. His clients are from the industrial and the public sectors. His research focuses on International HRM, Gender and Diversity, Auditing and Work time Flexibility.

Stephan Erlenkaemper completed his apprenticeship in banking before studying Business Administration at the RWTH Aachen and the Catholic University of Eichstaett-Ingolstadt. He majored in Marketing, Banking and International Management. During his studies, he gained practical experience in the retailing-sector, the telecommunications industry and in the field of strategy consulting. Furthermore, he received a scholarship from the Eberle-Butschkau foundation. He graduated with distinction as Diplom-Kaufmann in 2001. Subsequently, he earned his Ph.D.-degree in February 2005 from Prof. Bueschken, Professor of Marketing at the Catholic University of Eichstaett-Ingolstadt with summa cum laude. In his dissertation he examined the antecedents and determinants of auction prices – paying special attention to auctions being held on eBay. He developed an empirically-based, statistical model to forecast end prices in online auctions. Apart from his dissertation, he has worked for a large number of consulting and publishing projects, among them for Audi, BBDO-Consulting and miscellaneous German medium-sized companies on a freelance basis. Since March 2005, he has been Head of Marketing and member of the management of kaufeigenheime® Wohnungsbau-gesellschaft mbH in Ingolstadt. He is regularly involved as a censor in business plan competitions and serves as a referee in executive-education programs.

Sophie Gaïo joined LHH in 1995. She is currently Senior Consultant and Director of Professional Services for LHH France. Based at LHH's head office in Lyon, Sophie is nationally responsible for integrating LHH programs and processes, in addition to managing the quality level of delivery of individual services offered by 11 offices in France. She is also responsible for delivering the LHH Certification Process as a Masters Trainer for France and Europe and she plays an active role in business development, collaborating with General Management when new programs or services are being developed. Prior to this role, Sophie was an LHH Senior Consultant responsible for individual services and for the delivery of large career management projects. Before joining LHH, Sophie held a GM position within a key recruitment agency in addition to having significant operational and management experience within the HR functions of both Ellis Group and Tetrapack. She qualified as a Master Trainer and Facilitator for LHH Programs and Services, in addition to holding a Masters in Human Resources and a Masters in Law.

Michael Graubner is a management consultant with McKinsey & Company, Inc. in Frankfurt. He holds an M.Sc. in Mechanical Engineering and Business Administration from the University of Technology in Darmstadt, Germany. From 1997 to 1999, Michael Graubner studied at the University at Buffalo, New York, U.S.A., where he received a Master of Business Administration from the School of Management. From 2002 to 2005, he was a doctoral student at the Department of International Management and Consulting at the European Business School in Schloss Reichartshausen, Germany. At all three institutions, he taught masters-level courses on various subjects including Management Consulting and Economics. He has published on the organization and human resource management of professional service firms. Before entering management consulting, Michael Graubner gained work experience in different industries such as automotive, engineering, glass and light metal processing, construction, and financial services. He lives in Hofheim am Taunus near Frankfurt.

Kathrin Günther is currently working as a software consultant. In 1999, she completed training at a compulsory health insurance fund in Paderborn. After that she studied Business Computing, specializing in human resource management and IT consulting at the University of Paderborn. During her studies she gained extensive practical experience as a consultant at the Junior Enterprise Campus Consult in Paderborn. Her projects dealt mainly with marketing, market analysis and training. She instructed e.g. in Lotus Notes, presentation skills, SAP/3 HR and human relations. Moreover, she organized the training for the student consultants of Campus Consult. Since September 2004, she has worked as a consultant at the MACH AG. The MACH AG is a software consultancy in Lübeck which develops and distributes finance and personnel software. Their clients are the Civil Service.

Frederike Harms is now studying International Business Studies, specializing in Human Resource Management and Organization with the subsidiary subject of Work- and Industrial Psychology at the University of Paderborn. She obtained a university entrance diploma in 2002. Frederike Harms started as a visitor at the Junior Enterprise Campus Consult Paderborn in May 2003, then became a member in October and was part of the executive board as head of the Networking department for a year. Apart from the commitment in the Networking department, she was involved in the personnel team of Campus Consult, which designs and carries out solutions for all problems arising in the field of human resources in the Junior Enterprise. Frederike Harms has also conducted several projects for companies, mainly in the field of marketing. She plans to finish her studies in the beginning of 2006.

Tom Hinzdorf is presently working as a marketing consultant for BBDO Consulting, Munich. He deals extensively with brand and customer equity management in theory and consulting projects. Before he joined BBDO Consulting he was one of the co-founders of the marketing and coaching consultancy Sophus, Ingolstadt. Tom Hinzdorf holds a Ph.D. in Marketing from the Ingolstadt School of Management of Catholic University, Eichstaett in Germany. He teaches regularly in various university programs in Germany and is the author of several articles about pricing, commitment marketing and employer branding.

Elena Hristozova is a research assistant at the I.P.A. Institute for Human Resource and International Management, Helmut-Schmidt-University / University of the Federal Armed Forces, Hamburg. Her main research areas are human resource management in consultancies and crisis-driven personnel practices. She is currently working on her thesis on evolution and the success of crisis-driven human resource management in German consultancies. She holds a university degree in International Business Relations from the University of National and World Economy (UNWE) in Sofia and a masters degree in European Studies (M.E.S.) from Europa Kolleg in Hamburg. She gained consultancy experience in the area of training and development, organisational development and compensation and benefits.

Walter Jochmann joined the Kienbaum group in 1983. Since 1997/98, he has been Chairman of the Board of Kienbaum Management Consultants GmbH, in which the consulting activities of the Kienbaum group are bundled, and since 1999 he has been a board member of the Kienbaum Holding. He is head of the business unit Human Resource Management which comprises the competence areas HR-strategy, diagnostics, management development, HR programs and processes, change management and HR IT solutions. Jochmann has published numerous articles in the field of HR Management and is an expert in designing and implementing major reorganizations (strategic realignment, post-merger integration) as well as in restructuring HR departments. Amongst others, his expertise covers areas such as the development of HR visions, goal systems (i.e. HR balanced scorecard) and products and the alignment / optimisation of processes and organisational structures. Recently, his main area of interest has been the measurement of HR departments' contribution to corporate success as well as the integration of human assets into traditional financial evaluation methods.

Ildiko Kreisz is the HR Director for all German speaking countries within Accenture including Austria, Switzerland and Germany. She graduated from the Johann Wolfgang Goethe University of Frankfurt with a degree in Business Administration with an emphasis on Banking, Organization and International Trade. Her studies included a year at the think tank 'Center of Strategic and International studies' at the Georgetown University of Washington DC. She began her career at Accenture as a consultant in 1991 within the area of Financial Services, where she worked for more than 10 years before moving to human resources. Today, she is managing HR services for over 4,500 employees covering a broad range of services like human capital and compensation strategy, recruiting, people satisfaction, capability development and HR operations as well as HR outsourcing.

Uta B. Lieberum is assistant professor at the I.P.A. Institute for Human Resource and International Management, Helmut-Schmidt-University, Hamburg. She is also associated with the OTA-Hochschule, Private University of Applied Science in Berlin for Organization and Human Resource Management, where she is Head of Faculty for Business Administration. Her main research areas are special aspects of International Human Resource Management, Gender- und Age-Diversity and Career-Management. She obtained her doctorate from the Helmut-Schmidt-University in Hamburg with a thesis on cultural aspects of international alliances. Her practical experience is based on consultant activities in different sectors (flexible working hours, employee surveys, implementation of corporate policies and moderation).

Maida Petersitzke is a research assistant at the Institute for Human Resource and International Management at the Helmut-Schmidt-University/University of the Federal Armed Forces in Hamburg. Her research focuses on the management of psychological contracts, which is also the central theme of her PhD project. Related to that, she has also done work on employability and work-life balance. Maida holds a degree in Psychology from the University of Aberdeen and an MSc in Organizational Psychology from the Manchester School of Management (UMIST). She has worked in several organizations, mainly in personnel selection and assessment.

Katrin Priemuth is co-founder and CEO of the coaching consultancy Sophus, Ingolstadt. She studied psychology at the Universities of Dresden, Johannesburg and Oxford and earned her Ph.D. from Ludwig-Maximilian University of Munich. She is an accredited team and individual coach and executes coaching and organisational development projects with a wide range of German, Austrian and Swiss clients. Katrin Priemuth specialises in leadership development, enhancement of employee satisfaction and motivation and change management projects. She also lectures in Organizational and Industrial Psychology at the Ludwig-Maximilian University of Munich and is author of a wide range of articles about employer branding, employee commitment, absence from work and coaching in psychological journals and books.

Klaus Reiners has been the press officer of the National Consultants' Association in Germany BDU (Bundesverbandes Deutscher Unternehmensberater e.V.) since 1998. During this time he wrote several contributions regarding the occupational image of management consultants and regarding career development in management consultancies. Related to his work, he gives also regular lectures at Universities with the title "Career chances and selection criteria in management consulting". He holds university degrees both in history and in geography and a postgraduate degree in public relations (DAPR).

Ansgar Richter, Ph.D. holds the Chair of Management and Consulting at the European Business School (ebs), Schloss Reichartshausen, Germany. He is also co-director of the Institute of Industrial Services Management at the ebs. He studied Philosophy and Economics at the universities of Frankfurt and Bochum. From 1994 to 1999 he studied at the London School of Economics, where he completed a M.Sc. in Industrial Relations and Personnel Management and a PhD in Management. Following his studies, he worked as a management consultant with McKinsey & Company, Inc., pursuing projects in the area of corporate organisation and strategy for clients in Germany, Luxembourg, the UK, Finland, and the United States. Ansgar Richter has been at the ebs since 2002. His special area of interest is the organisation and strategy of consulting companies, and he has published extensively in these and other areas. He has received numerous awards for his teaching and research, including the Thomson-South Western Award in 2005 from the Management Consulting Division of the Academy of Management for the best research-based paper. He is a member of the advisory committee of the Network Consulting Rhein-Main e.V. and of the Executive Committee of the Management Consulting Division of the Academy of Management.

Mareike Schilling is currently working at BearingPoint in Frankfurt as a consultant in the Financial Services sector, focused on Business Process Improvement and Retail Banking. She holds a masters degree in Business Administration with an emphasis on International Business and Organization from the University of Paderborn. Before her graduation in April 2005, Mareike Schilling took part in the MBA International Case Competition in Montreal, Canada. In 2003, she spent a semester at the Dublin City University in Ireland. She has also gained extensive experience in the consulting business by working at the Junior Enterprise "Campus Consult". Before starting her academic career, she completed a professional bank training program at the Sparkasse Werl and worked there as assistant to the Board of Directors for another two years.

Lorraine Schneider currently works as a HR and Change Management consultant at Capgemini Deutschland GmbH. She is a graduate student of psychology with an emphasis on work and organisational psychology. Lorraine gained practical experience in Human Resources, Change Management, Global Marketing, Workplace Health Promotion, and research during various internships in Germany and Singapore, for example at Deutsche Telekom AG, Benteler AG, AOK, Bosch Rexroth AG, as well as at the Chair of Work and Organisational Psychology at the

University of Paderborn/Germany. She also extended her knowledge in consulting services working at the Junior Enterprise Campus Consult Projektmanagement GmbH where she completed several projects. In addition, Lorraine acted as a member of the student advisory council of the Springer publishing company, and finished her training as coach at the Institut für Innovationstransfer at the Universität Bielefeld GmbH.

Wolfgang Schnelle† was born in Danzig in 1930, and after he finished his schooling in Germany he trained to work in industry as a commercial clerk. He took an interest in psychology and taught himself about social psychology, organizational sociology and micro-economic organizational theory. In 1966, he attended the Carnegie Mellon University in Pittsburgh, where he met Herbert Simon, Igor Ansoff and Richard Cyert. In 1956, he became a consultant on 'office landscaping' and three years later he was one of the founding members of the consulting firm 'Organisationsteam Schnelle', which changed its name to 'Quickborner Team' in 1967. He left the 'Quickborner Team' in 1972 to set up Metaplan. He remained a partner there until 1999, after which he continued to work for the company on a free-lance basis. During the course of his life, Wolfgang Schnelle received assignments in a number of industries, including the automotive, electrical goods, machine construction, pharmaceuticals, TV, software, publishing, banking and insurance industries. He also received commissions from government institutions, public administrations, pension funds, medical practices and hospitals. His personal motto was "We should not try to change people's behavior. Let us instead come to an understanding of how conditions can be changed that determine our behavior!"

Burkhard Schwenker is Chief Executive Officer of Roland Berger Strategy Consultants. He studied Mathematics and Business Administration at the University of Bielefeld from 1977 to 1981. He launched his professional career at PWA Papierwerke Waldhof-Aschaffenburg AG, where he last worked as a board assistant. He started his Ph.D. thesis in Economics in 1986, and was awarded a doctorate by the University of Flensburg (final grade: summa cum laude) for his dissertation on competition in service companies in 1989. In the same year, he joined the Corporate Strategy and Organization Competence Center of Roland Berger Strategy Consultants and started to build up the Hamburg office. He was elected Partner in 1992 and appointed head of the Competence Center in 1994. Schwenker was a key figure in the management buyout negotiations with Deutsche Bank in 1998, the year in which the Partners elected him to the Executive Committee. In this capacity, Schwenker was in charge of corporate development, financial planning and analysis, product development and knowledge management. In July 2003, Schwenker was appointed Spokesman of the Executive Committee of Roland Berger Strategy Consultants, taking over from the company's founder Roland Berger. In September 2004, the Partners unanimously elected him Chief Executive Officer.

Angelika Sonnenschein is the Director of Human Resources for Europe and the Middle East at Booz Allen Hamilton and is based in Düsseldorf. She studied English and French in Bonn, Kalamazoo/USA, and Grenoble/France. After completing her degree, Angelika worked for 4 years as a Liaison Officer at the Council for Scientific and Industrial Research in Bonn. In 1987, she joined Booz Allen Hamilton, initially establishing the Recruiting and HR functions for Booz Allen in the German-speaking region and then expanding these Europe-wide. Angelika has been the Director of Human Resources for Europe and the Middle East since 1999. She also holds an Executive MBA from Kellogg/WHU and has significant experience in organizational psychology.

Christian von Thaden is presently working as a marketing consultant for BBDO Consulting, Munich. He deals extensively with customer relationship marketing in the automotive sector. Before he joined BBDO Consulting he was one of the co-founders of the marketing and coaching consultancy Sophus, Ingolstadt. Christian von Thaden holds a Ph.D. in Marketing from the Ingolstadt School of Management of Catholic University, Eichstaett in Germany. He teaches regularly in various university programs in Germany and is author of several articles about pricing, conjoint analysis and commitment marketing.